KU-022-436

AN INCONVENIENT GENOCIDE

WHO NOW REMEMBERS THE ARMENIANS?

GEOFFREY ROBERTSON QC

Biteback Publishing

This edition published in Great Britain in 2015 by
Biteback Publishing Ltd
Westminster Tower
3 Albert Embankment
London SE1 7SP
Copyright © Geoffrey Robertson 2014, 2015

Geoffrey Robertson has asserted his right under the Copyright, Designs
and Patents Act 1988 to be identified as the author of this work.

All rights reserved. No part of this publication may be reproduced, stored
in a retrieval system or transmitted, in any form or by any means, without
the publisher's prior permission in writing.

This book is sold subject to the condition that it shall not, by way of trade
or otherwise, be lent, resold, hired out or otherwise circulated without the
publisher's prior consent in any form of binding or cover other than that
in which it is published and without a similar condition, including this
condition, being imposed on the subsequent purchaser.

Material from *Rebel Land* reproduced by kind permission of Bloomsbury
Publishing. © Christopher de Bellaigue, 2010, *Rebel Land: Among Turkey's
Forgotten Peoples*, Bloomsbury Publishing plc.

Every reasonable effort has been made to trace copyright holders of material
reproduced in this book, but if any have been inadvertently overlooked the
publishers would be glad to hear from them.

ISBN 978-1-84954-897-7

10 9 8 7 6 5 4 3 2 1

A CIP catalogue record for this book is available from the British Library.
Set in Adobe Garamond Pro

Printed and bound in Great Britain by
CPI Group (UK) Ltd, Croydon CR0 4YY

MIX
Paper from
responsible sources
FSC
www.fsc.org   FSC® C020471

The Armenian massacre was the greatest crime of the war, and the failure to act against Turkey is to condone it; because the failure to deal radically with the Turkish horror means that all talk of guaranteeing the future peace of the world is mischievous nonsense; and because when we now refuse to war with Turkey we show that our announcement that we meant 'to make the world safe for democracy' was insincere claptrap.[1]

— Theodore Roosevelt, 1918

I have sent my Death's Head units to the East with the order to kill without mercy men, women and children of the Polish race or language. Only in such a way will we win the lebensraum that we need. Who, after all, speaks today of the annihilation of the Armenians?[2]

— Adolf Hitler, in Obersalzburg, 22 August 1939,

CONTENTS

Greece

Constantinople

Bilejik

Eskishehir

Kutahia

Izmir

Afion-Karahisar

Turkey

Konya

Adana

Ankara

Sepasti

Gurun

Aleppo

Cyprus

Syri

Mediterranean Sea

Lebanon

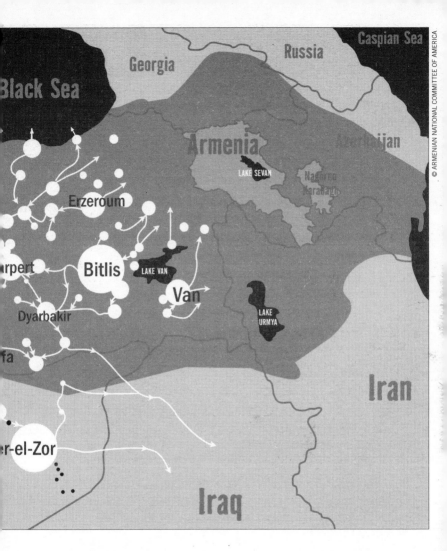

© ARMENIAN NATIONAL COMMITTEE OF AMERICA

THE ARMENIAN GENOCIDE

Massacre sites: The marker size represents the number of deaths.

Death March Routes: Turkish troops forced Armenians into the desert, without food or water, to die of starvation and heat exhaustion.

Concentration Camps

Deportation Checkpoints

Present day regional country borders

Historic Armenia borders

Current Armenia borders

PREFACE TO THE PAPERBACK EDITION

ADOLF HITLER SUMMONED his generals to a villa in Salzburg on 22 August 1939 and, in a shockingly brutal speech, urged them to show no mercy towards women and children when invading Poland. There would be no retribution, because 'who, after all, speaks today of the annihilation of the Armenians?' He was encouraging them to believe they would have the same impunity that the 1923 Treaty of Lausanne had allowed to Ottoman politicians who oversaw, in 1915, the extermination of over half the Armenian race, by rounding up and killing community leaders, executing their able-bodied men and then sending their women, children and old men to face death in the Syrian desert. The Ottoman Turks may not have used gas chambers, but they used death squads and death marches, starvation and typhus-ridden concentration camps situated in places we have only heard of today because they are being overrun by ISIS. The evidence of genocidal intent is plain from the laws passed in 1915–16 to seize and sell homes and lands and churches, because the government had decided the Armenians were not coming back. One hundred years later, the question of its responsibility for their torment returns.

This book, written for the centenary of the Armenian genocide, has the object of proving beyond reasonable doubt that what happened *was* genocide, as that concept is now defined in international law. Shortly after the Ottomans opportunistically threw in their lot with the Axis powers in 1914, they began to eliminate their minorities. First they came for the Greeks, who at least had a homeland to which they could be deported. Then for the Armenians, most of whom were slaughtered, and lastly for the Assyrians, a third of whom were killed. These people were not, as the present Turkish government would have the world believe, just some of the many victims of the First World War. Nor were hundreds of thousands of women, old men and young children an 'enemy within' which had to be eliminated to win that war. They were not casualties of war at all: the war was the cover for their mass murder by the state.

This book – the only extensive treatment of the question by an international jurist – sets out the undeniable historical facts, and applies to those facts the law as it is stated in the 1948 Genocide Convention and more recently by international courts. The result is clear: members of the Young Turk government committed genocide because it was their intention to destroy a substantial part of the Armenian people, which they proceeded to do. And even if Ottoman leaders did not have that special intent, they were all indubitably guilty of committing a crime against humanity. Turkey, neuralgic about use of the G-word, refuses to own up even to this, and maintains barefacedly that it was justified in 'relocating' (i.e. marching to death Armenian families after murdering their menfolk) as a matter of military necessity.

What has given the subject its importance is the obsessive and massively funded denialist campaign by Turkey, backed by threats to close its air bases to countries which use 'the G-word'. This puts the US and the UK in a quandary – saying the obvious, in order to console the Armenians, is politically inconvenient whilst the Middle East remains in conflagration. But Turkish denialism has other consequences – it amounts morally to the last act of the 1915 genocide, punishing the children and grandchildren by refusing to acknowledge that their forebears were victims of an international crime. It perverts the law of war, with arguments for the legitimacy of mass killing of civilians whenever the military end may justify the murderous means. And it underwrites a movement to confine the crime of genocide to events that are equivalent to the Holocaust – to which, of course, there is no equivalence. This movement is supported by diplomats and 'real-politicians' who are discomfited by the legal duty imposed on states by the Genocide Convention, namely the duty to enforce the law against genocide.

So the centenary, on 24 April 2015, was an important re-assertion of the concept of genocide as a crime for which there can be no impunity and which requires international enforcement. Pope Francis set the scene, creating a diplomatic rift with Turkey by describing the slaughter of the Armenians as 'the first genocide of the twentieth century'. The Pope is not infallible – it was in fact the second, after the German army massacres of the Herero people in 1905 – but genocide it certainly was. The Pontiff confronted Turkish denialism head-on: 'Concealing or denying evil is like allowing a wound to keep bleeding without bandaging it.' He received no intelligible response, other than a graceless withdrawal of Turkish envoys from the Vatican.

The centenary was marked by the publication of new historical scholarship verifying the racist motivation behind the slaughter, as well as artistic and literary attempts to bridge two nations that remain divided. 'That was then, this is now' was the message, but it has so far fallen on deaf ears in Turkey, which declines to apologise, and Armenia, which refuses to forget. A solemn commemoration in Yerevan was attended by Presidents Putin and Hollande, and other national leaders. President Obama, who knows that the slaughter was genocide (see p.10), did not show up or even dare to voice his opinion, although Joe Biden and Samantha Power, in their personal capacities, did subsequently attend a commemoration service with the President of Armenia in Washington.

There were by this time no shots left in the denialist locker – their small group of well-paid historians produced nothing new to counter the evidence, other than a short documentary film justifying death marches, euphemistically described as 'displacement of populations away from the war zone'. Turkey's main trick was to put back its own celebration of the Dardanelles victory (usually held in March) until 24 April, to combine it with 'Anzac Day' on the 25th. 'Anzac' is sacred to Australians and New Zealanders, who believe their national manhood was exposed on the bloody sands of Gallipoli in 1915 by their participation in the disastrous British invasion, so Turkey was able to welcome their prime ministers. This counter-commemoration served to distract those two countries from the more significant event at Yerevan, but elsewhere the intelligent world was not fooled: mourning the sacrifice of soldiers lawfully killed whilst fighting in a declared war is very different from remembering the victims of an international crime.

Although the centenary brought more evidence that Turkish denialism is unsustainable, it brought no change in heart or mind from Ankara – not even a concession of the obvious: namely, that what happened to the Armenians was at the very least a crime against humanity. There was no offer of an apology, no act of symbolic reconciliation, no plan for restitution of Christian churches or recompense for the Armenian property expropriated in the course of the genocide, nor any suggestion that school textbooks, which convey an anti-Armenian narrative, might be reconsidered. There was instead a truculent silence, broken by occasional expostulations about how everyone suffered in the war. That was true enough but not good enough: those who suffered from international crimes committed under cover of war are entitled to retribution, no matter how belated.

The centenary galvanised the Armenian Church to bring an action in Turkey's Constitutional Court for restoration of some of their stolen property, which will challenge the legal system of that country to afford some long-delayed justice, failing which the issue will have to be decided by the European Court of Human Rights. The Grand Chamber of that court will soon deliver judgment in the *Perinçek* case, discussed in Chapter 8, on the difficult subject of whether laws against genocide denial are compatible with freedom of speech. They are, but only when that denial is intended to foment race hate: from that, Armenians are entitled to the same protection as Jews, because they too have suffered one of history's holocausts.

The importance of recognising the slaughter of the Armenians in 1915 as genocide was realised by Raphael Lemkin, who coined the word and elaborated the concept, namely that extreme nationalism, engendered by a government for its political purposes and directed against racial or religious minorities, can produce a unique moral blindness towards their annihilation. Genocide scholarship, which Lemkin inaugurated, identifies recurring patterns in the build-up to murderous hatred: the Armenian genocide provides many lessons in how even 'progressive' politicians, by playing with the fire of ethnic resentments, can lay the ground for a state to direct, or enable, the mass murder of a group of its own people. Those with genocidal intentions stalk the world today: at the centenary, ISIS was decapitating Christians and Yazidis, whilst shortly afterwards the government of Burma ramped up its oppression of Rohingya Muslims to such an extent that many took to the open sea on voyages of death. The Armenian genocide – for genocide it certainly was – must be studied and analysed as such, one of all too many examples of how human nature can be manipulated and twisted into perpetrating the worst of crimes.

The overriding message of the centenary – and of this book – is that it is time to stop prevarication. The law is clear, and the historical facts are certain enough for that law to be applied to them and to produce, beyond any reasonable doubt, a verdict of genocide. What follows from that finding is now to be worked out, and I suggest some appropriate reparations in Chapter 9. But genocide denial is no longer an option, and nor is the 'genocide equivocation' favoured for strategic reasons by the US and the UK. These states wring their hands and invariably describe the events as a 'tragedy'. It was not a tragedy, but a crime – the worst crime of all.

The centenary has brought happier reflections, namely that the human spirit can recover from, and rise above, the greatest of catastrophes and the greatest of crimes. In the words of the American-Armenian writer William Saroyan:

> I should like to see any power of the world destroy this race, this small tribe of unimportant people, whose wars have all been fought and lost, whose structures have all crumbled, literature is unread, music is unheard, and prayers are no more answered. Go ahead, destroy Armenia. See if you can do it.

Send them into the desert without food or water. Burn their homes and churches. Then see if they will not laugh, sing and pray again. For when two of them meet anywhere in the world, see if they will not create a new Armenia.

We must thank Armenians for their laughter and songs and prayers and for their determination not only to remember the fate of their forebears, but to demand that it be requited, as some proof that they did not die in vain. Their persistence in this demand inspires us to maintain the rage about crimes against humanity inflicted on human beings anywhere in the world.

Geoffrey Robertson QC
Doughty Street Chambers
June 2015

INTRODUCTION

My firmly held conviction [is] that the Armenian
Genocide is not an allegation, a personal opinion, or
a point of view, but rather a widely documented fact
supported by an overwhelming body of historical
evidence. The facts are undeniable … as President,
I will recognise the Armenian genocide.

Senator Barack Obama, Campaign Statement on
the Importance of US–Armenia Relations
19 January 2008

L ET ME BEGIN with a declaration of disinterest: my only
personal connection with the history discussed in this book
is through a grand-uncle, William 'Piper Bill' Robertson
(he played bagpipes in the Leichhardt Town band), who happened
to be huddling in the bow of a British warship off the Dardanelles

on 24 April 1915. The imminence of the Allied invasion in which he participated triggered the order that went out that night in the Ottoman capital, Constantinople, to round up the Armenian intellectuals – professors, community leaders and political activists. Most were taken away and secretly killed, and a few weeks later came the orders to deport a whole community from Anatolia (now most of modern Turkey) to the deserts of Syria – death marches on which over half of the Armenian race was destroyed. The following day, 25 April, which Australians commemorate as Anzac Day, the ill-fated landing at Gallipoli commenced, and Bill was soon cut down by machine gun fire from Turkish defenders.

The ravages of the Great War brought untold suffering to families of all races and religions caught up in the conflict, and there is little point, a century on, in bemoaning losses occasioned by the stiff-necked and stupid behaviour of the political leaders who took their nations to war and refused, for four years of carnage, to contemplate a peace agreement. 'Piper Bill' was one casualty among millions; he had volunteered to fight and was lawfully killed by a Turkish soldier. Other than a generalised sadness at the futility of this war, he is entitled to no special mourning a century on. But the million or so Armenians who died, most of them civilians, were the victims of a crime against humanity. Should they be remembered, like my grand-uncle, just as victims of war? Or do victims of atrocious crimes in wartime, crimes that have never been punished then or later in peace, have a special claim on our memory – and on our thinking about how to avoid such atrocities in the future?

I believe that the descendants of the victims of unrequited international crimes do have legitimate grounds for demanding some form of retribution, however long delayed. Where crimes against humanity are concerned, we are all Armenians – the very fact that fellow humans can conceive and commit them demeans us all, as members of the human race, not just the Turkish or Armenian race. It becomes a matter of international concern if a country seeks to cover up such crimes, by blotting them out of school textbooks or prosecuting those who allege them, or worse, if denial takes the form of an insistence that they were justified in the first place. There can never be justification for genocide, even on the shoulder-shrugging grounds that it occurred in war when life was cheap and 'military necessity' or 'national security' required it to be risked. Any state that takes the lives of hundreds of thousands of women, of old men and young children on the grounds of their race must, in the absence at least of confession and apology, pay a price, as long as a century later.

The well-funded chorus of Turkish denialism shouts that these victims were simply casualties of a civil war within a world war in which they were either authors of their own misfortune (the view that the Armenian community got what it deserved since it harboured terrorists) or should simply be added to the common tragedy in this bloody Anatolian theatre where Muslims and Christians, Turks and Greeks, Russians and Assyrians all suffered. Both forms of denialism are objectionable, because they fail to comprehend the fact that Armenians were deliberately subjected by their state (then, the Ottoman Empire, run by the 'Young Turk' government) to unlawful and inhumane treatment. Genocide is the worst kind of crime against humanity, and it was inflicted with the intention and the effect of removing – from Anatolia, from Cilisia and from the world – most of the Armenian race. It also, beyond any doubt at all, amounted to the international crime of persecution – a widespread and systematic forcible transfer of a civilian population because of its political sympathies or its ethnic origin. Genocide denialists never admit that if the Armenians are not victims of genocide (which they deny on *faux*-legal grounds) they are certainly victims of the crime of persecution, and of other crimes against humanity. Instead, they claim that if the 1915 events did not amount to genocide they amounted to nothing at all: *c'est la guerre* – as if 'military necessity' in war can justify the marching of hundreds of thousands of civilians to their death. That this is a war crime of utmost gravity was confirmed by the American and Australian military courts which convicted Japanese generals for the death marches in the Philippines and at Sandakan. Their victims were soldiers who were prisoners of war: to subject civilians to the same treatment is a crime that 'military necessity' can never justify, any more than it could justify General Mladić's destruction of Muslims in Srebrenica on the ground of strategic advantage for his army and his cause.

Genocide, because it is the worst crime against humanity, calls for special study of its causes and for special precautions against its recurrence. There are lessons to be learned from the way in which a new and seemingly progressive 'Young Turk' government decided to solidify its support behind the banner of racial superiority and how this in turn led its intellectual theorists to demonise and dehumanise minorities from other races. Genocide scholarship serves a valuable purpose of identifying patterns that recur in the build-up to behaviour in which formerly happy neighbours can be incited to hack each other to death and to renounce the very notion of 'neighbourhood' as a living space which human beings of different creeds or colours can amicably occupy. Within living memory, murderous race hatred has been inflicted on the Hindus and Bengalis of Bangladesh, on the Tutsis in Rwanda, the Muslims of Bosnia-Herzegovina, the Tamils of Sri Lanka, the Chechens in Russia, the Mayans in Guatemala, the Chinese in Indonesia, the Darfurians in Sudan, and on other victim groups: the list is long and it will lengthen, unless the world now remembers the Armenians and rejects the claim that their killing was no more than cruel necessity.

The Armenians were Christians, but the genocide derived from racial more than religious motives, although at street level many were killed to cries of 'Allahu Akbar' and hatred of Christianity undoubtedly played its part. Religious fervour is an important factor in many genocides – there is nothing that people are not capable of if they think it will secure them a life after their own death. There is little to choose between major religious texts in their approval of the elimination of infidels: the Koran injuncts the faithful to 'slay the idolators wherever you find them',[3] whilst the God of the Old Testament is forever urging Christians to exterminate tribes that worship other gods: 'Thou shalt smite them and utterly destroy them.'[4] Echoes of these primitive injunctions can be found in modern murderous ideologies, of Bosnian Serbs and of ISIS and Boko Haram, and those who argue for recognition of the Armenian genocide must keep well clear of Christian evangelicals offering support more for the sake of Muslim-bashing than for the sake of historical justice.

Since Turkish treatment of the Armenians was on any view a crime against humanity which requires retribution, there is still a point in characterising it as genocide, the worst of all such crimes. What most concerns me about denialism is that it seeks to narrow the offence so that it would cover only the Holocaust. This is not what the legal architect of the crime, Raphael Lemkin, intended and it was not the purpose of the Genocide Convention, although its passage was speeded by the horrific revelations at Belsen and Auschwitz. Denialists insist that the Armenian genocide cannot be proved as a matter of law because a 'specific intent' to destroy all or part of a racial or religious group means that there must be proof of an extermination order. This legal mistake ('specific intent', in fact, is usually proved by inference from conduct) feeds denialist rhetoric: there is no proof, they say, that the Ottoman government ordered the *extermination* of all Armenians; it merely *relocated* them in circumstances where most were killed by brigands and disease and lack of food. This may have been negligence, but they built no gas chambers and held no meeting to arrange 'the final solution'.

But even Adolf Eichmann's spine-chilling minutes of the Wannsee Conference, where the Holocaust was planned, make no reference to a 'final solution' of extermination. Able-bodied Jews are to be despatched to labour camps where most are expected to die from hard work whilst the women and children are to be 'evacuated to the East'. 'Evacuation' for the Nazis, like 'relocation' for the Young Turks, is the euphemism for a procedure in which the existence of most of the condemned race will be ended – the 'final solution' that is devoutly wished is the 'destruction of part of a race' that is outlawed by the Genocide Convention. The Wannsee minutes provide a justification based on 'wartime necessity': they note that Jews are disloyal and most are breaching wartime currency regulations, and are dangerous anyway because interbreeding will poison the superior German race.[5] The Young Turks (and today's Turkish government) similarly rely on Armenian disloyalty and its danger in wartime, which provided them with the cover under which to solve 'the Armenian question' by eliminating the Armenians. Hence the deportation orders, and the acquisition by the state of their homes and property, because these deportees were not coming back. In both the Ottoman Empire and the Third Reich, actions which produced homogenous neighbourhoods amounted to genocide because it can be inferred from all the circumstances, from the race-superiority doctrines in the beginning to the property expropriation laws at the end, that the purpose of taking those actions was to achieve ethnic cleansing by destruction of the race that is to be 'cleansed'.

There can be no doubt, even from the work of denialist historians, that the crime committed against the Armenian population of the Ottoman Empire in 1915 was what today would be legally classed as genocide. At the time, it was a crime without a name: international criminal law did not exist and sovereign states and their leaders were not liable for killing their own people because of their race or religion or, for that matter, their red hair. The Entente allies – Britain, France and Russia – quickly declared it 'a crime against humanity', which it was, in rhetoric at least but not in law, because that generic crime did not come into existence until it was defined in the 1945 London Agreement, which set up the court at Nuremberg (the current definition is set out in Article 7 of the 1998 Rome Statute, which established the International Criminal Court). 'Genocide' was the word coined by Raphael Lemkin in 1944 to describe the crime that for the past twenty years he had been urging the world to punish, because of the particular ease with which racial and religious hatred could be stirred up in multicultural societies, a phenomenon he illustrated by analysis of historical massacres, emphasising in all his writings the fate of the Armenians. This was his exemplar of the need to end the impunity of statesmen who destroyed ethnic groups in their own state. They should, he argued, be prosecutable anywhere and everywhere, under a criminal law that applied universally. By 1944, Lemkin had the fate of the Jews in Germany and the East more urgently in mind, but he interpreted the Holocaust as a crime of the same kind as that visited upon the Armenians.

*   *   *

GIVEN THAT LEMKIN's view was enshrined in the Genocide Convention of 1948, and the destruction of over half the Armenian race in 1915 remains undisputed, how is it that the two most significant Western nations today continue to dispute it? The UK government condemned the massacres as a 'crime against humanity and civilisation' when they happened, but has in recent years been describing them as if they were no more than an un-blameworthy 'tragedy', repeating the crafty mantra that 'neither this nor previous governments have judged that the evidence is sufficiently unequivocal to persuade us that these events should be categorised as genocide'. The civil servants who crafted this dishonest statement (it turns out that no UK government since the Genocide Convention has ever judged the evidence) misun-derstood and misapplied the law relating to genocide, perhaps deliberately, because their policy memoranda reveal a shameful secret: the UK government's Foreign Office had decided that because Turkey was 'neuralgic' on the subject, the country was too commercially and politically important to upset by telling the truth. As one note to the Foreign Secretary put it, in respect of the government's equivocal position: 'HMG is open to criti-cism in terms of the ethical dimension. But given the importance of our relations (political, strategic and commercial) with Turkey … the current line is the only feasible option.'[6]

These and other policy memoranda were obtained in 2009 under the UK Freedom of Information Act. I had been asked by the Armenian Centre in London to provide an opinion on the legal correctness of the UK policy, which had abandoned the 'ethical dimension' in favour of what was thought would be commercial and strategic advantage for the UK. The documents provided a case study of how diplomats, like the witches in *Macbeth*, can 'palter with us in a double sense',[7] concocting phrases like 'insufficiently unequivocal evidence' for ministers to use, and thereby to mislead Parliament and the public. My opinion, 'Was There an Armenian Genocide?', analysed the reasons behind what I termed the UK's 'genocide equivocation'.[8] It was raised in Parliament[9] in 2010 and British government ministers have thereafter dropped the claim that the evidence is 'not sufficiently unequivocal'. They now accept that 'the treatment of the Armenians was horrific and caused the deaths of hundreds of thousands by force of arms, starvation and disease … They should not be forgotten…'[10] But instead of remembering them as victims of genocide, the UK is still determined to avoid upsetting Turkey, so it avoids any mention of the 'G' word and merely asks that nation to work with the Armenians 'to address their common history … in an open, honest and constructive manner'.

Unfortunately, this is not possible so long as Turkey maintains its obsessive denialism and uses Article 301 of its Penal Code to threaten those of its citizens who 'insult Turkishness' by referring to the treatment of Armenians in 1915 as genocide. It devotes massive resources to propagating a form of 'genocide justification', namely that the deportations and massacres were merely incidents in a civil war, which did not amount to a crime because they were impelled by 'military necessity'. Its 'neuralgic' reaction goes to absurd lengths: when the parliament of an Australian state (New South Wales) recognised the genocide, Turkey threatened to ban its MPs from attending the 2015 centenary commemoration for the loss of Australian life – including that of 'Piper Bill' – at Gallipoli. When the Swedish Parliament and the US Congressional Committee on Foreign Affairs used the 'G' word, Prime Minister Erdoğan responded by threatening to deport 100,000 Armenian guest workers – given that mass deportations were the vehicle for the genocide, this menace was particularly ugly.[11] The very fact that it could be uttered demonstrates the need for Turkey to understand that its predecessor, the Ottoman Empire, committed an international crime.

The British reluctance to alienate a resurgent and politically important nation parallels that of the US government, which had not hesitated to condemn the massacres in 1915 – they were fully covered in the *New York Times* and some of the evidence for

9

Ottoman government guilt comes from the cables and memoirs of US ambassador Henry Morgenthau and his consular officials. After 'genocide' was made the subject of a convention, the US in a submission to the International Court of Justice in 1951 cited 'the Armenian genocide' as a main example of it, alongside the Holocaust.[12] Presidents Ford, Carter and Reagan all went on record to condemn the massacres. But on Armenian Remembrance Day (24 April) in 1990, George Bush Snr suddenly dropped the 'G' word, and neither Bill Clinton nor George W. Bush picked it up, or went beyond the words 'mass killings' or 'massacres'. Barack Obama, a legal scholar who had studied the case closely enough to know what he was talking about when he spoke of 'genocide' during his campaign in 2008, reneged on his promise to use the word when he became President. In a transparent exercise in equivocation, he now uses the term *Meds Yeghern* to describe 'one of the worst atrocities of the twentieth century'.[13] *Meds Yeghern* means 'the great calamity' to Armenians, but it does not mean 'genocide'. Like the UK government, he falls back on pious hopes that the two countries might 'address the facts of the past as part of their efforts to move forward', despite the fact that in the present and in the foreseeable future, Turkey refuses to do so. Its continuing and indeed increasing strategic importance as an Islamic country that is a pro-Western gateway to a war-torn Middle East provides it with the clout to gag the US and the UK (although not France, which recognises this genocide and even tried to punish its denial) and to threaten prosecution under Article 301 of the Penal Code against any of its own people who 'insult Turkishness' by attributing this crime to the Ottoman Empire.

*   *   *

THE FIRST OBJECT of this book is to explain that, beyond

any reasonable doubt, genocide as defined by international law describes the process by which about a million Armenians lost their lives in 1915. This is a question that must, in the nature of things, be answered by lawyers, not by historians who profess no understanding of the law or experience in applying it. The historian's role is to establish the facts, not to attribute to them legal categories and consequences. The abiding illogic of the debate has been the notion (especially peddled by denialists) that the issue can be 'left to historians' or that 'historians are divided' over whether the massacres amounted to genocide. Historians, however eminent, are not qualified to answer this legal question. Denialists answer it wrongly, for example by thinking that genocide requires proof of a written order from central government to eliminate all members of a race or religion, or that there must always be an intention to kill everyone in that group rather than an intention to kill part of the group or an intention to create conditions where killing is inevitable.

This confusion over the meaning of the 'G' word is shared by the Turkish Prime Minister, who declared in 2014 that it was not possible for genocide to have been committed, 'because if such a genocide occurred, would there have been any Armenians living in this country (i.e. in Turkey)?'[14] He appeared to think that genocide means the actual extermination of a race, which of course it does not: there were Jews left in Germany after the Holocaust, Tutsi survivors in Rwanda, Bengalis in Bangladesh and so on. It is one of the tactics of genocide deniers to define the crime itself almost out of existence, narrowing its meaning so that it applies only to the Holocaust.

In this book I offer no original reading of Ottoman history, but rather an analysis of the existing evidence, much of which has been available for almost a century. I have applied to it the tests developed in my own trade for detecting bias and sniffing out hidden agendas. I have made allowances for the naivety of American missionaries, the excitability of foreign correspondents playing up to the image of the 'terrible Turk'; the deluded boastfulness of the Armenian revolutionaries like the Dashnaks, who imagine they are leading a popular insurrection. I have been mindful of the understatements in diplomatic discourse and the unreliability of diplomatic memoirs. I have read a good deal of genocide denialism, and hope I have been fair to its main historian propagators, especially when quoting their research when it scores an 'own goal' (some of their work actually confirms the actions and motives from which genocidal intention can be inferred). I have tried to ignore material upon which serious doubt has been cast by either side: the Talaat telegrams, whether ordering massacres or oozing concern for Armenian deportees, seem respectively too bad and too good to be true. In preparing my 2009 opinion I had declined to consult the 'Blue Book' – Arnold Toynbee's devastating collection of eyewitness testimony – because of the intensity of the Turkish belief that it was fraudulent. But denialists have failed to prove the fabrication of a single document so I have brought its contents into calculation as well as the devastating collections of German eyewitness evidence published at the end of the war by the Lutheran pastor Johannes Lepsius. There is a compelling corroborative power to the thousands of contemporary witness statements, although readers will have to turn to other books to appreciate their full horror: I have not dwelt on their grisly details of mass drownings and decapitations, or the rape of women and boys and the killing and abduction of children, or descriptions of the Euphrates not just running with blood but changing its course because its waterways were blocked by dead bodies. Bearing in mind that these accounts come from so many different positions and perspectives, they demonstrate, collectively, coherently and with overwhelming corroborative detail, the falsity of the claim that the Armenian Genocide is 'an international lie'.

That does not mean that there are not uncertainties – about the extent of the genocide casualties, for a start. Modern demographic techniques were lacking in 1915 and although church records counted 2.1 million Armenians in Anatolia, the Ottoman authorities reckoned 1.1 million – a figure denialists use to ridicule the claim that 1.5 million died. But that was the casualty figure repeatedly mentioned to visiting German politicians in 1915, and it might be thought that the church had a better idea of how many of its adherents lived in crowded Armenian quarters of Anatolian cities and towns. The Turkish government goes to great lengths to bring down Armenian deaths to 600,000 but (as it accepts) these were almost all civilians – women, children and old men – so the number does not really matter, other than to wonder about officials who can solemnly say 'we *only* killed 600,000'. (As these same people insist that there were only 1.1 million Armenians, they are admitting that over half of the race was killed.)The conservative likelihood is that about a million Armenians perished, and that is the figure I have accepted in this book for want of greater demographic certainty, although I would be unsurprised if the actual death toll were as high as 1.5 million, or as low as 800,000. Armenians constituted about 30 per cent of Eastern Anatolia; they were extirpated from their homeland in a manner that ensured they would not return. Most died, and their deaths were foreseeable and foreseen.

I set out the law of genocide in Chapter 4 and apply it to the generally accepted facts of what happened to the Armenians in 1915, which are summarised in Chapters 2 and 3. My conclusion that they were without doubt victims of genocide is strengthened by considering the arguments of denialist historians, many of whom do not appear to understand the law that they profess to be denying (Chapter 5). That does not, of course, solve the issue of how genocide – and this genocide in particular – should be remembered, and the second objective of this book is to examine what international justice requires in respect of a state responsible for a crime against humanity. I express doubts about the value of the laws in some states of Europe which threaten denialists – of the Holocaust as well as other genocides – with prosecution and even prison (Chapter 8). Recognition by parliaments (Chapter 6) gives some satisfaction to descendants of victims, and resolutions to this effect have been passed by twenty national legislatures. This helps with the building of monuments and museums, and guards against the sanitisation of school textbooks. But international law has further obligations in store for states that are responsible for crimes against humanity and remain complicit in those crimes by denying them, and in Chapter 9 I canvass ways in which Turkey and its compliant partner, Germany, may make – or may be obliged to make – just reparation. But in the meantime, for the centenary commemoration of the day when Armenian intellectuals and community leaders were dragged from their homes to their deaths, I offer these reflections on an unforgettable crime that, until Turkey can accept responsibility, will remain unforgivable.

CHAPTER I

THE ARMENIAN
QUESTION

The Issue

I N MAY 1915, the Ottoman government passed a law that
ordered the deportation of about a million and a half
Armenians from Anatolia: able-bodied men were massacred, if already conscripted, or sent to army labour camps,
whilst their families were marched towards Syria and hundreds
of thousands – over half – died en route from disease, starvation and armed attack, or else in un-provisioned camps in
Syria. The 'Young Turk' government was accused of responsibility for what the governments of Britain, France and Russia

jointly and formally declared to be a 'crime against humanity and civilisation'.[15] These allies solemnly promised to punish its perpetrators, and after the war special provision was made to do so in the Treaty of Sèvres. Some were convicted (the main defendants *in absentia*) in trials in Constantinople in 1919 and 1920. The United Kingdom rounded up sixty-eight Turkish officials suspected of ordering atrocities and took them for trial in Malta,[16] but they were eventually released, in part because of uncertainty over whether Britain had jurisdiction to punish officials of a foreign country for actions lawfully taken in that country. There was, until the Nuremberg Charter in 1945, no international criminal law to punish the political and military leaders of sovereign states for the mass murder of their own citizens.

The destruction of a substantial part of the Armenians in Turkey became, in the years before the Holocaust, the main example given by those who argued for the creation of a new international crime to be called 'genocide'. This came to pass with the UN's Genocide Convention of December 1948. Genocide scholars and international law experts, along with most historians and twenty national parliaments (and forty-three state legislatures in the US) have described the fate of the Armenians as 'genocide'. Recent US presidents have declined to apply this label, a reluctance shared by the UK governments, which until 2010 formally described the events of 1915 as no more than 'a tragedy' and which claimed that, 'In the absence of unequivocal evidence to show that the Ottoman Administration took a specific decision to eliminate the Armenians under their control at the time, British governments have not recognised the events of 1915 and 1916 as "genocide".'[17]

Lemkin's Answer

This answer would certainly have perplexed Raphael Lemkin, the architect of the Genocide Convention, since the Armenian massacres and deportations were uppermost in his mind when he coined the word – a hybrid of the Greek '*genos*' (meaning 'race' or 'tribe') and the Latin '*cide*' (from '*caedere*' i.e. 'to cut', 'to kill'). They had preoccupied him ever since he read about the case of Soghomon Tehlirian, an Armenian whose entire family had been killed and who in reprisal assassinated Talaat Pasha, the former Ottoman Interior Minister and 'Grand Vizier' who had been primarily responsible for them. The evidence called on Tehlirian's behalf at his trial, in Germany in 1921, had convinced Lemkin (and the jury) that the purpose of the Turkish authorities in deporting the Armenians was to destroy the race, but he was reluctant to approve of the acquittal of a vigilante who had acted as the 'self-appointed legal office for the conscience of mankind'.[18] He studied the abortive British proceedings against Ottoman officials in Malta, and the jurisdictional difficulties that had arisen from the fact that in the absence at the time of any *international* criminal law, there was no juristic basis for prosecuting officials of a foreign government for organising the deaths of their own nationals.

Lemkin's first paper on this subject, written for a conference in Madrid in 1933, argued that the world needed a new law to prohibit the murderous repression of racial and religious groups, warning that this was necessary in order to prevent the repetition, in other countries at other times, of the Ottoman slaughter of the Armenians. Presciently, he drew attention to Hitler's recent rise to power, but his first and subsequent drafts of this new law were always referable to the fate of the Armenians: the evidence, to his mind, was unequivocal. Lemkin's chief example of the kind of crime that he wanted the world to outlaw remained, until the outbreak of the Second World War, the Armenian massacres. He adopted Churchill's description of the Nazi Holocaust ('We are in the presence of a crime without a name') as his premise for urging the adoption of a convention against it, and his penultimate example was always the Armenians: he began with the Maronites (although he could have started with the citizens of Carthage) then the Huguenots in France, the Protestants in Bohemia, the Hottentots in German West Africa and then the Armenians, followed finally by the Jewish, gypsy and Slavic victims of the Nazis.[19] In 1944 the 'G' word made its first public appearance, in Lemkin's book *Axis Rule in Occupied Europe: Laws of Occupation, Analysis of Government, Proposals for Redress*. Chapter 9 was headed 'Genocide'.

It is important to understand what Lemkin meant, because his thinking is the surest guide to the definition of the crime in the Convention and its application to particular mass murders. Lemkin was a Polish Jew, much moved in his youth (so he explains in his autobiography) by tales of Nero's attempt to exterminate Christians, of Charles II of France gloating over the tortures of the Huguenots, of Catholics in seventeenth-century Japan 'being compelled to drink water, after which all the openings of their bodies were cemented and heavy loads put upon their bodies until they exploded'. The victims in his youthful chamber of horrors were not only Christians – they included 'the Muslims of Spain, crowded half naked on the decks of boats before their bodies are thrown into the sea' and he 'heard the screaming of Jews in the pogroms, when their stomachs had been opened and filled with feathers and tied with ropes'. Then, at age fifteen, he encountered 'contemporary examples of genocide, such as the slaughter of the Armenians'.[20] These nightmare visions of man's inhumanity to man and to women and children, born and yet unborn, Muslim, Jew, Catholic or Protestant, inspired his life's quest for an international law that would punish the most hideous persecutions of ethnic groups. His 1944 book explains that

> genocide is effected through 'a synchronised attack on the different aspects of life of the captive people', an attack that has a number of possible harbingers:
>
> - destroying institutions of self-government.
> - disrupting the group's social cohesion, e.g. killing or removing the intelligentsia (mindful of Hitler's statement in *Mein Kampf* that 'the greatest of spirits can be liquidated if its bearer is beaten to death with a rubber truncheon').
> - destroying cultural institutions and prohibiting cultural activities.
> - ending education in the liberal arts.
> - shifting wealth from the persecuted group to privileged nationals.
> - policies of de-populating areas inhabited by the group.
> - interfering with the activities of the churches catering to the religion of the group.
> - reducing the group numbers by starvation or murder.

These indicia of genocide had been notably present in Nazi Germany and, Lemkin argued, in Turkey under Ottoman rule in the persecution of the Armenians. Genocide, he stressed (and many genocide deniers – including the present President of Turkey – seem ignorant of this), does not necessarily mean extermination of a race:

> It is intended rather to signify a co-ordinated plan of different actions aiming at the destruction of essential

foundations of the life of national groups, with the aim of annihilating the groups themselves. The objectives of such a plan would be disintegration of the political and social institutions of culture, language, national feelings, religion and the economic existence of national groups, and the destruction of the personal security (liberty, health, dignity and even the lives) of the individuals belonging to such groups. Genocide is directed against the national group as an entity, and the actions involved are directed against individuals, not in their individual capacity, but as members of the national group.[21]

These descriptions by Lemkin of what he meant by genocide describe what happened to the Armenians. This is unsurprising, for Lemkin himself tells us that he had the fate of the Armenians exactly in mind when he coined the word.[22] Lemkin pressed the case of the Armenians on the Canadian ambassador in Geneva, who introduced him to Dr H. V. Evatt, Australian Foreign Minister (and later, President of the General Assembly in 1948), who took up his cause with powerful forensic and political intelligence. Lemkin's lecturing to and lobbying of the delegates to the UN legal subcommittee in Geneva during the drafting of the Genocide Convention leave little doubt that the Preamble statement, 'RECOGNISING that at all periods of history genocide has inflicted great losses on humanity', was intended to refer, *inter alia*, to that period in history in 1915 when over half the Armenians living in the Ottoman Empire were slaughtered or starved to death. Indeed, in the first case on the interpretation of the Convention, the United States government submitted to the International Court of Justice that 'the Turkish massacres of Armenians was one of the outstanding examples of the crime of genocide'.[23]

The UK's Answer – 1915

The UK government's recent description of these events as no more than a 'tragedy' would have astonished the leaders of that government in 1915 and during the post-war peace conferences. Contemporaneously, they were viewed not as a tragedy but as a monumental crime. A joint declaration by Britain, France and Russia in May 1915 vowed that all members of the Ottoman government would be held personally liable for what was, for the first time, described as a 'crime against humanity',[24] and the Allied governments announced publicly to the Sublime Porte (the main government office in Constantinople) that 'they will hold personally responsible for these crimes all members of the Ottoman government and those of their agents wherever implicated in such massacres'. Arthur Balfour, the Foreign Secretary, said, 'The massacres in Syria and Armenia are far more terrible than any that history has recorded in those countries,'[25] and the government replied to speeches in the Lords accusing the Turks of proceeding 'systematically to exterminate a whole race out of their domain'[26] with the promise that 'when the day of reckoning arrives, the individuals who have precipitated or taken part in these crimes will not be forgotten'.[27] Lloyd George, then Prime Minister, did not mince his words when recollecting his view at the time:

> By these atrocities, almost unparalleled in the black record of Turkish rule, the Armenian population was reduced in numbers by well over one million … If we succeeded in defeating this inhuman empire, one essential condition of the peace we should impose was the redemption of the Armenian valleys forever from the bloody misrule with which they had been stained by the infamies of the Turk.[28]

As Winston Churchill, himself no mean historian, saw it:

> In 1915 the Turkish government began and ruthlessly carried out the infamous general massacre and deportation of Armenians in Asia Minor … whole districts were blotted out in one administrative holocaust … there is no reasonable doubt that this crime was planned and executed for political reasons.[29]

Waiting for Nemesis

The allies had promised – to themselves, to the Armenians and to the world – that Turkey and its political leaders would be punished for their 'crime against humanity'. The question of who exactly would do the punishing had been left unresolved: 'international criminal law' as such did not exist in 1918, and the 'Westphalian' sovereignty principle required that a state's crimes against its own people would be punished either by the state itself, or not at all. There was no precedent for an international criminal court, although now was the time to create one – or two, since the clamour to 'hang the Kaiser' required the German leadership to be put on trial as well, at least for ordering the unprovoked and brutal invasion of Belgium and the policy of unrestricted submarine warfare which led to the sinking of passenger liners and hospital ships.

The 'crime against humanity' for which the allies had determined to punish the Young Turks back in 1915 was as yet undefined although the Hague Convention of 1907 might permit prosecutions for breaching 'the established customs among civilised peoples, the laws of humanity and the demands of public conscience'. This was thought sufficient at Versailles to write into the Peace Treaty an international tribunal to put the Kaiser on trial, although it never sat – ostensibly because Holland refused to extradite him, but really because America refused to participate. The US was a late entrant into the war and did not suffer the collective grief that fuels the demand for retribution. President Wilson and his Secretary of State, Robert Lansing, were opponents of any suggestion for international justice. They argued that trials would amount to retroactive punishment for actions that were not international crimes at the time they were committed, and would breach the sovereignty principle that states alone could punish for crimes against their own people. The Armenians were Ottoman subjects, and their sufferings at the hands of their own government would have to be punished by their own government – present or future – if they were to be punished at all.

The liberal government that replaced the Young Turks and their Congress of Union and Progress Party (CUP) at the end of 1918, after the empire's defeat, consisted mainly of their political opponents, who had no hesitation in putting their enemies in the dock. Those mainly responsible – Talaat, Enver and a few of their leading ideologists and officials – immediately fled to Germany for fear of being prosecuted for the Armenian massacres. Encouraged by Britain as the occupying power, the new Turkish government set up a military tribunal which tried them *in absentia*: they were convicted of mass murder, along with a number of their ministers, officials and district governors, three of whom were hanged. But by the end of 1920 the trials in Constantinople fizzled out, as the government crumbled and then fell to the nationalist party led by Mustafa Kemal (later called Atatürk), which comprised many former CUP members and opposed retribution for what Kemal himself conceded had been 'a shameful act'.[30]

At the Paris Peace Conference at Versailles, Britain demanded the indictment of the Turkish leaders responsible for the Armenian massacres, and submitted a list of those who deserved most blame, especially Interior Minister Talaat and War Minister Enver, 'who certainly ought to be hanged'.[31] A Commission on the Responsibility of the Authors of the War was established in January 1919 and it recommended the prosecution of the Turkish leaders for war crimes committed against their own citizens on their own sovereign territory because these were an example of 'primitive barbarism' and implemented by a 'terrorist system'. In the Treaty of Versailles the Allies reserved the right to bring suspected war criminals to trial and Article 230 of the Treaty of Sèvres, which followed on 10 August 1920, proclaimed in respect of the Armenian sufferings:

> The Turkish government undertakes to hand over to the Allied powers the persons whose surrender may be required as being responsible for the massacres committed during the continuance of the state of war on territory which formed part of the Turkish Empire … The Allied powers reserve to themselves the right to designate the Tribunal which shall try the persons so accused, and the Turkish government undertakes to recognise such Tribunal.
>
> Under Article 228 the Turkish government undertook to furnish all documents, the production of which might be 'considered necessary to ensure the full knowledge of the incriminating acts, the prosecution of offenders and the just appreciation of responsibility'.

Although other nations soon tired of this novel commitment to international justice, Britain was determined to keep its promise to bring the authors of the atrocities to justice. In mid-1919, irritated by the delays in the Constantinople trials and concerned that the rising nationalism would soon put an end to them, they seized sixty-eight prisoners who were awaiting trial, most of whom were suspected of involvement in the Armenian massacres, and shipped them to a military prison in Malta, then under British colonial rule. For the next two years they were held indefinitely, whilst the UK government, against US opposition, sought the support of its allies to set up an international court to try them for the mass murder of the Armenians. It was a long, and eventually fruitless, wait.

British Justice – Delayed and Denied

The jurisdictional difficulties of prosecuting foreign officials for killing their own people concerned Balfour: as early as December 1918 he had told an Allied conference that the perpetrators of the Armenian massacres,

> strictly speaking had committed no definite legal offences ...
> it was necessary to consider how they could be got at. Talaat
> had said that Armenians were constant trouble. He had made
> up his mind to get rid of them and, in consequence, he had
> massacred them *en masse*. That was merely the policy and the
> offenders could not be tried by court martial, as they had
> committed no definite legal offence.[32]

That was the problem: the massacres and deportations were not 'war crimes' (the Ottoman Turks were not at war with their own people) so were not able to be tried by the other side at a court martial, and the position at international law was unclear. The Treaty of Sèvres gave a basis for proceeding, but trials never proceeded. The US was opposed to the idea of international justice; France and Italy lost interest in establishing a court, because they wanted to get their snouts into the resource-rich trough of the new Turkey and did not want to alienate Kemal and his nationalists, who would soon be dispensing the riches. Russia was now ruled by Bolsheviks, distracted by defending their communist state. The UK, meanwhile, waited forlornly on its allies and did not appoint a prosecutor to collect evidence and draft indictments. Its diplomats cabled each other about the difficulties of obtaining access to Ottoman documents or even to the Constantinople court files; the Armenian intellectuals and community leaders had mostly been killed and survivors of the convoys had dispersed and were afraid to come forward for fear of reprisals and in any event did not speak English. These are problems faced by every international criminal court, and it is hard to believe that a good team of prosecuting lawyers would not have been able to obtain sufficient evidence against at least some of the prisoners.[33] The British legal officer at Constantinople had no doubt that they already had a *prima facie* case against potential defendants, but 'unless there is whole-hearted cooperation and will to act among the allies, the trials will fall to the ground and the direct and indirect massacres of about one million Christians will get off unscathed'.[34]

But the eventual reason why this first attempt at international justice failed was the strong opposition to it by Mustafa Kemal, the increasingly powerful leader of the Turkish nationalist movement, which in due course (and after a short civil war) took over the government and declared the Turkish Republic. It also captured a number of British officers and soldiers, and offered to swap them for the Turkish suspects in Malta, who had not yet been indicted. So they were exchanged for British prisoners held virtually as hostages. 'It is in a measure yielding to blackmail, but seems justified by present conditions' was the UK Foreign Office advice to accept the prisoner exchange[35] – the 'present circumstances' including the view among politicians that 'one British prisoner is worth a shipload of Turks'.[36] By this time, Kemal had another winning argument: the allies had accepted the Wilsonian position on sovereignty, and allowed the Germans to try their own war criminals at Leipzig. Why not allow Turkey to try these suspects in Ankara? In September 1921, Kemal's nationalist government in Ankara solemnly promised the UK that, when shipped back from Malta, 'the detainees will be marched from the port straight to their respective states, where they will be tried for crimes of which they are accused'.[37]

On the strength of this promise the detainees were shipped back to Turkey, where many of them marched from the port straight into positions in the nationalist government. None was put on any form of trial. In due course Kemal's rising power and his victory over the Greeks forced the Allies to abandon all the penal clauses of Sèvres and to replace it in 1923 with the Treaty of Lausanne. This Treaty featured a 'Declaration of Amnesty' for all offences committed between 1 August 1914 and 20 November 1922. Such blanket amnesties would not now be recognised in international law,[38] but since Turkey today relies on the Lausanne amnesty clause as a reason for avoiding accountability, it is important to note that it applied only to individual perpetrators, and not to the state itself, responsible because those perpetrators formed its government (or in this case, the government of its predecessor). In any event, an 'amnesty' in law does not operate to obliterate, much less to forgive, the crime, but merely to exonerate individuals from its penal consequences.

The Malta detentions were a British debacle. It is true that commitment to the trials was abandoned for selfish reasons by France and Italy, already negotiating with the rising nationalists for trade and revenue concessions, and by the Bolsheviks, who lost interest. But it was the British who kept the suspects in indefinite detention, awaiting agreement to a trial in an international court.

The enterprise in Malta was wound up, not because there was no evidence but because an international court had not been set up with a prosecution authority to secure witnesses; there were serious doubts about whether an English court in Malta would have jurisdiction to try the detainees, and because the British government bowed to its own public's pressure for a prisoner swap. As we shall see (pp 143–4), it is now a constant refrain in denialist propaganda that by setting the detainees free, the UK acknowledged that there was no evidence against them, and hence no evidence that there were massacres – they were 'acquitted' and 'exonerated'. Nothing, as they say, could be further from the truth, but truth is the first casualty of genocide denialism.

International Criminal Law Stops and Starts

The Sèvres Treaty – the embodiment of the Entente promise to punish 'crimes against humanity and civilisation', had been quietly superseded in the interests of business (oil concessions) and anti-Bolshevism (the need for Turkish support) by the Treaty of Lausanne, which dropped all references to retribution for the Armenian massacres (indeed, all reference to Armenians). It was a massive betrayal of all the promises made, during the war and afterwards, by Britain, France and America. It marked, moreover, the end of a moral vision which did not reappear until Nuremberg, namely the notion that political and military leaders who abuse their state power to commit international crimes should not do so with impunity or immunity: if not prosecuted at home they should face an international court.

The idea of an Armenian nation – Russian Armenia together with the Ottoman provinces of Van, Bitlis and Erzuram, with access to the sea at Trabzon (where so many had been drowned in 1915) – also proved a pipe dream once Kemal's nationalist army advanced in 1920, put paid to the liberal government and shrank Armenia into a tiny state carved out of a patch of Russian Armenia around Yerevan. Not even great Mount Ararat, the symbolic mountain overshadowing that city, was allowed to this poor state, which bravely claimed a brief independence until Turkish sabre-rattling on its borders forced it into the arms of the Red Army. There it remained, the most impoverished of the Soviet states, until the collapse of the USSR in 1991. It had been comprehensively betrayed by the Western allies. The only act of decency came from the US Senate, which refused to ratify the Lausanne Treaty – 'it ignores the solemn pledges that American statesmen have repeatedly made to the Armenian people and recognises by implication calculated murder as policy of government' – as the former US ambassador to Germany put the case against betrayal by 'dollar diplomacy'.[39] The Treaty of Lausanne drew a legal veil over any form of international retribution for the crimes of 1915, and left the Armenians as the worst losers of the First World War.

*   *   *

THE ARMENIANS DID not suffer the first genocide of the twentieth century – that fate befell the Herero and Nama ('Hottentot') peoples in south-west Africa in 1905–7, mostly massacred (the survivors were enslaved) by a brutal German army, with the Kaiser responsible for an expropriation order authorising seizure of the 'entire moveable and fixed property of the tribe'.[40] The only glimmering of international law against such barbarity was in the Hague Conventions of 1899 and 1907, which purported to regulate international wars, and had a sweep-up provision ('the Martens Clause') which obliged belligerents to obey the rules of international law 'as they result from the usages established between civilised nations, from the laws of humanity and the requirements of public conscience'. The problem for the Hottentots and for all the previously massacred Indian and Aboriginal peoples in Africa and America and Australia was that no rules at all had resulted from civilisation, humanity or public conscience. It took the Armenian massacres of 1915 to produce the first, a solemn undertaking by Britain, France and Russia to ensure that this 'crime against humanity and civilisation' would be punished. The reference to a 'crime against humanity' was rhetoric, and remained so until the London Agreement of 1945 established the Nuremberg Tribunal to punish 'crimes against humanity', defined for the first time in Article 6(c) to include 'murder, extermination, enslavement, deportation, and other inhumane acts committed against any civilian population, before or during the war, or persecutions on political, racial or religious grounds … whether or not in violation of the domestic law of the country where perpetrated'.

Not for the last time, a hopeful development in international law – the international justice provisions in the Sèvres Treaty – had been stymied by *realpolitik* and US opposition. Sèvres was a candle briefly lit – another, the Versailles Treaty Articles 227–30 providing for the trial of Kaiser Wilhelm II by an international tribunal, was scuppered when the Netherlands, whence he had fled, refused to extradite him. Germany similarly declined to give up the Young Turk leaders. The only way to put Talaat on trial, it seemed to some vengeful Armenians, was for Soghomon Tehlirian to assassinate him, and explain to the jury that this war criminal deserved to be convicted and executed under the Sèvres Treaty anyway, and that his assassin should be acquitted because he had acted in the grip of a trauma that required him to seek retribution for the death of his entire family. There were other assassinations, the rough justice meted out by 'Operation Nemesis' (named after the Greek goddess of retribution) serving in the absence of any other form of justice.

It was this despairing resort to vigilante vengeance that inspired Raphael Lemkin in the search that would result in his invention of the word 'genocide'. It was quickly picked up by Allied leaders in 1944 to describe what Churchill had called 'the crime without a name' and found its way into several of the 'lesser' Nuremberg trials. In one indictment, for example, genocide was said to be a 'master scheme ... devised by the top-ranking Nazi leaders in pursuance of their racial policy of establishing the German nation as a master race and to this end to exterminate or otherwise uproot the populations of other nations'.[41] It was not treated as a specific crime in the main trial, however, because that took place in 1946 before the existence of the Genocide Convention, which was introduced in the UN on 9 December 1948. In 1951 the International Court of Justice confirmed that the Convention had '*jus cogens*' force (i.e. it was binding in all nations) and remarked on its 'purely humanitarian and civilising' object and purpose,[42] confirming a US government submission which had identified the Armenian massacres as an archetypal example of genocide.

That is where the Armenian question rested, partly because Armenia, which had emerged with valiant independence in 1918 as a tiny land-locked nation bordered by Turkey, Iran and Azerbaijan, soon needed Soviet troops for protection against its neighbours and became one of the satellite states of the Soviet Union (which showed no interest in promoting any law about past or future genocides). There was no fuss in 1943 when Turkey (a neutral in the Second World War) brought Talaat's body back from Germany and ceremonially reburied him on the 'Hill of Liberty'. In the '70s and early '80s 'Operation Nemesis' was revived, not this time for justice but for unjustified terrorist attacks against Turkish consulates and airlines – they began when an old Dashnak in retirement in California invited the Turkish consul to dinner, and killed him.[43] This murderous campaign raised the profile of the issue but hardly in a way which helped Armenia (Turkish propaganda today makes use of it to garner sympathy and support). The only UN 'judgment' on the issue was delivered in 1985, by a special rapporteur, Ben Whitaker, a highly respected British barrister and former MP. He concluded:

> At least one million, and possibly well over half of the Armenian population, are reliably estimated by independent authorities and eyewitnesses to have been killed or death-marched. This is corroborated by reports in the United States, German and British archives and of contemporary diplomats in the Ottoman Empire, including those of its ally, Germany.[44]

Meanwhile, the Genocide Convention had gone into cold storage during the Cold War, with the exception of the trial in Israel of the captured administrator of the Holocaust, Adolf Eichmann, convicted under an Israeli law which reflected the Convention definition of genocide. The court decided that his guilt came when the 'final solution' was conceived at the Wannsee Conference in June 1941. Before that time, Germany's anti-Semitic policy had been to persuade the Jews to leave, by discriminatory laws and public obloquy, and ghetto-isation – and impunity for those responsible for *Kristallnacht*. This was evidence of the build-up to genocide, but because their living conditions were not intolerable, Eichmann was in this period guilty of a crime against humanity, but not yet of genocide.[45] Had the refugee exodus been at gunpoint under conditions where most would have met with death, there would have been a conviction for genocide in this earlier period. It is a crime against humanity (the crime of 'persecution') to engage in 'ethnic cleansing' by way of forcing a race to depart, and another crime against humanity (genocide) to subject members of the race to forced departure by death march, when it is foreseeable that a substantial part will die.

It was not until the 1990s that the United Nations began to deliver on the Nuremberg legacy, by setting up international courts to punish genocide in Rwanda and the Balkans. The former was easy enough – evidence of the 'Hutu power' campaign and the photographs, from a distance, of Hutu gangs, machetes aloft, slaughtering their Tutsi neighbours, left little doubt about the 'specific intent' of commanders whose radio station transmitted the call 'the grave is only half full, who will help us fill it?'[46] The International Criminal Tribunal for Rwanda (ICTR) delivered the first modern genocide verdict (in the case of *Akayesu*) in 1998 and has punished eleven government ministers and a number of generals and colonels. Its jurisprudence has clarified the expression 'deliberately inflicting on the group conditions of life calculated to bring about its physical destruction in whole or in part' as meaning 'methods of destruction by which the perpetrator does not immediately kill the members of the group but which, ultimately, seek their physical destruction'. Such methods include 'subjecting a group of people to a subsistence diet, systematic expulsion from homes and the reduction of essential medical services below minimum requirement'[47] – all features of the Armenian deportations.

There has been no international court determination of whether the massacres and deportations in Turkey in 1915 would today amount to the crime of genocide. In the *Perinçek* case in the European Court of Human Rights, four judges were sure that they did whilst three expressed doubts, although the point was not in issue and there is now an appeal (see Chapter 8). The only contested proceedings were held by the International Centre for Transitional Justice pursuant to an agreement by American

Turkish and Armenian associations to obtain 'an objective and independent legal analysis'. The verdict, in 2003, was that,

> notwithstanding the efforts of large numbers of 'righteous Turks' who intervened on behalf of the Armenians, at least some of the perpetrators of the Events knew that the consequence of their actions would be the destruction, in whole or in part, of the Armenians of eastern Anatolia, as such, or acted purposively towards this goal, and, therefore, possessed the requisite genocidal intent ... the Events, viewed collectively, can thus be said to include all of the elements of the crime of genocide as defined in the Convention, and legal scholars as well as historians, politicians, journalists and other people would be justified in continuing to so describe them.[48]

This verdict was not binding and was ignored by Turkey, which currently funds a massive campaign to justify the Ottoman attacks on Armenians in 1915, claiming that they constitute no international crime, and to oppose democratic parliaments throughout the world which recognise these attacks as genocide. So it remains of importance to put them in unchallengeable historical perspective (Chapter 2), to consider at least some of the credible corroborative evidence (Chapter 3) and then to apply the Convention test to that evidence to decide (Chapter 4) whether the attacks should be characterised as genocide, or as any other international crime.

CHAPTER 2

THE HISTORY

The Build-up to Genocide

....

THE OTTOMAN EMPIRE radiated its power from Constantinople (now Istanbul). It once rivalled imperial Rome, especially under Suleiman the Magnificent in the sixteenth century, when it stretched from the Balkans, eastern Europe and Greece over to the Caucasus, through north Africa and Egypt and across to Iraq, Syria, Yemen and the Horn of Africa. During the reign of Sultan Abdul Hamid II, from 1876 to 1909, however, this empire was crumbling. The 'sick man of Europe' was losing many of its provinces to independence movements backed by Western powers anxious to pick up spoils like Cyprus or to influence newly liberated nations like Romania and Bulgaria. Although multilingual and multicultured, it was essentially a Muslim empire, governed from the Sultan's Sublime Porte mainly in the interests of the fifteen million Turkish Muslims living in Anatolia (now a large part of modern Turkey). There were Christians in this land – mainly two million or so Armenians, who once ruled themselves and were the first to convert to Christianity as long ago as 301 AD, a decade before Constantine made it the religion of the Roman Empire and hundreds of years before they had been absorbed by the Ottomans. There were also half a million Assyrians and the same number of Greeks, as well as Jews, and they were permitted to organise themselves in communities dominated by their religious leaders and known as *millets*. But Christians and Jews remained second-class citizens ('infidels' to the Turks) who were forced to wear distinctive clothing, were discriminated against in Sharia courts, whilst suffering educational and property restrictions, and were expected to remain at all times subservient to their Muslim superiors. Some *Tanzimat* reforms in 1839 and 1859 relaxed restrictions on Christian schools and businesses, and the ironic result, by the end of the century, was that the better-educated and commercially thriving Armenians became the subject of Muslim envy and malice. Social resentment was one factor which encouraged vengeful mind-frames, especially from the *Muhacirs* – several million Muslim refugees from the shrinking Ottoman Empire who had to be resettled, and the *Hamidiye,* light cavalry regiments formed from fierce Kurdish tribesmen, willing to plunder and kill Armenians because these depredations usually went unpunished by the central government.

* * *

IT HAS BECOME a fundamental feature of Turkish denialism

– one of the first 'facts' propagated on its Foreign Ministry website (see Chapter 5) – that Turks and Armenians lived in harmony for 800 years until, at the end of the nineteenth century, Armenian terrorist and separatist groups, with help from foreign governments and foreign missionaries, took up arms against the Turks, and so became the author of their community's 1915 misfortune. This website, purporting to explain 'The Events of 1915', refers to an eight-century relationship 'predominantly about friendship, tolerance and peaceful co-existence'. In so far as this refers to relations during Sultan Abdul Hamid's reign, it is simply untrue. 'The Great Assassin' as Gladstone dubbed this Caliph, was wont to describe Armenians as 'a degenerate community' and banned the very word 'Armenia' from newspapers.[49] He oversaw the slaughter of some 200,000 Armenians between 1894 and 1896, at the hands of his Ottoman forces and his loyalist *Hamidiye* militias. It was no coincidence that these massacres took place at a time when some educated Armenians were demanding changes in their centuries-old relationship with Muslim power, a relationship characterised by insult, subservience, discrimination and, at best, by sufferance.

The Sultan, the empire's absolute political ruler, was also endowed with religious supremacy as the Caliph – the spiritual successor to Mohammed, who in the Koran enjoins the faithful to 'wage war against the unbelievers and be severe to them'. But he also enjoined tolerance for 'people of the book' (Jews and Christians, but not atheists and apostates) and Ottoman common law reflected this compromise by tolerating infidels but relegating them to a class inferior to Muslim citizens.[50] They were *dhimmi* – people living under Muslim sovereignty, protected against violence and dispossession and with freedom to practise a Christian religion, but otherwise subject to legal discrimination. Their testimony in court was accounted of much less value than that of

Muslims and they were not permitted to marry Muslim women and, unlike Muslims, were prohibited from carrying weapons. Petty discrimination was endemic: the bells of their churches and synagogues had to be muffled lest the noise disturb the Muslim faithful; Christians had to give way to Muslims on footpaths and could not ride horses in their presence; Armenians had to wear red headgear, whilst the Greeks were required to wear black and the Jews, turquoise. Their houses had to be lower in height than the abodes of their Muslim neighbours – a rule symbolising their lower status.[51] They paid special taxes to central government, which notably failed to protect Armenian farmers from further exactions made at gunpoint by Kurdish gangs – and the Kurds, as Muslims, were permitted to carry guns.

Why had the Armenians put up with prejudice and indignity for so long without complaint? The answer had much to do with the passive religious leadership required by the *millet* system, and with the overwhelming power of the Sultan and his army, who showed little willingness to follow through with the *Tanzimat* reforms and end discrimination against racial and religious minorities. Inevitably, later in the century, young Armenians travelled to, or were brought up in, Europe and Russia and became acquainted with ideas of liberty and equality: they returned and by the 1890s had formed underground cells, as *Hunchaks* (socialists) or *Dashnaks* (radicals), influenced by the ideas of Marx and Bakunin. The world began to notice in 1895 when a group of Dashnak youths took over the Ottoman bank in Constantinople in protest against failure to implement reform and parleyed the release of hostages in return for their own safe passage abroad. At this point they were idealists: from the hoard of gold and currency notes in their control on bank premises, they took nothing. This would change, as they developed revolutionary theories and began to publish them in Geneva and Paris.

The battle of Navarino, back in 1827, when Britain led France and Russia to defeat the Ottoman fleet and liberate Greece, had served notice on the Sublime Porte that its hegemony over ethnic groups was dependent upon allowing them some basic rights. When religious enmities within the Empire erupted in 1861, 40,000 Catholic Maronites were slaughtered in Lebanon, and the Great Powers launched an invasion that led to autonomy for Lebanon. Butchery of Christians in Bulgaria in 1876 inspired Gladstone's pamphlet on 'the Bulgarian Horrors', demanding the expulsion of the Turks from Europe, and the Treaty of Berlin in 1878 partly achieved that objective by securing the independence of the Christian states of Serbia, Romania and Montenegro. The treaty went further: Article 61 provided: 'The Sublime Porte undertakes to carry out, without further delay, the ameliorations and reforms demanded by local requirements in the provinces inhabited by the Armenians, and to guarantee their security against the Circassians and the Kurds…'

Had the Great Powers held the Sultan to this undertaking, the genocide forty years later might have been avoided, especially if he had honoured Article 62, which guaranteed to his minorities 'civil and political rights, public employment, free exercise of professions and industrial pursuits' irrespective of 'religious differences'. This prototype human rights guarantee was ignored, however, and discrimination continued as ever before.

The Hamidian Massacres

The Hamidian massacres of 1894–6 began with a tax revolt by Armenian peasants in Sassoun, in the mountains of eastern Turkey. They resented paying exactions to the local government as well as having money extorted from them (with government permission) by Kurdish chiefs. The provincial governor urged local Muslims to teach the insubordinate Armenians a lesson, and they did so by killing thousands of men, women and children, whilst government troops and *Hamidiye* regiments stood by – or joined in.[52] The refusal to pay tax was dubbed an 'uprising' by the Ottomans – they blamed the Hunchaks, although the British vice-consul at nearby Van reported that these self-proclaimed revolutionaries had made no significant contribution to the unrest and non-payment of tax obviously provided no justification for a reprisal of mass murder. The vice-consul's reports are stomach-turning:

> Eighty tons of petroleum were utilized for burning the houses together with the inhabitants inside them … a number of young men were bound hand and foot, laid out in a row, had brushwood piled upon them and were burned live … some sixty young women and girls were driven into a church, where the soldiers were ordered to do as they liked with them and afterwards kill them, which order was carried out.[53]

This was to become an all too typical description, repeated by many diplomats, missionaries and eyewitnesses over the next three years, of incidents which were blamed by the Ottoman officials on the 'military necessity' to use force to put down Armenian insurrections or provocations. In this case, as in many others, diplomats said the excuse was bogus. 'There was no insurrection' at Sassoun, the British vice-consul reported. Turkish claims that they had killed soldiers 'I found after careful enquiry to be false'. A whitewash inquiry was set up by the government – its terms of reference gave its game away by stating that it was to report on 'the criminal acts committed by a body of Armenian insurgents'. The British vice-consul H. S. Shipley concluded that, on the contrary, 'Armenians were absolutely hunted like wild beasts, being killed wherever they were met ... I am compelled to say that the object was extermination, pure and simple.'[54]

The Sassoun massacres moved many ordinary Armenians in Constantinople to attend a peaceful protest organised by the Hunchak party, demanding civil rights, fair taxation and protection from the Kurds (or alternatively, permission to bear arms). Police opened fire, and then charged the protesters with clubs, killing many of them. The Hamidian massacres reached their hideous apogee at Christmas in 1895 in Urfa when Turkish soldiers and civilians invaded the Armenian quarter of the town to pillage and to kill any who resisted. Several thousand sought refuge in the cathedral, but Ottoman troops broke through the doors and gunned down the women and children in the gallery. They gathered up bedding and straw, over which they poured thirty cans of kerosene, then set the church ablaze. The British consul, G. H. Fitzmaurice, reported:

> The gallery beams and the wooden framework soon caught fire, whereupon, blocking up the staircase leading to the gallery with similar inflammable materials, they left the mass of struggling human beings to become the prey of the flames.
>
> During several hours the sickening odour of roasted flesh pervaded the town, and even today, two months and a half after the massacre, the smell of putrescent and charred remains in the church is unbearable ... I believe that close on 8,000 Armenians perished in the two days' massacre of 28 and 29 December.[55]

This outbreak of violent racial and religious hatred did not last. The government, fearful of foreign intervention, restrained its soldiers, as the grisly details had been widely reported in the West, and especially in America, where the *New York Times*[56] described them subeditorially in the same word that now describes the Nazi genocide: 'ANOTHER ARMENIAN HOLOCAUST'.

According to British consuls on the ground, there had been many incidents of mass conversion to Islam by Armenians under threat of massacre. A typical report, from Charles Hampson, the vice-consul for Bitlis province, concluded that 'no Christians remained ... 15,000 had been killed, 19,000 converted to Mohammedanism, and 2,500 women carried off'. It was the same throughout the affected areas: families 'converted' by force or from fear (although many reconverted when the danger had passed). Christian churches and monasteries had been razed to the ground (Johannes Lepsius, the German Lutheran pastor and journalist, counted 645 in ruins after an inspection in 1896) and others were converted to mosques.[57] The Ottoman government, in order to avoid the foreign intervention threatened for its breaches of Article 61 of the Treaty of Berlin, now pioneered and practised a denialist rhetoric: these killings were local and isolated military actions *necessary* to put down revolts that had been instigated by Armenian terrorist groups (the Dashnak seizure of the Ottoman bank had proved a propaganda windfall in this respect). Impartial observers (including several British consuls) refuted this explanation, and studies of particular districts showed that the great majority of Armenians remained loyal and passive. Nonetheless it was a chicken and egg question: the very ferocity of the massacres convinced leaders of the small revolutionary movements that hope of Great Power intervention was idle – there could be no more blatant breach of Article 61 of the Treaty of Berlin than the Hamidian massacres, yet no gunboats had appeared on the horizon to protect them. That would only be achieved by Armenian independence – nothing would succeed like secession.

For all their horrors, and the religious and ethnic hatreds that made them horrible, the Hamidian massacres did not amount to genocide. They were not planned by central government, although its troops sometimes participated and their officers went largely unpunished. But they did serve notice of the depths of racial and religious hatreds that existed within the Empire and imposed a duty on the government to do nothing to rekindle them, and a positive duty to take the actions which had been required back in 1878 by Articles 61 and 62 of the Treaty of Berlin, i.e. to extend civil rights to disadvantaged minorities. That did not happen – instead, in the years preceding the genocide, these hatreds were exacerbated by an extreme Turkish nationalism promoted by a new government – the Committee of Union and Progress (CUP) – made up of seemingly progressive nationalists, 'the Young Turks'. They were led by a triumvirate: Talaat Pasha, the Interior Minister and later Prime Minister (Grand Vizier); Enver Pasha (War Minister); and Cemal Pasha, and they were initially joined, in their reformist fervour, by the underground Dashnak party, hopeful that the overthrow of the Sultan might end Armenian woes.

Turkification

The Sultan remained as absolute ruler until 1908, when he was briefly forced to become a constitutional monarch and then sent into exile. The most powerful of the political forces pitted against him by the end of his reign was the Young Turk (*Ittida-hist*) movement, which had begun as a progressive underground party that was revolutionary enough to work with the Dashnaks, although it never ceded equality to Armenians. It led the Union and Progressive Party, the committee of which, the CUP, was in control of the government after the Sultan's exile. The Young Turks had strong support in the army at the time, although it was that same army which, in 1909, would perpetrate a massacre when sent to restore order after Armenian unrest in the city of Adana. The British vice-consul, an eyewitness to the killing in the city, estimated the loss of life at between 15,000 and 25,000; 'of these, very few, if any, can be Muslims'. The new government this time denounced the atrocity, but few were punished. The death toll served to remind the CUP of the vulnerability of the lives of its Armenian citizens and the danger of allowing racial hatreds to fester. Armenian leaders still looked to the Great Powers for protection and in early 1914 they at last obtained intervention of a sort: Turkey was reluctantly forced to sign the Armenian Reform Agreement, by which two foreign 'Inspector Generals' would oversee the security of the two million Armenians in eastern Anatolia, who formed about 30 per cent of the local population. The outbreak of war aborted this agreement, but not before it had provoked government hostility towards the Armenians for seeking foreign intervention and was added to a populist dislike of their wealth and success as merchants and money traders. The suggestion began to be officially propagated that Armenians were not part of a 'Turkish' nation.

An extreme nationalism entered the political soul of the CUP, which led to the development of the kind of race supremacy theories that are particularly associated with the prelude to genocide. At first called 'Ottomanism', and then 'Turkification', these theories argued for the cultural homogenisation of the country under an Islamic/Turkish identity with the pre-eminence of Sharia law and the Turkish language and a commitment to a 'Turkish strength' in schools and youth movements and the army which would end 'national decay'. The Young Turk government preached the racist idea that Turanian nationality was a badge of superiority, to the exclusion of non-Muslims and especially Christians; and this led to the public subhumanising of minority groups like

Armenians ('tubercular microbes') and Greeks. Its extreme nationalist fervour demanded a 'warrior nation' to prevent 'the decay of
the Turkish race'; a 'Turkification' programme for language and
culture; and the banning of Armenian organisations. The British
ambassador noted at this time the emergence of a violent 'Turkey
for the Turks' campaign: 'For them [the Young Turks] "Ottoman"
evidently means "Turk" and their present policy of "Ottomanisa-
tion" is one of pounding the non-Turkish elements in a Turkish
mortar.'[58] Others noted an added virulence in the language of
Turkish race theorists – Christians and Jews were 'cancers' and
'internal tumours' that needed to be 'cleansed'. There can be no
doubt that the 'Turkification' campaign stirred race hate, and it
was followed by government directives from Enver Pasha ordering that villages, rivers, towns etc. should be renamed if they
bore Christian or Armenian names.[59] A law of 1909 had banned
associations bearing the name 'Armenian' (or any other minority
race) and the Turkish language was made mandatory in private
as well as state schools.

'Turkification' certainly paved the way for the extirpation of
Armenians from Anatolia, and Turkish historian Taner Akçam
argues that after Enver's appointment as Minister of Defence
in January 1914, a series of secret meetings were held to discuss
ethnic cleansing. There came other straws (indeed, bricks) in the
wind in this countdown to genocide. After a secret agreement
to enter the war on the side of Germany (2 August) there was
a general mobilisation and Armenian men between fifteen and
forty-five were conscripted into the Ottoman army. In February
1915, all these soldiers were disarmed and transferred to labour
battalions,[60] where most were subsequently massacred, after doing
menial jobs behind the lines. Plans were made for resettling Muslim refugees from the 1913 Balkan defeats in areas 'cleansed' of
Armenians. A 'Special Organisation' was geared up to carry out

work which could not be publicly linked to the government. This was a secretive paramilitary body, led by regular army officers, charged with counter-terrorism: it kept files on Armenian leaders and intellectuals, and was blamed in the post-war trials for organising, under the direction of the CUP, some of the worst massacres of Armenian deportees.[61] These were committed by Muslim prisoners (*chettis*) it had released from jails and organised into squads for murders that would not be directly linked to the government or the army.

24 April 1915

Turkey formally entered the war on the side of Germany in November 1914, pursuant to the secret agreement in August, and immediately fired the first shots against Russia. It could have remained neutral, but Enver calculated that Germany would win, and the Empire would benefit from the alliance, especially if the victory neutralised Tsarist Russia. Shortly after entry, the Sunni Muslim religious head, a recent CUP appointee, declared *jihad* (holy war) against Christians (although the government's allies, Germans and Austro-Hungarians, were specifically exempted). Talaat and Cemal endorsed his *fatwa* by threatening reprisals against Armenians if Muslims were killed by Allied naval bombardment. Meanwhile, Enver mobilised the army and, like Napoleon, foolishly marched to do battle with Russia, in winter. After the army's disastrous defeat at Sarikamish (75,000 dead out of an army of 90,000) at the end of the year, its Armenian conscripts were publicly blamed for disloyalty.[62] Police were ordered to search Armenian homes for illegal arms and to arrest on any suspicion of treason. At this time it is likely that there were further CUP discussions on how to solve 'the Armenian question' because it called a conference on 26 February which planned to attack 'the enemy within'. An order on that date from the Interior Ministry required the deportation of some Armenian communities 'into the Anatolian desert'. This outraged the Armenian intellectuals and political leaders in Constantinople, where the Dashnak party had several MPs. Two months later, on 24 April, it was decided that removals would be to the more empty and more distant desert in Syria, and that Armenian leaders in Constantinople should no longer be in a position to protest – they were arrested, conveyed to army prisons, and in due course almost all were killed.

The deportations became official government policy in May, but they had begun, perhaps as test runs, as early as March. At Zeytun, for example, there had been an anti-government uprising in that month by army deserters and Hunchak party members, but the majority of the community had refused to join and its church leaders had in fact informed on the rebels. Nevertheless many were massacred and the whole community was deported, at first to barren salt lakes in the west, and then to the Syrian desert: most were killed or starved to death. Muslim refugees (*Muhascirs*) from the Balkan defeat and other Muslim families were moved immediately into the forcibly vacated homes, Armenian carvings and inscriptions of historic value were destroyed, and names of streets and places were 'Turkified'. This mini-genocide is significant because it happened in late March and early April, shortly before the uprising in Van which denialists use as evidence of a 'civil war'. The fate of the Armenians at Zeytun became a precedent for every other community in Anatolia as this fateful year progressed.[63]

Meanwhile, the war situation had become threatening. On the eastern border were Russian troops that had defeated the Ottoman army in January, whilst from the west the armies of

Britain and its Commonwealth were preparing their ill-fated attempt to storm the Dardanelles. It is no coincidence that on 24 April British warships hovered off Gallipoli in preparation for the landing on the 25th: this was the trigger for plans drawn up some time before, by those in the Special Organisation who compiled with lethal accuracy the lists of the names and addresses of Armenian intellectuals, priests and community and Dashnak leaders throughout the country. In Constantinople that night several hundred were seized and transported to military prisons near Ankara, where they were joined by several thousand of similar position arrested in the provinces. Most were subsequently executed without trial. One of the few survivors of the initial arrests describes how

> it seemed as if on one night, all the prominent Armenians of the capital – assemblymen, representatives, progressive thinkers, reporters, teachers, doctors, pharmacists, dentists, merchants and bankers – had made an appointment in those dim cells of the prison. More than a few people were still wearing their pyjamas, robes and slippers.[64]

Over eighty Armenian novelists and poets, together with hundreds of teachers, lecturers and professionals, were slaughtered over the coming months in one of the surest indicia of genocide: the killing of an ethnic group's writers and thinkers.

The date of 24 April is given another fateful significance by the fact that it was the day that Talaat ordered a change of direction for the deportations that had already been underway from Zeytun and elsewhere. He ordered the long, despairing columns to leave Anatolia and snake into the Syrian desert, to the south-east of Aleppo. From this day onwards, Anatolia was to be ethnically cleansed,[65] and most of those expelled from their home and homeland were to suffer a drawn-out torture before their deaths.

Another trigger – although its extent is much disputed – was an Armenian uprising in Van, the province bordering Russia, from which some local Armenians had left to join the Russian army. The trouble seems to have started with the hanging of a local Armenian schoolteacher and became inflamed when the district governor, who 'undoubtedly expected that by killing the leaders of the revolutionary parties, he would destroy the cohesion of the rebels',[66] by treachery had two Dashnak leaders assassinated. It escalated, and over several weeks of fighting there were heavy casualties on both sides – Christian missionaries who were eyewitnesses generally speak of massacres by the Ottoman troops and defensive fighting by the Armenians. The Russian army advanced and temporarily secured the city. It was the only example in 1915 when Armenian resistance was successful (and only for a few months – the Ottomans returned with a vengeance to retake the town in July): in other cities and villages throughout the country, rebellion seems to have been low level or non-existent. In Urfa the Armenians, alive to the memory of the cathedral massacre in 1895, barricaded themselves in their quarter within the city and held out for several months until the inevitable massacre, whilst at Musa Dagh on the Mediterranean, the townspeople refused their deportation orders and held out in the mountains for forty days until they could be rescued by a French warship.

The Deportations

Otherwise, from May to September, Anatolia was emptied of up to two million Armenians, pursuant to emergency deportation laws passed at the end of May. The Temporary Law of Deportation authorised army officials to deport populations on suspicion of treason, or for 'military necessity'. In the year of 1915, the government found it 'militarily necessary' to empty the whole of Anatolia – including many places which were far from the front-line towns which had no record of treacherous behaviour – and send the population on death marches to the desert. A decree in May 1915, dishonestly entitled *Administrative instructions regarding moveable and immoveable property abandoned by Armenians reported as a result of the war and the unusual political circumstances*, required registration of deportees' homes and properties, and in September came the first of the notorious laws providing for confiscation of their goods and properties and other assets. Many of their forcibly abandoned homes were quickly allocated to Muslim refugees from the Balkans and the Caucasus. Other property – bank accounts, buildings (homes, barns, mills), land (cultivated and uncultivated), farm equipment, personal possessions (jewellery, clothes, furniture and paintings), livestock and capital – were decreed 'abandoned' and seized by liquidation commissions. They were put up for sale – often at an undervalue, and often to CUP henchmen. The proceeds, when not embezzled or sent to secret bank accounts in Germany, went to the Ottoman Treasury.[67] At the same time, cultural property was destroyed or used for other purposes. The Armenian delegation at the Versailles Conference in 1919 claimed the loss of 1,860 churches, 229 monasteries, 1,438 schools, 42 orphanages and 29 seminaries.

The deportations – 'relocations' as the Turkish government euphemistically terms them – caused massive loss of life. Denialists generally admit 600,000 deaths, whilst Armenian scholars (and contemporary politicians) place the losses at 1.5 million. One objective historian concludes that they were not less than 800,000 and not more than 1.2 million.[68] The evacuations of Armenians were ordered by central government – it passed the law in May, although Talaat and his Ministry of the Interior gave the first order as early as February, and four months later – on 24 June – ordered the deportation of 'all Armenians without exception' to distant places where they were forbidden to open schools and could not settle if by doing so they would count as more than 10 per cent of the local Muslim population. Most ended up in disease-ridden starvation camps in the desert around Der Zor, reached after hundreds of miles marched to Aleppo (the much-battered city in modern Syria). This area was well known for the harshness of its climate, and for the savagery of the Bedouin tribes who then roamed it. There was no possibility of agriculture or any sustainable crop: only recently the government had been told of its utter inhospitality for resettling the *Muhacir* refugees from the Balkans – 'they would all be dead of hunger', Talaat had told Parliament in 1914.[69] He and most of the CUP leadership (some of whom were themselves refugees from the Balkans) well knew that deportation was likely to mean death, and those who did not were soon apprised of the fact that death usually came even before the barren destination was reached. The deportee columns of women and children and old men were guarded by a few Turkish policemen who did not protect them from looting, rape and kidnap by *chettis* (released prisoners under Special Organisation control) or marauding Kurds, who carried off many of the girls to sell into sexual slavery and killed the young children. In the desert camps outside Der Zor and Aleppo, many died from starvation, others from typhus and dysentery. The government continued to disrupt relief efforts by American and German missionaries: Talaat ordered that any Turkish official assisting them to relieve misery and starvation in the camps should be severely punished.[70]

The deportations from Anatolia ordered by Talaat in May were followed by deportation orders for all other Armenian groups throughout eastern Turkey. A few local officials refused to carry out the orders – an indication that some government agents realised their deadly consequences and were prepared to face punishment for disobedience. The homes and property of Armenians were pillaged or seized. Little or no food was made available to those ordered to march through the desert or forced aboard packed trains and tens of thousands were to die from starvation and disease. There was no security, and columns of people were set upon, their members robbed, raped, abducted or killed – by Kurdish brigands, by Special Organisation death squads, by paramilitaries and by police under the control of party officials or local governors. There were no safe havens already prepared to receive them: a credible US fact-finding mission in 1919 (the Harbord Report) concluded that

> the women, old men and children were, after a few days, deported to what Talaat Pasha called 'agricultural colonies' – from the high cool breeze-swept plateau of Armenia to the malarial flats of the Euphrates and the burning sands of Syria and Arabia.[71]

Hundreds of thousands were killed on these marches, because they were Armenians and because they had been deliberately ordered to suffer what the Genocide Convention describes as 'conditions of life calculated to bring about their destruction in whole or in part' – a very substantial part on any calculation. Talaat's orders, in cables to local officials, were to bring the Armenian problem to 'a final end, in a comprehensive and absolute way'.[72] Morgenthau cites telegrams from Talaat ordering orphanages to reject Armenian children whose parents died on the marches because 'the government ... considers the survival of these children as

detrimental'. Many thousands of women were abducted or acqui-
esced in conversion to Islam in order to save their lives, or the
lives of their children.[73] Forcible religious conversion is another
indicator of genocide.

In 1915, the extent to which racial hatred had been whipped
up by the ideology of 'Turkification', and to an extent by ancient
religious hatreds, became very clear. There are credible eyewitness reports of whole communities being liquidated – by means
including mass burnings, drowning and asphyxiation at desert
camps. Most Armenian conscripts had been taken out of Ottoman army units in February 1915 and consigned to labour camps:
later in the year, in many camps they were executed. So too were
able-bodied men left in the Anatolian villages, victims of the
notorious ex-prisoner killing squads (*chettis*) organised by the
Special Organisation. Meanwhile, old men, children and women
were the vulnerable victims of the marches through the desert.
Some young women were able to survive by offering themselves
as brides whilst others were spared by converting to Islam. Some
children were forcibly removed and placed with Muslim families (Article II(e) of the Genocide Convention identifies 'forcibly
transferring children of the group to another group' as an act of
genocide if committed with the requisite intent). British historian Cathie Carmichael provides an accurate summary of facts
that today's Turkish government cannot dispute:[74]

> Deportations from different locations, initiated by govern-
> ment telegrams, involved the rounding up and killing of some
> Armenians on the spot. Many were also subjected to the wrath
> of their neighbours and put on the open road with no pro-
> tection. Although they were nominally 'deported', most of
> the Armenians died of exposure, disease, starvation or violent
> attack, either from gendarmes or from bands of Kurds in the

mountains. In the Black Sea port of Trebizond [Trabzon], the local community was taken out to sea and drowned. Many women were violated and murdered in front of their families. At least two-thirds of the 'deportees' did not survive this treatment; those few who did eked out a precarious existence in refugee camps in Syria or in Russian-controlled areas … Within a few weeks, an entire community had effectively been destroyed forever. About one million Armenians died, approximately half of the pre-war population, but their community was never reconstructed within Anatolia itself … The deportations and massacres had effectively used violence to solve what European diplomats had been calling 'the Armenian question' for decades. As Donald Bloxham has argued the massacres 'enabled the Committee of Union and Progress to secure Anatolia as an ethnically 'purified' core area for the development for the Turkish people'.[75]

Many 'survivors' of the death marches lost their lives in the disease-ridden 'refugee camps' in Syria, which were not supplied with food or medicine or shelter other than tents. Aleppo became the crossroads for the deportee caravans, ordered south-east into a network of camps along the Euphrates River towards the town of Der Zor.

Witnesses speak of unburied corpses along the road by a river down which floated dead bodies roped together. One recalls the scene that met her when her convoy reached the camp at Katma:

> The sight before me was horrible beyond description. Hundreds and hundreds of swollen bodies lay in the mud and puddles of rain water, some half-buried, others floating eerily in rancid pools, together with rotted bodies and heaps of human refuse accumulated during the week-long rain. Some

victims – only the upper torsos emerging from the mud and puddles – were breathing their last. The stench rose to the heavens. It was nauseating beyond belief. The scene was like a huge cesspool laid bare and made to stink even more under a hot sun. There was no chance of finding safe drinking water. Any water in the area would have been contaminated. It was the ideal breeding ground for the incubation of typhus, typhoid, cholera, smallpox, dysentery and other scourges resulting from such unsanitary conditions.

The two German consuls at Aleppo frantically called Berlin about the scale of the disaster and the danger that by promoting Ottoman denials, Germany might itself become complicit. 'Against the assurances of the Sublime Porte to the contrary, all comes down to the destruction of the Armenian people,' said Walter Rössler. He explained that the Ottoman 'justification' was nonsense: 'Does the Sublime Porte consider the continued shipment of sick people and children as a political and military necessity?'[76] He called 'indescribable' the scenes at Katma, some of which were indelibly caught on the camera of Armin Wegner, a German paramedic. Others were described in horrific detail by German and Swiss nurses and aid workers, not to mention bankers and railway supervisors (Deutsche Bank was financing the railway to Baghdad, which was used to carry deportees from western provinces). Franz Gunther, a Deutsche Bank executive, even sent a photograph of a deportation train to his directors, as an example of the 'bestial cruelty' of the Ottoman government – cruelty that the bank was funding.[77] Rössler's vice-consul, Hoffman, reported that allowing rape of the deportees had become an official policy that the government did not bother to hide. By October 1915 he estimated the death toll at 600,000 and rising, and quoted one CUP official, with whom he had interceded, replying, 'You still don't understand what we want: we want to eradicate the Armenian name,' whilst another had said, 'We want an Armenia without Armenians.'[78] The deportations and massacres continued until July 1916, when the German ambassador, Metternich, informed Berlin that 'the Armenian persecutions in the eastern provinces have entered their last phase' – their object was 'the elimination of the Armenian question through the extermination of the Armenian race'.[79]

Much of the racial hostility towards the Armenians, as with the Jews later in Germany, derived from their wealth and their disproportionate representation in the ranks of merchants, bankers, lawyers and doctors. What then became of their money, after all of their property fell into the hands of 'liquidation commissions' set up for the purpose of acquiring their assets? Talaat infamously asked US Ambassador Morgenthau for a list of all Armenians holding policies with American life assurance companies: 'They are practically all dead now and have left no heirs to collect the money. It of course all escheats to the state. The government is the beneficiary now.'[80] The ambassador angrily refused, but the episode demonstrates the mentality of CUP nationalists who believed themselves entitled to the wealth that the crafty Armenians had in some way purloined from the Turkish people. Assets and properties (houses, shops, bank deposits etc.) expropriated without compensation under the Abandoned Properties Act would be worth trillions today. Not a penny has ever been paid in recompense to survivors or descendants: it went to the state, for the rehousing of Muslim refugees and into the pockets of CUP officials. Some funds were embezzled, it is alleged, by *Ittihadist* leaders, and ended up in their secret bank accounts in Berlin.[81] Norman Stone writes of these 'grubby tales': 'In Ankara or Kayseri, there were substantial Armenian populations, doing no one any harm. They had prosperity, sometimes substantial. They too were deported and associates of the CUP stole the properties, to their families' subsequent and often significant enrichment.'[82]

There are some reported cases, upon which denialists place great emphasis, of charges brought and sometimes punishment inflicted upon low-level Turkish officials and Kurdish brigand leaders for unlawful actions in relation to Armenian property. But some of these defendants were selected because they were hostile to the central government, whilst the crimes were cases of embezzlement and profiteering kept secret from the state, or from higher-up officials who might have expected to benefit. There can be no denying that it was 'lawful' – because laws specifically provided for the seizure of the 'abandoned' goods and land of extirpated Armenians, and for 'liquidation commissions' that confiscated and consigned to the state and its cronies whatever they could grasp. What remains palpable is that no denialist historian has come up with evidence of a single judgment or official decision which ordered the return of property to an Armenian owner – then or indeed in the century that followed. This fact speaks for itself.

CHAPTER 3

THE EVIDENCE

Witnesses

....

THE FACTS SET out starkly in Chapter 2 are supported by a mass of compelling evidence from the most reliable sources in the place and the period and have been confirmed by US investigators immediately after the war and by trials in Constantinople at which CUP officials were convicted of mass-murdering Armenians. This chapter marshals some of this material, which any forensic investigation would find credible. For example, there are hundreds of contemporary accounts of these appalling events. Many were by eyewitnesses: journalists (notably from the *New York Times*), German bankers, missionaries (including German Christian missionaries), aid organisers and consular officials (especially US vice-consuls reporting as anxious neutrals and German officials reporting as anxious allies). Some of the most telling accounts, which attest to the genocidal intentions of Talaat and other high-ranking political figures, were written in despatches or in subsequent books by Western diplomats. Few eyewitnesses to any crime are unaffected by what they see or the eyes through which they see it. German diplomats and businesspeople and army officers were the most obviously impartial, because their nation was an ally of the Turks, whilst Christian missionaries tended to see events through Armenian eyes for the very good reason that they had been mainly teaching Armenians and were often hostages in barricaded Armenian quarters of towns under attack by Ottoman forces. They testify with honest eloquence to the terror, although less certainly to Turkish motivations.

The American ambassador Henry Morgenthau (whose cables alerted Washington to the 'race extinction' by 'terrible tortures, expulsions and massacres') repeatedly interceded with Talaat and says that he was told to mind his own business: 'Let us do with these Christians as we please.' He had no doubt that what he described as 'this attempt to exterminate a race' was not a response to fanatical popular demands, but was a policy 'directed from Constantinople'.[83] His opinion of the 'military necessity' justification, advanced by the Ottomans at the time, was dismissive. As he telegrammed the State Department,

> Reports from widely scattered districts indicate systematic
> attempts to uproot peaceful Armenian populations and
> through arbitrary arrests, terrible tortures, wholesale expul-
> sions and deportations from one end of the Empire to the
> other accompanied by frequent instances of rape, pillage,

> and murder, turning into massacre, to bring destruction and destitution on them. These measures are not in response to popular or fanatical demand but are purely arbitrary and directed from Constantinople in the name of military necessity, often in districts where no military operations are likely to take place.

German diplomats had no motive to lie when reporting on the behaviour of an ally. The German ambassador in the latter part of 1915, Count Wolff-Metternich, reported to Berlin that 'the CUP demands the extirpation of the last remnants of Armenians … and the government must yield. Turkification means a licence to expel, to kill or destroy everything that is not Turkish, and to violently take possession of the goods of others.'[84] The German vice-consul in Erzurum reported that the cruelty of CUP measures would mean 'the certain death' of the Armenian deportees. He said that the CUP 'are bluntly admitting that the purpose of their actions is the total obliteration of the Armenians. As an authoritative person word-for-word declared, "We will have in Turkey no more Armenians after the war."'[85]

Examples abound from diplomats – having met with Talaat and other leaders – reporting conversations redolent of genocidal intent. Talaat told the German ambassador, for example, on 17 June 1915 that he wished 'to use the world war as a pretext for cleansing the country of its internal enemies – namely the Armenian population'.[86] The German government delivered several protest notes over what it correctly termed 'the systematic slaughter of the Armenian people who had been deported from their homes … which the [Ottoman] government apparently supported'.[87] Evidence from German diplomats counts a great deal: Germany was the Ottoman government's close ally, and its generals commanded sections of the Ottoman army and were in regular contact with their nation's consular officials, who had no motive to distort or exaggerate. Their fear of being tarnished by an alliance with those guilty of what they described as 'systematic slaughter of Armenians' would today be termed a fear of complicity with genocide.

That Germany was complicit is beyond doubt. It continued to support the Ottoman government whilst its diplomats and consuls were reporting to Berlin not only on the facts of the massacres and deportations but on the intention behind them, an intention plainly stated in meetings they held with Talaat and other ministers. Until August 1915 its ambassador in Constantinople was Hans von Wangenheim, who reported as early as 17 June that Talaat 'wanted to use the war in order to thoroughly clean out its domestic enemies – the native Christians'. The ambassador made clear his assessment that the attacks on Armenians were not motivated or justified by military considerations. On 7 July, he confirmed this assessment, pointing out that deadly deportations were extending to provinces not threatened with invasion and that the Ottoman claim of 'military necessity' – Turkey's argument today – was bogus. The government was 'in fact pursuing the aim of destroying the Armenian race in the Turkish Empire'.[88] His replacement later in the year was Count Wolff-Metternich, who complained so insistently to the Ottoman government about its treatment of Armenians that it demanded his recall (Berlin complied with this request the following year).

The German embassy in Constantinople was receiving reports from German bankers, builders, engineers, teachers and doctors, as well as Catholic and Lutheran missionaries and a large consular staff throughout the country. German visitors to Turkey had no doubt about the intention: as the head of Deutsche Bank put it, 'The Jewish pogroms in Russia, which I know, are comparative child's play.'[89] Visiting German politicians were left in no doubt either: Gustav Stresemann, a future Weimar Chancellor, was told there had been about 1.5 million Armenian deaths, as was Matthias Erzberger, leader of the largest party in the Reichstag. Even General Ludendorff, the German arch-nationalist, described Armenian suffering as 'not to be justified by anything' and German government documents published at the end of the war were full of the horrors perpetrated under the eyes and noses of its diplomats and their sources.[90] As the Erzurum consul put it, when asked whether there was not some general uprising by the Armenians which might justify their slaughter, 'Any proof whatsoever, in my view, is lacking.' This consul was actually an undercover military officer, Max Erwin von Scheubner-Richter, whose job was to infiltrate Muslims and encourage them to spy on the Russian forces. He was in a position to judge the Ottoman claim of military necessity, and was no bleeding heart – he subsequently became Hitler's lieutenant and died in the Munich Beer Hall Putsch. His concern to save the Armenians came from a nationalist's desire to protect 'the honour of Germany's escutcheon'.[91]

The German diplomatic despatches also identify some of the perpetrators of the barbaric violence visited upon the Armenians in outlying districts of Anatolia by provincial governors, accountable to a central government which must have known and approved of their actions. To take but one notorious example, Dr Mehmed Reşid was a close associate of Talaat and governor of Diyarbakır province. He was the subject of a cable to the Reich Chancellor, reporting that he 'has begun the systematic extermination of the Christian population in his province, without distinguishing between race or creed'. On 12 July, Wangenheim lodged an official protest with Talaat against his 'regular massacres of Christians' and in particular his round-up of 700 Armenians, including their bishop, whom he had driven away at night and 'slaughtered like sheep'.[92] But Reşid was Talaat's protégé – and his mistake was to have killed Assyrian Christians along with the Armenians and to have been found out by the Germans.

A trained medical doctor, Reşid was fond of dehumanising Armenians as 'microbes' within the 'organism of the fatherland'. He wrote, 'We will liquidate them before they liquidate us … My Turkishness triumphed over my identity as a doctor … The Armenian bandits were a load of harmful microbes that had afflicted the body of the fatherland. Was it not the duty of the doctor to kill the microbes?'[93]

Reşid boasted that he had 'removed' 120,000 'microbes' in massacres or by death from typhus in his prisons or on deportation death marches. There was no uprising in his province, and his systematic persecution of Armenians began before the uprising in Van. 'Self-defence' and 'military necessity' could be no excuse for this barbarism, and the Germans knew it: they complained of the 'incomprehensible irresponsibility' of his vendettas, which were causing 'growing unrest among the local population'.[94] The atrocities continued as Dr Reşid busied himself supervising the seizure of his victims' property and the transfer of their homes to Muslims. He was the subject of an interesting cable sent to Berlin on 10 September, pointing out that he was different to most other provincial governors, whose policy was to massacre the Armenian men and send the women and children on deportation convoys to Syria, where they had some chance of survival. Reşid, however, was happy to massacre them all.[95] For him, they were lice on the body politic, referred to as 'tumours' and 'bloodsuckers' – the language of dehumanisation which routinely flourishes in the course of genocide (in Rwanda, the Tutsis were usually described as 'cockroaches', whilst leaders of the Serb Republic regularly referred to their Muslim neighbours as 'tubercular microbes').

America in 1915 was neutral, but its diplomats were shocked to the core by what they witnessed. US vice-consul Leslie Davis, an experienced lawyer, had no doubt in his cables in 1915 and his subsequent autobiography *The Slaughterhouse Province* that the government was bent on destroying the Armenian race along with repositories of its culture. On one trip through eastern Anatolia he counted 'the remains of not less than 10,000 Armenians ... nearly all of them women, lain flat on their backs and showing signs of barbarous mutilation by the bayonets of the gendarmes'.[96] Jesse B. Jackson, the hardened US diplomat who served as consul in Aleppo, 1915–16, described in his despatches the local towns and districts 'where Armenians have already been practically exterminated' and called the Turkish government's scheme (misdescribed as a law relating to 'abandoned property') as 'a gigantic plundering scheme as well as a final blow to extinguish the [Armenian] race'.[97] Both American and German consular officials remarked on the government policy of encouraging those who survived the death marches to obtain protection by converting to Islam – in circumstances which amounted to forcible religious conversion, an all too familiar indicum of genocide.[98] They tell how officials were content for many of the girls to be kidnapped and sold into sexual slavery, although orphaned boys under thirteen were taken to state orphanages to be brought up as Muslims.

There are many statements corroborative of genocide from Christian missionaries and aid workers, not to mention the books and other writings and correspondence of survivors. Common to most of these 'first person' accounts is a depiction of a race-hate element in the killings, the beatings and the rapes, sometimes emanating from officials, sometimes from attackers who were connected with the army or the Special Organisation, and sometimes from the marauding Kurds. There can be no doubt, from all these sources, that there was a systematic pattern of racial attacks on vulnerable and starving columns of displaced Armenian women and children and old men as they trudged through the eastern provinces towards Syria. This result could and should have been foreseen and in any event it took place over a number of months without any official intervention to stop the killings or to protect the deportees.

Further corroboration of the evidence of diplomats from all major countries, and the reports of the missionaries and the journalists and the businessmen, comes from interned English residents and prisoners of war. Captured Australians taken to Akroinos recall in diaries how 'thousands of Armenians were turned out of these big towns to starve and thousands were massacred'.[99] Another Australian's prison was a neighbourhood of empty houses of Armenians 'murdered or driven out of town in the name of "ethnic cleansing" and the grounds of the prison camp were repeatedly sown with the remains of some of those victims'.[100] Other POWs saw out the war in Armenian churches that had been turned into prison camps: the common estimate was that one million Armenians had perished.[101]

The Blue Book

The number and consistency of newspaper reports and photographs in 1915 could leave little doubt that the Armenians were at the mercy of a government-instigated process that doomed them to death or gave them a less than 50 per cent chance of surviving a life-threatening environment. That was the news, even under repressive wartime censorship in Turkey, and in Germany, where the government did not want to have its ally criticised. The earliest compilation of first-hand accounts, from Red Cross nurses and missionaries and visiting businessmen, as well as from journalists, was produced by and for the British government in 1916. *The Treatment of the Armenians in the Ottoman Empire, 1915–16*[102] was a large collection of documents edited by the distinguished historian Arnold Toynbee, and endorsed by two other eminent British historians, H. A. L. Fisher and Gilbert Murray. The 'Blue Book' (as it came to be known, by the name given to such government publications) had been commissioned by Viscount Bryce, head of British wartime propaganda, who was notorious for publishing lurid and apparently invented claims about German atrocities in Belgium. His association with the Blue Book has been used to discredit Toynbee's work, and Phillip Knightley, author of *The First Casualty*, points out that the plethora of invented atrocity stories about the Germans meant that the true accounts from Turkey by war correspondents were discounted. Both *The Times* and, in Paris, *Le Journal* published horrifying stories about the atrocities the Turks were committing against the Armenians, but 'their detailed and damning accusations were lost in the welter of false and exaggerated propaganda of the period'.[103]

Recent scholarship has somewhat rehabilitated Bryce's reputation, because it has shown that some of his 'propaganda' attacks on the Germans were all too true (the Kaiser's army did execute, with utter ruthlessness, 6,500 innocent French and Belgian civilians between August and November 1914).[104] The Blue Book cannot be written off as the Turkish government would wish by claiming that Toynbee himself admitted it was propaganda. He did no such thing and insisted throughout his long and distinguished life that it was genuine, despite mentioning in one book the irony that it 'was duly published and distributed as war propaganda!' The Turkish government does not understand British irony or the purpose of Toynbee's use of an exclamation mark. In the same book Toynbee speaks of 'an attempt to exterminate the Armenians in 1915. In this case hundreds of thousands of people were done to death and thousands turned into robbers and murderers by the administrative action of a few dozen criminals in control of the Ottoman Empire.'[105]

The Turkish government in 2005 went so far as to demand an apology from Britain for publishing this 'anti-Turkish propaganda'. This extraordinary request, signed by both its Prime Minister and the leader of the opposition, may have been gestated by Justin McCarthy, the main denialist historian, who claims that the Blue Book evidence comprises 'false documents produced by the British propaganda office'[106] with some of its sources traced to Dashnak newspapers which 'had a tradition of not telling the truth'.[107] (The last point is not necessarily a criticism, since McCarthy often relies on Dashnak news and conference papers).[108] McCarthy's attack on Toynbee fails to demonstrate that the Blue Book is fictitious or that any single one of its accounts was invented by British propagandists.[109] Ironically, McCarthy's investigations actually showed that Toynbee *rejected* some reports because he could not establish the source, or because the source had relied on hearsay.[110] It may be that Toynbee should have done more checking and was too ready to provide anonymity, but he did not fabricate and there is certainly no good reason to ignore the fifty eyewitness testimonies he collected from identified people who were there at the time.

Witnesses to one side of the truth are useful if their testimony is corroborated, and statements issued as propaganda are not, for that reason, necessarily false (the more truthful the statement, the better it serves the propagandist's cause). Back in 1915, there was no cover-up of the fact that the Blue Book was compiled on behalf of the British government, which openly published it, and over one third of the statements were attributed by name to missionaries, consuls and journalists. Toynbee, as editor, said that he anonymised the rest in order to protect those who might suffer reprisals or whose work in Anatolia might be closed down if their identities were revealed. This is certainly a problem in any country where dissidents can 'disappear' and their relatives and organisations are at risk of being targeted. Although Toynbee can be criticised for using terms such as 'traveller' or 'foreign resident' to disguise the fact that the author was a missionary, in this he was guilty of excess of caution rather than deliberate untruth.

The Blue Book is a voluminous repository of evidence, carefully edited, province by Anatolian province, so the reader can appreciate the overall picture as well as the detail of particular incidents. Some contributions have been translated into English, but none has been shown to be invented and all are internally consistent. If they had been fabricated by British Intelligence then it would have done a better job – it might, for example, have forged cables and conversations in which Talaat and his henchmen speak clearly and crudely of extermination. The reason Toynbee was convinced that a few dozen CUP officials were criminally responsible for mass murder was that they intentionally directed and supervised arrests and deportations which they knew would produce a massive death toll of the targeted race, in circumstances which no 'military necessity' or civil war could justify.

What emerges from 150 statements by journalists, eyewitnesses, missionaries, Red Cross nurses and diplomats is that in most towns and villages where Armenians had a significant presence (they comprised about 30 per cent of the local population) there was no predisposition by community leaders to rebel or cause trouble. That came in a few places as a result of official corruption, especially where young Armenians were forced to pay a special tax to exempt themselves from conscription, or had other grievances. These grievances became more heated in consequence of the orders that went to all provincial authorities on 24 April 1915, directing them to arrest suspected 'subversives' – a group that came to include bishops and apolitical community leaders as well as members of the Armenian nationalist societies such as the Dashnaks. These societies were lawful – the Dashnaks had been on good terms with the Young Turks before the war, having cooperated with the CUP in overthrowing the Sultan, and even had a number of elected MPs, although they were readily suspected of disloyalty by the Special Organisation. In May came the official deportation orders, usually implemented by arresting the able-bodied men who had not been conscripted and having them either killed (often by ex-prisoner gangs under the direction of the Special Organisation) or moved to army labour camps to join the Armenian conscripts. The old men, the women and the children would be sent packing, marching hundreds of miles into the desert, in long columns guarded by only a few policemen. The columns set out on foot for Der Zor, in a desert near Aleppo, but were subjected en route to banditry, rape and murder by gangs of Kurdish brigands, whilst disease (typhus and dysentery especially) or starvation killed many who survived the marches. The Blue Book makes no secret of the CUP's fears that Armenians would rebel in order to achieve an independent state but, as the United Press correspondent pointed out,

> The terrible feature of this deportation up to date is that it has been carried out on such a basis as to render it practically impossible in thousands of cases that these families can ever again be reunited … This has been decided upon as necessary to secure the supremacy of the Turkish race in the Ottoman Empire, which is one of the basic principles of the Young Turk party.[111]

By July, everyone knew what the deportations meant: 'It is simply a scheme for extermination of the Armenian nation wholesale, without any fuss. It is just another form of massacre, and a more horrible form.'[112] By August, there were estimates of one million deportees. In Constantinople, the Armenian elite had been arrested and disposed of by the round-up on 24 April, and the rest of the intelligentsia were deported later in the year – this time by train (the Anatolian Railway) to the Arabian Desert.[113] The Blue Book contains heart-rending accounts of forced conversions and marriage of young girls to Muslims, either through threats or simply through the realisation that there was no other way to save their lives. Some teenage girls captured from the convoys were sold at auction. There were credible German reports of mass drownings in the Tigris and Euphrates rivers, and lengthy reports from American missionaries based in Van, pinning responsibility for the unrest on the local governor, Djevdet Bey, who had summoned local leaders to discuss peace and then had two of them killed, whilst the men who resisted conscription were shot.[114] There was evidence from Red Cross nurses that the convoys were left defenceless to attacks by marauding Kurds, who robbed their cargoes and killed or carried off their occupants.

The drownings at Trabzon (also spelled Trebizond) were described in harrowing detail,[115] especially by the Italian consul general, who lived there and tried vainly to save some of the victims. He spoke to an Italian newspaper in August 1915:

> There were about 14,000 Armenians at Trebizond – Gregorians, Catholics, and Protestants. They had never caused disorders or given occasion for collective measures of police. When I left Trebizond, not a hundred of them remained.
>
> From 24 June until 23 July, the date of my own departure from Trebizond, I no longer slept or ate; I was given over to nerves and nausea, so terrible was the torment of having to look on at the wholesale execution of these defenceless, innocent creatures.

The passing of the gangs of Armenian exiles beneath the windows and before the door of the consulate; their prayers for help, when neither I nor any other could do anything to answer them; the city in a state of siege, guarded at every point by 15,000 troops in complete war equipment, by thousands of police agents, by bands of volunteers and by the members of the 'Committee of Union and Progress'; the lamentations, the tears, the abandonments, the imprecations, the many suicides, the instantaneous deaths from sheer terror, the sudden unhinging of men's reason, the conflagrations, the shooting of victims in the city, the ruthless searches through the houses and in the countryside; the hundreds of corpses found every day along the exile road; the young women converted by force to Islam or exiled like the rest; the children torn away from their families or from the Christian schools, and handed over by force to Moslem families, or else placed by hundreds on board ship in nothing but their shirts, and then capsized and drowned in the Black Sea...[116]

The Blue Book papers also deal with Zeytun, where conscription rather than Dashnak revolutionary fervour caused an Armenian protest which was brutally put down.[117] Time and again, these statements insist that the villages in eastern Anatolia were peaceful, with no community support for revolt, until their leaders were arrested as a result of the 24 April order, or until local police began searches and seizures of Armenian property, or after announcement of general deportation orders in May and June. Then the Armenians would retreat to their quarter in the town, barricade it and wait for the attacks, which were usually successful, other than in Van, where the Ottoman troops fled from the Russian army but returned two months later after that army had withdrawn.

The Blue Book was not just a massive compilation of

72

contemporary documents: it concluded with a lengthy and masterful interpretation of their contents by Arnold Toynbee – the first authoritative analysis of what had happened in Anatolia in 1915. It was followed, and to similar effect, by two books of evidence compiled by the Lutheran missionary Johannes Lepsius, published in Germany in 1918. These contemporary reports were made available long before 'genocide' was identified as an international crime, although Toynbee's conclusion reads like an indictment:

> There is no dispute as to what happened in 1915. The Armenian inhabitants of the Ottoman Empire were everywhere uprooted from their homes, and deported to the most remote and unhealthy districts that the Government could select for them. Some were murdered at the outset, some perished on the way, and some died after reaching their destination. The death toll amounts to upwards of six hundred thousand; perhaps six hundred thousand more are still alive in their place of exile; and the remaining six hundred thousand or so have either been converted forcibly to Islam, gone into hiding in the mountains, or escaped beyond the Ottoman frontier. The Ottoman Government cannot deny these facts, and they cannot justify them. No provocation or misdemeanour on the part of individual Armenians could justify such a crime against the whole race.[118]

Toynbee refuted the two justifications for the deportations which the Turkish government uses today:

> 1. The Armenians at Van took up arms and joined the Russian enemy forces: the deportations were therefore necessary to forestall uprisings elsewhere in Anatolia.

The Armenians at Van did not revolt – they defended their quarter against aggression by troops under orders from the Turkish governor, Djevdet Bey. The local Armenian leaders were opposed to any uprising. In any event, the deportations from Zeytun and other parts of Cilicia had begun before the so-called 'revolt' at Van, and the deportations continued from places that were nowhere near the front line and which no 'military necessity' could justify.

> 2. There was a general conspiracy throughout the Empire to bring about Armenian independence. Prompt government action in disarming and deporting the whole people averted such an outcome.

This cannot stand with evidence that the great majority of religious and community leaders in the villages remained loyal. The 'revolutionary' Dashnak party had initially supported the Young Turks, to such an extent that the ban on Armenians obtaining arms had been lifted, and large numbers of Armenians had fought in the Turkish army in the Balkans in 1912/13. Toynbee noted Talaat's reference to 'the sad events that have occurred in Armenia … we have been reproached for making no distinction between the innocent Armenians and the guilty; but that was utterly impossible, in view of the fact that *those who were innocent today might be guilty tomorrow*' (my italics). Preventative detention and removal of a whole people was, by this admission, Talaat's objective. In the same interview, he said, 'Our acts have been dictated to us by a national and historic necessity. The idea of guaranteeing the existence of Turkey must outweigh every other consideration.'[119] The Nazis would feel much the same, thirty years later, about the 'necessity' for the Holocaust.

Toynbee was himself no propagandist: he went out of his way to pay tribute to the humanity of the Turkish troops at Gallipoli and recorded acts of kindness by individual Turks. Nor did his head-count conform to the 1.5 million that pro-Armenian groups, then and now, estimate as the toll of victims. He noted the uncertainty of contemporary demographics (the Ottoman government counted only 1.1 million Armenians in Anatolia, whilst the Armenian Patriarchate, more likely to be accurate, counted 2.1 million) and was prepared to accept a conservative figure of 600,000 casualties from massacres and deportations (ironically, the figure the Turkish government concedes today) with a further 600,000 who saved themselves, under duress, by conversion to Islam, or escaped to Russia or Egypt. Toynbee had no hesitation in holding the central government, and in particular the leaders of the CUP, responsible for an extermination policy. The 'fundamental uniformity of procedure' in all the various districts provided 'damning evidence' of pre-planned and systematic ethnic cleansing, beginning with the decree that ordered disarmament of all Armenians, followed by the round-ups of their leaders in April and the deportations which began tentatively in March but were formalised by the law passed in May. Those laws required surrender of the able-bodied men (who were killed or placed in army labour battalions), seizure of property, and the despatching of the old men, women and children on the death convoys, which in turn were beset by infectious deadly diseases – typhus especially – and set upon by brigands – Kurds from the mountains – and *chettis* released from the prisons. Those who survived were marooned without food or shelter, and without able-bodied menfolk, in the harshest of climates and in places where typhus, cholera and dysentery were rife. The central government, Toynbee argued, bears overall responsibility: it passed the deportation law, for implementation by its local governors, overseen by the chairman of the local branch of the Committee of Union and Progress in every town, and there were a few police charged with supervising the convoys – they often joined in the looting and did nothing to deter attackers. The general plan was clear:

> The months of April and May were assigned to the clearance of Cilicia; June and July were reserved for the east; the western centres along the Railway were given their turn in August and September; and at the same time the process was extended, for completeness' sake, to the outlying Armenian communities in the extreme south-east. It was a deliberate, systematic attempt to eradicate the Armenian population throughout the Ottoman Empire and it has certainly met with a very large measure of success.[120]

Photographic Evidence

A mainstay of the evidence for human rights violations is the picture worth a thousand words – of raped and executed bodies naked on a Sri Lankan beach or Bosnian Serb firing squads being blessed by Orthodox priests before liquidating Muslim men and boys at Srebrenica. The first – and most impactful – film proving war crimes was shown in court during the Nuremberg trial, when grainy pictures of conditions at Auschwitz and Belsen caused Goering and other defendants to hang their heads in shame. Photo-journalism can encapsulate a crime against humanity – the iconic examples from Vietnam, of a young Vietcong suspect having his brains blown out and a naked girl fleeing from her napalmed village, are in Armin Wegner's phrase 'images that horrify and indict'. Such images can also be manipulated and fabricated, although the techniques for doing so were rudimentary in 1915. That is reassuring in relation to the authenticity of photographs from the period, although this was a time when 'photography meant still photography and involved the arduous, time-consuming adjustment of photographic plates'.[121] Moreover, war photography was dangerous: coming up close to refugees infected with typhus was a health hazard, and the commander of the Fourth Ottoman Army in Syria had in any event banned any photography of the deportees out of concern they would expose Turkish cruelty. Neither danger deterred Armin T. Wegner, a German hospital orderly whose conscience did not allow him to lower his camera:

> I have taken numerous photographs. They tell me that Jamal Pasha, the hangman of Syria has forbidden the photographing of the refugee camps on pain of death. I carry these images that horrify and indict under my cummerbund … I do not doubt for a moment that I am committing an act of high treason and yet the knowledge of having helped those most wretched people at least in a slight respect fills me with a feeling of greater fortune than could any other deed.[122]

The twin deterrents – disease and a prosecution for treason – cancelled themselves out. Turkish officials and German army superiors were afraid to venture into typhus-ridden camps, so Wegner was not caught for some time, and was able to smuggle his pictures back to Germany where he later gave lectures deploring his own nation's passivity over the Armenian annihilation. His photographs of the disease-ridden tent cities outside Aleppo, of half-starved women, alive at the end of the death march and carrying their few possessions and their small children, provide a moving testimony to the awful truth of the deportations. Other relevant photographic evidence has been provided by the work of Near East Relief – an American Christian initiative which concentrated upon the rescue of Armenian orphans (it harboured some

30,000 of them in a vast orphanage at Alexandropol, just over the Russian border). Another conscience-stricken German, a high-school teacher in Aleppo named Dr Martin Niepage, worked with the consul, Hoffman, in order to report the atrocities direct to the German parliament. Niepage wrote about the appalling conditions of the deportees who managed to reach the high school, and Hoffman photographed 'the piles of corpses, among which still living children crawled or heeded the call of nature'.

The American Inquiries

In 1919, the year of the Paris Peace Conference at Versailles, the United States seemed a much more likely candidate to save the Armenians than the bickering British and French or the Russian Bolsheviks, immersed in their own civil war. There was a proposal that America should hold a mandate over Anatolia, so President Wilson sent two fact-finding commissions to investigate. The first was led by Henry King (a theologian) and Charles Crane, formerly secretary to the Committee on Armenian Atrocities (and to that extent biased) although the other commission members were independent and took care to interview all sides. Their report did not mince words about 'the great and lasting wrongs in Turkey which must be set right ... because of the adoption of repeated massacres as a deliberate policy of state; because of almost complete lack of penitence for the massacres'.[123] Much of eastern Anatolia, it reported, should be handed over to the tiny new state of Armenia as 'just reparation'.

The next US mission, conducted by General James Harbord assisted by a large contingent of military experts and fact finders, spent thirty days in the villages ravaged by pillage and denuded by deportations. The mission listened 'to the personal experiences of many witnesses to the atrocities of 1915'[124] – at a time when witnesses were unlikely to have been primed to lie or exaggerate. It certainly had no bias in favour of the Armenians, reporting on some reprisal massacres they had recently committed and noticing that

> the Armenian stands among his neighbours very much as the Jew stands in Russia and Poland ... he incurs the penalty which attaches among backward races to the banker, the middleman and the creditor. Unjust it may be, the sentiment regarding him is expressed by this saying current in the Near East: 'The Armenian is never legally in the wrong: never morally in the right'...The Armenian is not guiltless of blood himself...[125]

On the subject of the 1915 massacres, the Harbord Commission came down firmly against the Turks on the question of intentional guilt: 'Testimony is universal', it reported, 'that the massacres have always been ordered from Constantinople ... the 1915 order for deportation is universally attributed to the Committee of Union and Progress, of which Enver, Talaat and Djemal Pasha were leaders.' Harbord and his team visited every village from which deportations were ordered, and noted that official Turkish records indicated 1,100,000 had been deported 'from the high, cool breeze-swept plateau of Armenia to the malarial flats of the Euphrates and the burning sands of Syria and Arabia'. The death toll from what Harbord described as 'this wholesale attempt on a race' was usually estimated at 800,000[126] – 75 per cent of the race according to Turkish statistics. He concluded that the massacres and deportations in the countryside were carried out pursuant to a 'definite system':[127] in the areas he studied, soldiers would go from town to town, summoning all available Armenian men, aged fifteen to forty-five, to government offices and then marching them off to execution. The women, children and old men were then sent off at bayonet point on long marches, where 'starvation, typhus and dysentery', as well as armed attacks, took an incalculable toll. Harbord and his team were shocked at the desolation and destruction of the Armenian quarters, at the orphanages full of small boys, and at the experiences related by Armenian girls who had been raped or had run away after converting to Islam in order to save their lives. His report summarised the deportation through the eyes of these witnesses:

> Driven on foot under a fierce summer sun, robbed of their clothing and such petty articles as they carried, prodded by bayonet if they lagged; starvation, typhus, and dysentery left thousands dead by the trail side. The ration was a pound of bread every alternate day, which many did not receive, and later a small daily sprinkling of meal on the palm of the outstretched hand was the only food. Many perished from thirst or were killed as they attempted to slake thirst at the crossing of running streams. Numbers were murdered by savage Kurds, against whom the Turkish soldiery afforded no protection. Little girls of nine or ten were sold to Kurdish brigands for a few piastres, and women were promiscuously violated.[128]

Harbord was writing as an outraged American, but he found evidence, as soon as the war ended, for what he termed 'the most colossal crime of all the ages'.[129] He did not demand retribution for it, or insist that the ruined villages be given over to Armenia. He appended to his report a dignified letter from Mustafa Kemal, explaining why the new state of Turkey could not concede its sovereign land. Harbord's report reached Congress as Wilson was flailing in his attempt to obtain its support for the League of Nations and the 'American mandate' proposal was lost. But the report itself remains of great value as a fact-finding exercise conducted by military experts from a disinterested power, interviewing witnesses on all sides at an early time after the war. It reached the same conclusion as Toynbee in his Blue Book.

The Constantinople Trials

At the end of the war, after Turkish capitulation and British occupation, there was a reckoning of sorts for the 'Young Turk' leaders in their own capital, under a new Sultan and a parliament where liberal party members who had opposed the CUP were now prepared to speak out about the Armenian massacres, in terms that would have them prosecuted in Turkey today. Mustapha Arif, the new Minister of the Interior, said, 'Unfortunately, those who were our leaders during the war have applied the law of deportation in a manner that would rival the most bloodthirsty bandits. They decided to exterminate the Armenians, and they were exterminated.'[130] The new President of the Senate stated that the mass killing of Armenians had been 'officially' approved.[131]

Parliament condemned the CUP ministers over the deportation laws and the creation of the paramilitary gangs of *chettis* (the released criminals), 'whose assaults on life, property and honour rendered the ministers guilty as co-perpetrators of the tragic crimes that resulted'.[132] It set up a 'commission for investigation of crimes' to interrogate CUP ministers and officials and gather documents for their prosecution, and a military tribunal began to conduct trials from February 1919 onwards. The prosecutor, summarising the evidence against Talaat, Enver and Cemal that had been gathered by these inquiries, stated:

> The disaster visiting the Armenians was not a local or iso-
> lated event. It was the result of a pre-meditated decision
> taken by a control body composed of the above named,
> the immolations and excesses which took place were
> based on oral and written orders issued by that control
> body.[133]

In the first trial, in February 1919, Young Turk functionaries in Yozgat, from where 31,000 of its 33,000 Armenians had been deported, were accused of mass-murdering them, plundering their goods and raping some members of the convoys. The court heard evidence from local Muslim leaders testifying to the slaughter, evidence from eighteen survivors, and from a military commandant who admitted that 'underlying the entire scheme of deportations' was 'a policy of extermination'. Evidence from the cables, said the prosecutor, showed that 'deportation' meant 'massacre', and the tribunal judgment agreed that the real purpose of the deportations was as a cloak for pre-planned massacres.[134] The court convicted Kemal Bey and his police chief of 'crimes against humanity and civilisation' because they

> issued awesome orders to their subalterns at the time of the
> deportations of the Armenians. Acting under these orders,
> their underlings first fell on the Armenians and, without
> regard to ill health, treating men, women and children alike,
> organised them into deportation caravans ... Illegal orders
> were handed down for the murder of the males ... They were
> premeditatedly, with intent, murdered, after the men had had
> their hands tied behind their backs ... Nor did they make
> any attempt to prevent further killings ... Moslem supreme
> justice considers these events as murder, pillage, robbery and
> crimes of enormous magnitude.[135]

Talaat, Enver and Cemal were tried *in absentia*. They were afraid of retribution from the new government, and Germany, in an action that underlined its complicity, sent a gunboat on which they escaped with several of their 'Turkification' ideologues. Dr Reşid, whose enthusiasm for killing Armenian 'microbes' has been described earlier, committed suicide rather than face the court. The Young Turk leaders were found guilty of pre-meditated 'first-degree mass murder' carried out by the Special Organisation, which had arranged for the release of dangerous criminals and formed them into gangs to kill the Armenians; the deportations and massacres constituted a comprehensive attempt 'to radically solve the Armenian question' by (as the indictment put it) 'the extermination of an entire people constituting a distinct community'. This is so clearly a finding of what is now termed genocide (in one case the court even concluded that the CUP measures had the characterisation of a 'final solution') that it is difficult for deniers to deny it.

But of course they do, by pointing out that British were in occupation and pressing for trials, and the liberal government was anxious to comply so that Turkey would not be dismembered by the Allies at the impending Versailles Peace Conference. This does not alter the fact that the five initial judges were professional and independent; the procedures they employed, familiar to inquisitorial systems at the time, were neither unusual nor unfair by local standards; and their decisions were rational and evidence based. Claims by genocide deniers that defence counsel were not allowed are mistaken – sixteen participated, led by the president of the Turkish Bar Association, and their submissions were considered in the court judgments.[136] However, the Turkish public was alienated by the tribunal's disastrous decision to hang Kemal Bey: nationalists allowed his funeral to turn into an *Ittihadist* mass memorial to 'the innocent martyr of the Turks'. However foolish it was to make Kemal Bey a martyr (he was formally if farcically 'pardoned' posthumously by the nationalist government a few years later), that does not mean that the trials themselves were unfair or the verdicts unjustified by the evidence. At the time, the British criticised the court for what they thought was prejudice in favour of the CUP, especially because it released a number of prisoners – which may instead be an indication of its fairness.

The real problem with the Constantinople trials is that the transcript has mysteriously disappeared, together with much of the prosecution evidence collected by the two inquiries (although some documents from the 1918 Commission for Investigation of Crimes have survived). Parts of the trials have been painstakingly put together from contemporary press reports and accounts in the *Daily Gazette*, published by the government, but a good deal of original documentary evidence submitted to the tribunal is missing, presumed destroyed, or withheld by those with an interest to withhold documents that would support the indictment charge that 'the deportations represented neither a military necessity nor a punitive disciplinary measure'.[137] Also missing is some evidence about all the communities remote from the war zone which were denuded of Armenians (for example, documents presented to the tribunal showed that 61,000 of a 63,605 Armenian community in Ankara – a city very far from the war zone – were deported).[138] The trials, for this reason rather than for any proven bias or lack of independence, failed to serve the purpose of Nuremberg, namely to lay down an imperishable record to confound the genocide deniers of the future.

Nonetheless, the surviving records do serve as a reminder of a time when Turks were prepared to confront their criminal past with an honesty that demonstrated to the world and to Versailles that the perpetrators of the crime against humanity committed by the deportation of the Armenians were a handful of CUP ministers and their local apparatchiks, responsible for the criminal gangs who massacred the men and for the undefended convoys of women and children who were assaulted by brigands and disease and starvation. It is sad that Turkey can never take pride in this moment in its history, and tends either to portray the liberals as 'quislings' (Justin McCarthy's description of the liberal Prime Minister) or to see the trials as little more than a cunning attempt to gain an advantage at Versailles. The trials struggled on after the British, annoyed by the delays and the prisoner releases, took most of the remaining indictees to Malta, and two death sentences were carried out in 1920, after which the nationalist movement formed under the leadership of Mustafa Kemal stepped in and closed the tribunal down. Not, however, before it had delivered verdicts of guilt for crimes against humanity that would today count as convictions for genocide.

The Ottoman Archives

Newly discovered material – especially cable traffic, some of it coded – from the prime ministerial Ottoman archive in Istanbul has been analysed by Taner Akçam in his 2012 book *The Young Turks' Crime against Humanity*, to demonstrate the racial motivation behind the deportations, directed against Armenians as such rather than Christians generally. It appears that Talaat himself was sending a stream of secret cables from his home, a few of which have survived, whilst he and other leaders were being fully informed by provincial governors and then by their officials of the Armenian death tolls. It is clear from the cabled instructions that even those deportees who reached a tolerable location alive were to be subjected to race discrimination and were to be prevented from establishing their own schools or publishing their own newspapers,[139] whilst their 'abandoned' property (i.e. the houses from which they had been forcibly removed) was allocated by the government settlement office to Muslim immigrants who had arrived as a result of the loss of the Balkans. There is telling evidence from cables sent by the settlement office to provincial administrators in June 1915, even *before* local Armenians were extirpated but in expectation that they would be forced imminently to leave, identifying Muslim refugees who would be 'sent at a later time to resettle areas ... that were left devoid of Armenians'.[140] It was the central government that issued the notorious decree of 5 January 1916 requiring that 'all of the provinces, provincial districts, villages, towns, mountains, rivers ... within the Ottoman domains which have been given non-Islamic names, such as Armenian, Greek and Bulgarian, shall be changed to Turkish'[141] – an indication of genocidal intent from the heart of the CUP, which wanted to destroy all traces of the Armenians by removing signs of their former presence.

The cables, ciphers and correspondence, recently accessed in the Ottoman archives, contain further evidence of genocidal intent. For example, there is a witness statement given to the 1918 pre-trial commission by Vehip Pasha, who was commander of the Third Ottoman Army in February 1916. He averred that

> the massacre and annihilation of the Armenians and their looting and pillaging by the killers were the result of a decision made by the Central Committee of the [Committee of] Union and Progress ... these specific acts of violence ... carried out in accordance with a comprehensive program and with a clear intent, were performed upon the instruction and urging, and with the supervision and follow-up of government functionaries, who were the tools of, first, the Central Committee of the CUP and its plenipotentiaries, and

> second, the wishes and aspirations of the CUP itself, which
> had discarded [all considerations of] law and conscience.[142]

The consequences of the genocide were referred to with brutal frankness by its main progenitor, Interior Minister Talaat Pasha, in a secret cable to the province of Ankara, dated 29 August 1915: 'The Armenian question in the eastern provinces has been resolved … there is no need to sully the nation and the government['s honour] with further atrocities.'[143] This cable would be an important exhibit in any trial in which a prosecutor sought to establish genocidal intent – in this case of the sender, the very minister in charge of the deportations, who was evincing his satisfaction that the 'the Armenian question' had been answered in the east by eliminating enough Armenians. If genuine, this telegram betrays Talaat's knowledge of the dishonourable and atrocious means being used, at the government's instigation, to destroy the Armenians.

In the course of the main killing months, May–July 1915, Talaat had become concerned that his orders to act against Armenians were being interpreted in some provinces as orders to kill all Christians. Three days after Wangenheim's protest on 12 July about Dr Reşid, governor of Diyarbakır province, (who had been indiscriminately killing Christians instead of confining his lethal attention to those he described as Armenian 'microbes') Talaat cabled Reşid: 'Since the disciplinary and political measures adopted vis-à-vis the Armenians do not in any way apply to the other Christians, an immediate end should be put to such events, which will have an extremely negative effect on public opinion…'[144]

Akçam points out that 'Talaat's complaint was that a policy formulated specifically for the Armenian population was being implemented indiscriminately for other Christians as well, and his demand was that the killing operations against the Armenians not be carried out in a manner that would involve other Christian populations'.[145] Talaat's assumption was clearly that the government-ordered killing operations, under the euphemism of 'disciplinary and political measures', would continue in respect of Armenians, but would not be visited upon other Christian groups.

Akçam interprets material from the Ottoman archives as indicating that government decisions and operational instructions were delivered on two tracks: one official and public in respect of the deportations, the other secret and communicated orally by private courier, giving orders to annihilate groups of Armenians. Evidence of this two-track system comes, for example, from Reşid Akik Pasha, briefly a government minister:

> There are certain secrets that I learned in my most recent, brief service in the cabinet … Among these, I came across one peculiar thing. This deportation order was given openly and in official fashion by the Interior Ministry and communicated to the provinces. But after this official order [was given], the inauspicious order was circulated by the Central Committee to all parties so that the armed gangs could hastily complete their cursed task. With that, the armed gangs took over and the barbaric massacres then began to take place.[146]

Giving brutal orders in code or by secret courier would have been necessary so as not to provide fodder for Allied propaganda and particularly to avoid embarrassing Germany, which formally protested twice in 1915 about the treatment of Armenians. There is abundant evidence that prisoners were released into paramilitary gangs and directed by the Special Organisation to kill Armenians: testimony like that from Reşid Akik Pasha would go to prove state responsibility for genocide.

Akçam argues that genocidal intent can also be inferred from a CUP 'demographic policy' that in every resettlement area, no more than 5–10 per cent of the population could be non-Muslim, which resulted in specific orders to reduce drastically the number of Armenians in areas which they populated heavily: 'The 5 to 10 per cent rule is found in ciphered and top secret correspondence at the highest level of the state … this can be considered as a concrete indication that the policy towards Armenians was indeed genocidal. The 10 per cent ratio seems to have been the operational goal in implementing that policy…'[147] So it may have been, but a demographic goal of this kind is not *per se* genocidal unless there is an intention to destroy part of the race in order to achieve it. The important fact is that the deportations inevitably and foreseeably imposed conditions of life that meant death for people selected on account of their race: a policy of transmigration was privately acknowledged and publicly known to mean the destruction of a substantial section of the Armenian population.

Conclusion

The above evidence is sufficient to prove beyond any reasonable doubt that the Ottoman state was responsible, on the legal principles set out in the next chapter, for what would now (and would ever since the word was coined by Lemkin in 1944) be described as 'genocide'. The sheer weight of evidence and the consistency of witness accounts, including those by respectable people who could have no axe to grind or reason to fabricate (the German missionaries and diplomats, for example, whose country was in alliance with Turkey and the neutral US vice-consuls like Davis and Jackson) really does put paid to any suggestion that there has been some massive, international anti-Turkish conspiracy to align false statements and so suppress the truth. As for all the Armenian accounts, whilst some may be exaggerated, they do collectively have a ring of truth: as one historian comments, 'For the Armenian diaspora, flung around the world, speaking different languages, it would require a stupendous concert of deceit to fabricate the descriptions of massacres, to dream up reminiscences. Such a conspiracy would be without precedent.'[148] Such a conspiracy, given the hundreds of eyewitness observations to similar effect by neutrals and by allies, would have been impossible. The intentions of the CUP leaders in 1915, evidenced for example by Talaat's conversations and cables, was to destroy a substantial part of the Armenian race as such. This is a clear inference from all the contemporaneous evidence, and history confirms that they succeeded, whether they killed 600,000 or 1.5 million. As a matter of law – and as the matter in primary dispute between Turkey and many other democratic governments – should their conduct, if repeated today, amount to the crime of genocide?

CHAPTER 4

THE LAW

The Significance of Genocide

'GENOCIDE' IN COMMON parlance is the word that comes to mind whenever a massive death toll results from a state-backed onslaught on people of a disliked, demeaned and different ethnic group. This is not its legal definition, and nor is the cataclysmic meaning offered by the *Oxford English Dictionary*: 'the deliberate and systematic extermination of a national or ethnic group'. As a matter of international law, a state is responsible for genocide when its agents, with the intention of destroying in whole or *in part* a national, ethnic, racial or religious group, kill or cause serious mental or bodily harm to,

91

or inflict destructive conditions of life on, such a group. There is never much doubt about the sufferings undergone by the group – the question of responsibility generally hinges on whether there is proof that political or military leaders intended to rid the country of the group as a social unit. It is not sufficient just to disperse its members, but it is certainly not necessary (as the *OED* editors seem to think) to liquidate them all. Size, in fact, does not matter – the World Court (the International Court of Justice – the ICJ) held that there was genocide at Srebrenica, which involved the killing of 7,000 Muslim men and the deportation of 18,000 women and children.

The annihilation of political or social groups does not count as genocide, although it would amount to the second worst crime against humanity, namely 'extermination' or, if most of the group survived, the crime of 'persecution'. These crimes against humanity are committed when racial or religious groups are massacred but 'genocidal intent' cannot be proven. General Pinochet did not commit 'genocide' by killing thousands of left-wingers, and the Taliban would not be guilty of genocide if it succeeded in exterminating all homosexuals. Klaus Barbie's attempt to destroy the French Resistance was not genocide – he was convicted of the crime against humanity of 'persecution' on political grounds (a crime that has been termed 'politicide'). So 'genocide' as the worst example of a crime against humanity does raise some logical questions – why does it cover Hitler's racist extermination of six million Jews but not Stalin's class-hating extermination of ten million Kulaks and other middle classes? Do atheists constitute a 'religious' group?[149] Given the difficulty created by courts which have insisted on proof of 'specific intent' to destroy, and unnecessarily but portentously dressed this requirement up in Latin (*dolus specialis*), some lawyers favour the abandonment of 'genocide' as a separate crime, since all who are guilty of it can be convicted more easily by charging them with a crime against humanity which requires an intention to kill or mistreat civilians, but without any proof of a 'special' intention to do so because of their race or religion.

This view has something to be said for it, in terms of saving time and money: prosecutors of suspected *génocidaires* always charge a crime against humanity as a fall-back in case they fail to persuade the court to draw an inference of special genocidal intent. But there is a particular obloquy attached to a conviction for genocide, which may offer a psychological deterrent to leaders tempted to incite racial hostility towards minorities. Moreover, there is force in the argument that ethnic and religious feelings are a tinderbox, much more readily inflamed than social or political passions, and the Genocide Convention is still necessary to put all states under special obligations to prevent the harbingers of genocide from taking hold. That obligation, incidentally, is placed on states irrespective of the fact that they are at war: they are entitled to kill the soldiers of an enemy state, but not to use war as an excuse to eliminate an inconvenient ethnic group within their own borders because that group might welcome the enemy as liberators or because some of its members may be fighting for the enemy or be perceived as 'fifth columnists'. It is during war that the law of genocide is most necessary to protect minority groups, and it is ironic that the Turkish government denies genocide of the Armenians on the pretext that they were 'the enemy within' during a war – the very circumstances in which special obligations on a state to protect racial and religious groups are essential. Leaders of such groups may, of course, be apprehended if suspected of treason or sabotage, and followers may be spied upon or interned if reasonably believed to be disloyal, but the object of genocide law is to protect the group from having its ethnic or religious identity 'destroyed' – whether by mass murder or 'ethnic cleansing' or forcible religious conversion or assimilation into the dominant ethnic group.

Genocide is not always the most heinous crime – cold-blooded liquidation of a political (or, in Cambodia, apolitical) class may involve more moral wickedness in conception and planning. It is, however, certainly the most dangerous crime – the easiest to foment by theories about the superiority of a dominant racial group, or the 'uncleanliness' of adherents to minority religions. That is why maintaining genocide as a separate crime assists in identifying its causes and in requiring states to guard against their recrudescence. However, if 'genocide' is to be retained as a distinct crime for these purposes, it must not become too difficult to prosecute, or too easy to get away with.

This is the danger of modern genocide denial by Turkey, which argues that the attack on a race must be virtually equivalent to the Holocaust before the crime of genocide can be proved. But requiring an 'extermination determination' on the Nazi level would render 'genocide' virtually useless as a criminal concept, because the Holocaust was unique. When Professor Bernard Lewis invidiously contrasted the Armenian genocide claim with the reality of the Holocaust, he was convicted in France for genocide denial: what he failed to understand was that there can be different gradations in, and distinct ways of committing, this most dangerous of crimes. Just because the Jews had not taken up arms against the Nazis does not meant that a group which fights back is disentitled to cry 'genocide' when it is, 'as such', in the process of being wiped out. The Nazis moved to eliminate the Jews because they *believed* they were a threat – morally, culturally, financially – to German hegemony, and the Ottoman government moved to eliminate the Armenian population because it thought they were a threat because many of them would welcome an Allied invasion. Deniers of the Armenian genocide obsess about the threat from revolutionary Dashnaks compared with the 'passivity' of the Jews in Germany, but a race is protected from destruction, even if among its members there may be found some terrorists (or freedom fighters) who want liberation from the rule of the would-be destroyers.

Jews themselves have not been tempted to lay exclusive claim to having been the victims of genocide: their organisations have usually been quick to condemn denials of the Armenian genocide and their 'Holocaust' museums acknowledge it. They recognise that something valuable may come from their own suffering from genocide if its definition is extended to other groups whose existence has been, or might in future be, put in the balance by the poison of racial hatred fed by state agencies. This is one reason why 'genocide' is useful as a separate criminological category, which focuses on its early causes, located in political rhetoric, school syllabuses, censorship of embarrassing historical facts, discriminatory property and language laws, and so on. In a world where racial and religious aversion abounds, identifying the harbingers of the most dangerous crime is a reminder to governments of their duty to discourage them, or to combat them once they have taken hold.

This chapter will proceed to apply the law relating to genocide to the facts and evidence set out in Chapters 2 and 3. It may not be an easy read for non-lawyers. International law has no police force or parliament and its rules develop from treaties and the accepted practice of states, assisted by court decisions and textbook writers, so its development needs to be explained in some detail to appreciate how it applies in a specific situation. It imposes duties on states, for which they can be held to account by the International Court of Justice (if they accept its jurisdiction) whilst their political or military leaders may be prosecuted, in certain circumstances, before the International Criminal Court (ICC) or special UN tribunals like that for the Balkans (the ICTY) or for Rwanda (the ICTR). In the case of genocide, the treaty which sets out the basic law is the Genocide Convention, the provisions of which have been interpreted in recent judgments delivered by these tribunals in applying international criminal law. It is to the Convention and the case law that we must turn, therefore, to answer the question of whether the massacres and deportations of the Armenians in 1915 amounted to genocide. This depends on identifying the constituent elements of the offence, deciding how and whether 'genocidal intent' can be proved, and whether 'military necessity' avails as a defence. The answer is, in my opinion, very clear but the legal reasoning behind that opinion must be elaborated in some detail, in order to confound the genocide deniers who do not know the law of genocide.

The Genocide Convention

A rticle 1 of the 1948 Convention on the Prevention and Punishment of Genocide simply states that 'genocide, whether committed in time of peace or time of war, is a crime under international law'. This treaty has been ratified by so many states (146 at present count) that it is now considered *jus cogens*, a rule of modern customary international law binding on all states (whether they have ratified the Convention or not) and requiring them to prosecute acts of genocide. The Convention is particularly important because it has US backing – it was ratified by President Reagan in 1986 to appease Jewish fury over his visit to Bitburg cemetery. (The outrage was fanned by a hitherto unknown young man, fat and bearded, who flew from

Michigan to stage a demonstration at the cemetery to embarrass the US President by pointing out he was honouring SS graves. It was film-maker Michael Moore's first, and most effective, protest).

As the International Court of Justice has explained, the origins of the Convention show that it was the intention of the UN to condemn and punish genocide as 'a crime under international law ... involving a denial of the right of existence of entire human groups, a denial which shocks the conscience of mankind and results in great losses to humanity, and which is contrary to moral law and the spirit and aims of the UN'.[150] The objective of the drafters of the Convention was to lay down a law clear enough to deter potential *génocidaires*: that principle should guide its interpretation and has done so, apart from some confusion over the requirements of 'specific intent'.

Article II of the Convention, repeated in Article 6 of the Rome Treaty of the ICC, decrees that

> genocide means any of the following acts committed with intent to destroy, in whole or in part, a national, ethnical, racial or religious group, as such:
>
> - Killing members of the group;
> - Causing serious bodily or mental harm to members of the group;
> - Deliberately inflicting on the group conditions of life calculated to bring about its physical destruction in whole or in part;
> - Imposing measures intended to prevent births within the group;
> - Forcibly transferring children of the group to another group.

Elements of the Crime: the *Actus Reus*

This crime – like all other serious crimes – has a factual element (*actus reus*) and a mental element (*mens rea*). The *actus*, described in the list above, involves the causation of harm – physical or mental – to members of a group, targeted by discrimination on national, ethnic or religious grounds. Importantly it includes 'deliberately inflicting on the group conditions of life calculated to bring about its physical destruction in whole or part' – and this Article II(c) was clearly drafted with the fate of the Armenians in mind. The Ottoman government had ordered their deportation under conditions that were known to expose them to disease, starvation and lethal attack by Special Organisation paramilitaries and marauding Kurds. As the leading legal textbook on genocide notes:

> The treatment of the Armenians by the Turkish rulers in 1915 provides the paradigm for the provision dealing with imposition of conditions of life. These crimes have often been described as 'deportations'. But they went far beyond mere expulsion or transfer, because the deportation itself involved deprivation of fundamental human needs with the result that large numbers died of disease, malnutrition and exhaustion.[151]

Destruction of the Group in Whole or Part

The object does not have to be the extermination of the entire group: a part of it will suffice, even a small part, defined geographically. Thus the International Court of Justice has held that genocide was not committed generally by Serb troops in

Bosnia, other than at Srebrenica – by the killing of 7,000 men and boys and the deportation of 18,000 women and children who resided in that area.[152] The International Criminal Tribunal for the Former Yugoslavia (ICTY) examined the requirement that there must be an intention to destroy a group 'in whole or in part' in the case of *Krstić*, and concluded that the intent to eradicate a group within a limited geographical area, such as a region of a country or even a municipality, could be characterised as genocide.[153] As William Schabas (*Genocide in International Law*) notes, 'Destroying all members of a group within a continent, or a country, or an administrative region or even a town, might satisfy the "in part" requirement of Article III. The Turkish government targeted Armenians within its borders, not those of the diaspora.'[154]

What is required is that the 'part' should be an identifiable part or else a *significant* part of the whole (the ICJ in its *Bosnia v Serbia* decision, incorrectly in my view, considered that a 'substantial' part must be targeted).[155] There is no doubt, however, that a very 'substantial' part of the Armenians in the Ottoman Empire were targeted by the deportations and at least 800,000, perhaps 1.5 million, were killed. On any view, even with the 600,000 estimate that most genocide deniers accept, this is a substantial proportion of the Armenian population and of course the survivors – several hundred thousand – only survived with serious physical and psychological damage. The evidence shows that Armenians were targeted as such, i.e. as a racial group, and not merely because they were Christians and thus part of a wider religious group.[156] (See earlier the example of Dr Reşid, the provincial governor in Diyarbakır, who began killing all the Christians he could apprehend, but was ordered by Interior Minister Talaat to restrict his lethal attentions to Armenians.)

In the case of *Akayesu*, the first genocide conviction by the

International Criminal Tribunal for Rwanda (ICTR), the trial chamber held that the term 'deliberately inflicting on the group conditions of life calculated to bring about its physical destruction in whole or in part' included subjecting a group of people to 'systematic expulsion from homes',[157] such as the deportation orders to which the Armenians were subjected in 1915. In the case of *Kayishema and Ruzindana*, it was held this also included 'the deliberate deprivation of resources indispensable for survival, such as food or medical services'[158] (again, witnesses confirm that this was a feature of the 1915 deportations). The International Criminal Tribunal for the Former Yugoslavia (ICTY) has ruled that the definition also covers the creation of circumstances that lead to a slow death, such as lack of proper housing, clothing, hygiene or excessive work or physical exhaustion[159] – another feature of the 1915 death marches.

Article III of the Convention extends the definition of genocide to conspiracy (an agreement to participate in a genocidal act), incitement to commit genocide (a crime committed e.g. by radio broadcasts in Rwanda: 'the grave is only half full – who will help us fill it?') and 'complicity' in genocide – a concept that involves not only aiding and abetting but being an 'accessory after the fact', i.e. helping to cover it up or taking its benefits. The ICJ found that Serbia had breached its obligations under Article IV of the Convention by failing to prevent the Srebrenica massacres and by failing to prosecute those responsible for the genocide.[160]

The Kaiser was certainly complicit in the Armenian genocide, perhaps to a greater extent than Milošević in the *Srebrenica* case. German diplomats notified Berlin immediately and explicitly that its Ottoman allies were bent on exterminating the Armenian race, but the Kaiser and his Reich Chancellor and ministerial advisors decided to turn a blind eye in the interests of the alliance and in 1916 even removed an ambassador (Wolff-Metternich) who was complaining too loudly to Talaat. Germany had sufficient power and influence to stop the genocide: Turkey was reliant on German arms supplies and on German generals, both on the Dardanelles and the Russian fronts. It was Germany that snatched the perpetrators from the jaws of justice after the war ended, and later refused to extradite them. Germany should share the blame, the shame and the responsibility, in a way that will be considered later (see Chapter 9). When German missionaries at Aleppo begged the German commander at the Russian front to take pity on the Armenian deportees dying of typhus in a camp outside the city, he viewed it through his field glasses at a distance of two kilometres and directed that they should die in isolation, lest the disease spread and infect his soldiers.

There is no immunity for genocide: it covers 'constitutionally responsible rulers, public officials or private individuals' (Article III). This is an important article, because pro-Turkish historians and some Western government officials seem to think that genocide can only be carried out as a matter of declared state policy, and demand 'unequivocal' documentary evidence of a high-level government decision. This is not a necessary element of the crime: responsibility may be inferred from approval by political or military leaders of actions that are known to have led to death or have been taken for racial or religious reasons, even if the actual perpetrators were freelance paramilitaries or bandits motivated only by greed. As the International Centre for Transitional Justice found in 2003 (earlier, pp 33–4), responsibility for the Armenian genocide devolved on the Ottoman government because it directed the deportations and knew that the marches would kill – and were killing – most of those who marched.

Genocidal Intent

....

Genocide law is still in a state of development: international criminal courts have only recently handed down convictions of perpetrators of genocide in Rwanda and Srebrenica, and the International Court of Justice in *Croatia v Serbia* (February 2015) confirmed the law applied in these cases. The need to prove a 'specific intention' to destroy part or all of a group has been a cause of confusion, as denialists wrongly assume that this requires evidence of some formal government order to exterminate a racial group. This would be absurd, as no government or its political or military leader would be brazen or foolish enough to promulgate such an order: Hitler never did so – the case against Adolf Eichmann was based on inference, from the elliptical notes he took at the Wannsee Conference. The truth is that 'specific intention', in the case of genocide, must be gathered firstly from the fact that mass murder, or mass torture, or group destruction through deportation or inadequate living conditions, has deliberately been visited upon a group selected by their race or religion. And then the 'special' intent to destroy them can be inferred from all the circumstances – including knowledge of the likelihood that the conditions in which they had been forced to live would cause a substantial number of the group to die. If the alleged perpetrators have been previously involved in whipping up hatred against the race, or in political rhetoric or policies which tout the superiority of their own race, or have deliberately turned a blind eye to killings they could have stopped, then the requisite intention may be inferred. Those who give orders for deportation, fully aware of the genocidal consequences that are likely to ensue, cannot plead successfully that they lacked the 'specific intent' for race destruction if that must have been the reason why they gave the order. Even if the immediate motive for the action was some military exigency, realisation of its real and probable lethal consequences fixes them with an intent to bring about those consequences. A defendant who says 'I sent a million Armenians into the desert but I didn't know they would all die and after all, 200,000 survived' has the specific intent necessary for the crime of genocide against Armenians.

This is clear from the cases already decided by international courts. In *Akayesu*, the ICTR confirmed that the commission of genocide requires proof of 'special intent', meaning the perpetrator clearly sought to bring about the act charged as a crime. The court noted that in the absence of a confession it is difficult to prove this intention, and consequently ruled that it could be inferred from a number of other factors.[161] For example, the intent can be inferred from words, or deeds, or by a pattern of purposeful action.[162] The intent can also be inferred from the general context in which other culpable acts were committed systematically against the same group, regardless of whether such acts were committed by the same perpetrator or by others. Further factors, such as the scale of atrocities committed, their general nature, in a region or a country, or the deliberate and systematic targeting of victims on account of their membership of a particular group, whilst excluding the members of other groups, can also enable the inference of genocidal intent to be drawn.[163]

In the case of *Akayesu*, the court inferred that the accused had the necessary intent from the speeches he had made, and the deliberate and systematic atrocities committed against the Tutsis in Rwanda.[164] Similarly, in the case of *Musema*, the ICTR inferred the necessary intent to destroy Tutsis from the numerous atrocities committed against them, the large-scale attacks against Tutsi civilians, and from the widespread and systematic perpetration of other criminal acts against members of the Tutsi group.[165] Such elements were also present during the Armenian deportations.

The requirement of an 'intention to destroy' part of a group 'as such' does not necessarily mean an intention that a lot of group members be physically exterminated. Genocide requires a finding of double intention – firstly, an intention to kill or cause some serious physical or mental harm or to impose inhumane conditions of life, or forcibly transfer children. That is the 'intention' necessary for a crime against humanity. But if these acts are done with the object of getting rid of the group *as a group*, it is that objective which amounts to the specific intent that elevates the crime to genocide. It need not be accomplished by extermination – group members may live on *after* being caused serious mental harm, or having had to endure life-threatening conditions, or after being prevented from giving birth, or being forced to have children adopted. In all these situations they survive as human beings – traumatised, but alive. For the purposes of proving genocide, the actions must be done deliberately, and with an intention to destroy the group as an entity, not necessarily by killing most of its members. There can be no doubt about the intention of the CUP government and its officials to destroy the group of Armenians in Anatolia by extirpating them, with the full knowledge and intention that they would suffer inhumane conditions and be harmed in body and mind, even if some of the group survived at the end of the massacres and the marches, or escaped to other countries.

The ICTY (the International Criminal Tribunal for the Former Yugoslavia) has so far convicted five Serbian defendants of genocide, for participation in the killings in Srebrenica (General Mladić, the commander who bears most responsibility, remains on trial). The cases are important in demonstrating that a 'group' may be a subset of a much larger ethnic presence. Srebrenica was a Muslim city surrounded by a predominantly Serb-populated countryside, in the racially jumbled geography of Bosnia. It was attacked by Bosnian Serb commanders (not by the army of Serbia) who did not, merely by taking the town (a UN 'safe area'), commit genocide. That happened shortly afterwards when Mladić ordered the deportation of all Muslim women, children and old men, whilst at the same time about 7,000 able-bodied men and boys were separated and detained, ostensibly to 'screen' them for war crimes but in fact for them to be carted off, killed and buried in mass graves which later yielded their corpses, with hands tied behind backs, shot from behind. Incriminating footage came from a private camcorder, with grainy images of Muslim men and boys huddled in fields, surrounded by soldiers who wait impatiently to be blessed by Orthodox priests so they can with easy consciences shoot their prisoners before nightfall. The ICTY and the International Court of Justice have concluded that the operation – the deportations and the massacre taken together – proved that

> the ultimate objective was to eliminate the enclave ... all these acts constituted a single operation executed with the intent to destroy the Bosnian Muslim population of Srebrenica ... the Bosnian Serb forces not only knew that the combination of the killings of the men with the forcible transfer of the women, children and elderly would inevitably result in the physical disappearance of the Bosnian Muslim population of Srebrenica, but clearly intended through those acts to physically destroy this group.[166]

The evidence from a number of towns and villages in Anatolia is of a similar character: the 'ethnic cleansing' began by rounding up the able-bodied Armenian men, on the basis that they might have evaded conscription, and either killing them or despatching them to labour camps (where they were soon killed anyway). Then their families were forced to set out in columns on the long march to the Syrian desert. The law deemed their houses 'abandoned' and provided them with no right of return, should they survive a march on which over half would die and then a 'relocation' to camps where life was barely sustainable because they were not provided with food or with medicines and medical help to combat the raging diseases of typhus and dysentery.

The mental element (*mens rea*) is often difficult to prove against public officials (who destroy incriminating records) and against private individuals, who must be proved to have a 'discriminatory intent', i.e. to be acting out of a conscious determination to participate in a programme which aims to destroy the group. Rarely will such a heinous intention be spelled out in any document: it must be inferred from circumstantial evidence. There will be little difficulty in proving mass murder, often from photographic evidence or the opening of mass graves. The discriminatory intent to destroy can be deduced from a range of evidence that demonstrates malice aforethought towards the group – usually there will be some history of its persecution, and the persecutors will themselves be in the grip of nationalist fervour which boasts their own racial supremacy and demeans the victim group (e.g. the 'Turkification' programme of the CUP, which was designed to diminish rival ethnic identities, especially those of the Armenians, the Greeks and the Assyrians). Other familiar indicia of genocidal intent are attacks which single out the intelligentsia or cultural leadership of the victim group (such as the arrests and subsequent killings of hundreds of Armenian intellectuals, lawyers, writers and cultural figures in Constantinople on and immediately after 24 April 1915)[167] and attacks on the groups' religious and cultural symbols (e.g. the destruction or expropriation of Armenian churches and monuments).[168]

'Genocidal intent' is a construct by inference from circumstance and public statements, but it must not be confused with motive, which may not be racial but strategic or political. This would not exclude the intention necessary for genocide. The international court dealing with Rwanda (the ICTR) has delivered rulings that put paid to denialist claims that the Armenians had to be extirpated because of their pro-Russian sympathies or their political wish for independence.

> The requirement that an ethnic group be targeted 'as such' does not prohibit a conviction for genocide in a case in which the perpetrator was also driven by other motivations … The prescribed acts must be committed against the victims *because* of their membership in the proscribed groups, but not solely because of such membership.[169]

Thus a Hutu defendant who claimed that he could not be convicted of genocide for killing Tutsis because he was motivated not by race hate but by the fact that they were his business competitors, had this defence rejected – his intention was to destroy the group, and his motive was irrelevant.[170]

Those who deny the Armenian genocide often do so on the mistaken ground that the crime of genocide requires a government policy or plan. However the appeal chamber of the ICTY held in the case of *Jelisić* that 'the existence of a plan or policy is not a legal ingredient of the crime'.[171] To the extent that 'deliberately inflicting on a group conditions of life calculated to bring about its physical destruction in whole or in part' involves some kind of order that amounts to an 'infliction', then that is satisfied by the Interior Minister's orders for deportation of Armenians in circumstances where their physical destruction by starvation, exhaustion and armed attack was foreseen. Collective or organised action may follow, as when others pursue a common plan, e.g. to rob or rape or murder the deportees. However, this does not need to be a government policy: it can be conduct which has the acquiescence of the authorities.[172] There is no doubt that in 1915 the Ottoman government continued the deportations in the knowledge that many of the deportees would die, and that it passed laws and regulations that enabled it to seize their property on the pretence that it was 'abandoned' – i.e. they would not be allowed to return and reclaim it.

Inferring Genocidal Intention

The main mistake made by genocide-denying historians and by 'genocide equivocators' (those whose primary interest is avoiding offence to Turkey, hence their grasping at any excuse for avoiding the 'G' word) is to think that the law of genocide requires specific evidence of political intent to annihilate a race. This is not what the law requires at all. 'Specific intent' does not call, as they seem to think, for 'specific evidence' – documents or orders – proving a racist motivation for mass killings. The law in this area works by inference: the process of logically deducing a leader's guilty knowledge from his position and his connection to and knowledge of the consequences of what can be proved to have happened. Crucially, the court must look to see whether there has been 'a pattern of purposeful action'[173] from which a genocidal intent may be deduced – and it is precisely that pattern of CUP action – dehumanisation, ethnic hatred fuelled by nationalist fervour, preparation, persecution, massacres, deportation laws, extermination followed by expropriation of property and afterwards (and still) denial – from which the CUP's guilty intention may be deduced.

The most recent leading case on genocide law – the decision of the appeals chamber of the ICTY in *Prosecutor v Radovan Karadžić*[174] delivered in July 2013, describes the importance of inferential proof:

> By its nature, genocidal intent is not usually susceptible to direct proof … in the absence of direct evidence, genocidal intent may be inferred from a number of facts and circumstances, such as the general context, the perpetration of other culpable acts systematically directed against the same group, the systematic targeting of victims on account of their membership in a particular group, the repetition of destructive and discriminatory acts, or the existence of a plan or policy.[175]

In other words, all the circumstances must be taken into account to determine whether the particular defendant, if a political or military leader, knew of and ordered or at least approved of racist measures by his forces. The court made clear – and this is important in the Armenian context – that is it not necessary for the actual physical killers – like the *chettis* or the Kurdish brigands – to have genocidal intent. They may just be following orders, or have no idea of the overall plan or no hostility to the race or religion of the victims because they just want to rob them of their money or rape their women or sell their girls into slavery. They will perpetrate the acts that will be construed as genocide if those who order and approve them do so for reasons of racial or religious hatred. The point made by denialist historians, that some of the killing was carried out by bands of marauding Kurds, is nothing to the point: the government deportation policy was directed against Armenians and conducted quite deliberately in ways which exposed them to murder and rape and enslavement by those Kurds, as well as by *chetti* death squads, connected secretly to the government through the Special Organisation.

The *Karadžić* decision is significant for proving guilty intention in cases of complicity to commit genocide. There was such complicity, between Young Turk leaders and their district commanders, just as there was between Karadžić (the highest military and civilian authority in Republika Srpska) and his commanders like General Mladić. Karadžić has been charged with involvement in a criminal enterprise, together with others in the Bosnian Serb leadership, to 'ethnically cleanse' municipalities in Bosnia and Herzegovina by killing groups of Bosnian Muslims and Croats – because they were Muslim and Croat. The trial court had ordered his acquittal on this genocide charge because it mistakenly thought that the physical perpetrators of the killing needed to have genocidal intent and there was no direct evidence against those who were accused of having it when they approved their actions. The appeal chamber restored the charge, and made clear that indirect and circumstantial evidence was sufficient to permit an inference of genocidal intent, which could in any event be deduced from private admissions Karadžić had made (similar to those made by Talaat to US Ambassador Morgenthau) that he wanted the offending race to 'disappear' from Bosnia. Although the court was at this point only concerned to find a *prima facie* case against Karadžić, its use of inference illustrates the way in which proof of genocide would be established in the case of the CUP leadership in 1915.

The importance of proof by inference for establishing genocidal intent has recently been underlined by the appeals chamber of the International Criminal Court in its decision to restore the genocide charges against the Sudanese leader Omar al-Bashir.[176] The pre-trial chamber had wrongly thought that the prosecution, which relied exclusively on inference to substantiate its allegations of genocide against Bashir, could not proceed to arrest him unless it could show that the inference of genocidal intention was the only reasonable inference from the evidence. This, the appeal chamber pointed out, was the test to be applied at the end of the trial: if there was no other reasonable inference, then the case would be proved beyond reasonable doubt. In order to obtain an arrest warrant, however, the prosecution had merely to present sufficient evidence to show that genocidal intention was one reasonable inference. There could be others, but these might be negatived from evidence forthcoming later. Both the *Bashir* and *Karadžić* decisions, from the appeal chambers of the two most important international criminal courts, confirm a method of inferential proof of genocide which denialists and equivocators alike fail to understand. What appears from the evidence of the consequences of the deportations summarised in Chapters 2 and 3 – evidence of killings, torture and imposition of conditions of life where death for a substantial number is inevitable, all directed against Armenians because they are Armenians – leads to an inescapable inference that those political leaders who gave the orders intended that a substantial part of the Armenian population would be exterminated in consequence. There is no other inference that is 'reasonable', and in any event genocidal intent is amply proved by Talaat's statements to diplomats and by cables and correspondence from government leaders.

Genocidal intent may be inferred from the very scale or proportion of the casualties – 'their massive and/or systematic nature, or their atrocity'.[177] To kill, for example, 600,000 of an ethnic group of 1.1 million (the lowest Turkish government estimate of the scale of the Armenian genocide) is on any view so disproportionate as to permit an inference of genocidal intent, as well as the systematic nature of the arrests and deportations across most of Anatolia, and the extreme cruelty of the massacres and the starvation and the untreated diseases, and the laws requiring expropriation of Armenian property. Notwithstanding the war, something had to be done – and the very fact that nothing was done suggests that those in a position to do something did nothing for a reason. In the *Karadžić & Mladić* case, the court said that intent should be inferred from 'the general political doctrine which gave rise to the acts'[178] and from a pattern of discriminatory conduct. Here the 'Turkification' campaign which preceded the deportations must come into play – the constant drum-beat of Turanian superiority, together with 'the use of derogatory language towards members of the targeted groups'[179] – the Tutsis were 'cockroaches', the Bosnian Muslims and the Armenians were 'tubercular microbes'. The court may also infer 'specific intent' from the combined effect of political speeches or projects laying the ground for genocidal action.[180] The Young Turks made serious threats to the Armenians, changed the names of their towns and streets and denied the use of their language. The government religious mouthpiece, a tame ayatollah, even issued a *fatwa* against Christians (Germans excepted).

Perhaps the most conclusive evidence of genocidal intent comes from the laws themselves, promulgated by the CUP in late 1915 and early 1916, which permitted the state to expropriate the 'abandoned' homes and property of deportees, and which set up 'liquidation commissions' to dispose of their assets. This is proof positive of an intention that Armenians should never return – survivors of the death marches would have nothing to return to, or for.

Although destruction of a group's culture and history, and museums and monuments and churches, is not (as Lemkin would have wished) listed among the Article III acts of genocide, evidence of their destruction can certainly support an inference of genocidal intent, by evincing a hatred that is clearly directed against the race or religion of the victim group. As the ICTY courts have held, in a passage endorsed by the ICJ in *Bosnia v Serbia*, 'attacks on the cultural and religious property and symbols of the targeted group ... may legitimately be considered as evidence of an intent to physically destroy the group'.[181] The way in which over 1,000 Armenian churches were burned down, and others were turned into mosques or munitions depots, whilst schools were taken over and cultural monuments destroyed, is highly relevant, as of course is the selection of its cultural elite – novelists and poets, professors and schoolteachers – for early annihilation.

For all the legalistic quibbles over 'specific intent', it can really be blindingly obvious. As the World Court said of Srebrenica, 'the Bosnian Serb forces not only knew that the combination of the killing of the men with the forcible transfer of the women, children and elderly would inevitably result in the physical disappearance of the Bosnian Muslim population of Srebrenica, but clearly intended through these acts to physically destroy this group'.[182] So it may be said that the CUP leadership not only knew that the combination of the arrest and 'disappearance' of Armenian intellectuals and leaders, followed by call-ups of its men and their massacre after transfer to labour battalions, and the killing of able-bodied men remaining in the villages followed by the forcible transfer of the women, children and elderly under conditions where hundreds of thousands of them would die, would inevitably result in their physical disappearance from eastern Anatolia, but it 'clearly intended through these acts to physically destroy this group'.

'Ethnic Cleansing'

This phrase has no legal meaning, although it is often used as a euphemism for genocide, just as 'relocation' is used as a euphemism for ethnic cleansing. On any view it will amount to a crime against humanity, defined by Article 7 of the Rome Statute for the International Criminal Court as the crime of 'deportation or forcible transfer of populations', meaning 'forced displacement by expulsion or other coercive acts from the area in which they are lawfully present without grounds permitted under international law'.[183] This form of 'ethnic cleansing' is a crime against humanity when committed 'as part of a widespread or systematic attack directed against any civilian population'.[184] There can be no doubt at all that the Armenian deportations were exactly that. Ethnic cleansing will amount to genocide if there is an intention that the 'cleansed' group should be substantially destroyed, in the course or consequence of the extirpation process. In the *Bosnia v Serbia* case, the ICJ interpreted the phrase 'ethnic cleansing' to mean 'rendering an area ethnically homogenous by using force or intimidation to remove persons of given groups from the area'.[185] To amount to genocide, this must be accompanied by an intention that a significant part of the group should be destroyed. The court accepted that ethnic cleansing, if accompanied by killing, torture or debilitating living conditions, 'may be significant as indicative of the presence of a specific intention inspiring those acts'.[186]

There is no dispute that the Ottoman government was responsible for 'ethnic cleansing' by ordering the Armenians removed to Syria. This amounts to genocide if it was accompanied by the infliction of conditions of life calculated to destroy the group. (Without such intent it would still amount to a crime against humanity, given that it was committed on a widespread and systematic scale against civilians.) The ICJ in its *Bosnia v Serbia* decision,[187] reaffirmed in its 2015 decision in *Croatia v Serbia*, cautioned that ethnic cleansing will in some circumstances constitute genocide, but is not necessarily or always carried out with a destructive intent. Whether or not it does amount to genocide will depend on whether those who order the deportations or those who carry out the orders are aware that the manner and circumstances of the deportations would inevitably involve physical or mental destruction of whole or part of the group. It would be unrealistic to suggest, in the circumstances of the Armenian deportations, that those involved, at ministerial, departmental and local CUP levels, did not have foreknowledge of the lethal consequences of their policy.

In any event they were well aware, throughout the year during which they were underway, that the deportations had turned into death marches. It was well known, and publicised throughout the world (especially in the neutral United States) that Armenians were dying in their hundreds of thousands, and those who put them in these conditions did nothing to extract them or bring the conditions to an end by, for example, providing homes at the end of the march, or supplying sufficient food and medical services, or protecting the deportees or punishing all of those who attacked them. (A number of Kurdish leaders and Turkish officials were prosecuted, ostensibly for killing Armenians, but closer analysis suggests that this was to placate Germany and that those chosen for prosecution posed a threat to the government or were really guilty of keeping for themselves property seized from Armenians.)[188] There is ample evidence that the CUP leadership knew of the massacres. The US ambassador, Henry Morgenthau, complained several times to Interior Minister Talaat Pasha about his government's 'extermination' policy, and quotes Talaat as replying, 'We have already disposed of three quarters of the Armenians; there are none left in Bitlis, Van and Erzurum. The hatred between the Turks and the Armenians is now so intense that we have got to finish with them. If we don't, they will plan their revenge.'[189] In a modern war crimes trial, the ambassador's testimony would be relied upon as evidence of an admission by Talaat to the specific intention necessary for his guilt of genocide, under the 'command responsibility' principle that is a central doctrine of international law, namely that commanders are guilty of international crimes committed by their soldiers or subordinates if they know about them, and do not act either to stop them or at least to punish the perpetrators.

Can 'Military Necessity' Be a Defence?

G enocide can occur in a war, whether international or local, or in peace (so it is not regarded as a 'war crime'). This is of some significance since denialists claim that there was a civil war in Anatolia, with a pro-Russian resistance movement spear-headed by Dashnak separatists. It is, however, settled that the Genocide Convention applies to repressive military action by one side within a civil war: Yugoslavia (when it still existed) argued that its actions against Bosnian Muslims could not amount to genocide because it was entitled to suppress their insurrection, but this claim was roundly rejected by the ICJ.[190] It can never be justifiable to commit genocide as a reprisal for an uprising. As Professor Schabas has explained, 'Reprisal as a defence must be proportional, and on this basis its application to genocide would seem inconceivable.'[191] 'Necessity' may be a defence for some extreme measures in war, but never to genocide or indeed to the massacre of civilians. Mladić and his generals may well have perceived it as 'necessary' strategically to destroy the Mus-lims in Srebrenica and so remove an enemy in the Bosnian Serb midst: this on no moral or legal calculus justified the killings and the deportations. Nor could the presence of Dashnak revolutionaries among the Armenian population of eastern Anatolia justify the deportations and massacres set in train by Ottoman government order.

International courts have rejected 'military necessity' as a defence to crimes against humanity like genocide[192] – so the Turkish argument that the deportations were necessary, whatever their toll in human life and spirit, in order to remove potential support for the Dashnaks, must be rejected. Nor does it permit any defence based on a right of 'reprisal' against terrorist attacks or local uprisings. The ICTY has been clear about this when refuting arguments that Serb and Croat forces were in such circumstances entitled to attack civilians:

> The rule which states that reprisals against the civilian population as such, or individual civilians, are prohibited in all circumstances, even when confronted by wrongful behaviour of the other party, is an integral part of customary international law and must be respected in all armed conflicts.[193]

'Necessity' in war can never justify the deliberate killing of civilians: if they are suspected of treason or loyalty to the enemy they may be detained or interned, or prosecuted, but not sent on marches from which they are not expected to return.

State Responsibility

The Republic of Turkey is not being accused of genocide in 1915 – it did not come into existence until 1923. But as it must carry the burden of its predecessor's duties, its 'responsibility' for the genocide is not because the republic was guilty of the atrocities, but because they were ordered and implemented by ministers or bureaucrats of its predecessor, the Ottoman Empire, a state governed at the time by the Committee of Union and Progress Party. Many members of that party re-emerged as ministers and officials in Atatürk's 1923 government, and of course the republic to this very day defends its conduct in 1915 and refuses to accept that the massacres and deportations constituted any international crime. This is sufficient, along with other factors, to make it responsible in international law for its predecessors' actions if they *did* constitute such a crime.[194]

Turkey, however, also denies that a state, as such, can commit the crime of genocide. This was Serbia's argument before the ICJ in *Bosnia v Serbia* and the court rejected it, firstly because all states have an obligation, under Article I of the Genocide Convention, to prevent genocide and that obligation logically implies that states as well as persons are prohibited from committing the crime 'through the actions of their organs or persons or groups whose acts are attributable to them'.[195] This legal responsibility does not depend on proof that the state itself, i.e. the government, intended the destruction of a race, nor whether any of its agents to have actually been convicted of genocide. But 'if an organ of the state, or a person or group whose acts are legally attributable to the state, commits any of the acts proscribed by Article III of the Convention, the international responsibility of that state is incurred'.[196] Article II identifies the genocidal acts as killing or torturing members of a racial or religious group, or inflicting on them unsustainable conditions of life or preventing births. It follows that once these Article II crimes are committed, the state becomes 'responsible' for stopping them and punishing them.

Secondly, the prohibition on state commission of genocide logically proceeds from the state agreeing to the categorisation of genocide as 'a crime under international law' in Article I. Finally, the text of Article IX is clear that 'responsibility for genocide' is contemplated for a state, and not merely for its failure to prevent or punish the crime. The court further held that the prohibition on state genocide not only extends to those acts enumerated in Article III (conspiracy, incitement, attempt and complicity), but a finding of state genocide can occur in the absence of any individual convictions.[197] The state will be responsible if it has 'effective control' over those who carried out the genocidal acts,[198] although a lesser standard, that of 'overall control', has been preferred in war crimes courts.[199] The Ottoman government was certainly in 'overall control' of Anatolia in 1915 and of those who carried out the atrocities there. That control was effective enough, in most of the areas where the killings took place, to shepherd into Anatolia tens of thousands of Muslim refugees from the Balkans, and many of these émigrés were resettled in houses from which Armenian owners had been forcibly expropriated.

Under the laws of state responsibility, the liability of the state for genocide may be engaged:

- If the orders are given and implemented by *de jure* organs of the state i.e. by ministers or government officials, police or regular army officers;[200]
- If the killings are done by *de facto* organs of the state – namely irregular bodies (such as the Special Organisation and its *chetti* gangs of released prisoners), or by death squads and paramilitaries connected with the state agencies;[201] or
- by persons or bodies acting under orders of state organs in a particular set of circumstances.[202]

The standard of proof for state responsibility is not quite the same as the 'beyond reasonable doubt' test that must be satisfied before an individual can be convicted. The claim against a state 'must be proved by evidence that is fully conclusive ... the court requires that it be fully convinced that allegations have been clearly established'.[203] This is a higher standard than the 'balance of probabilities' test that suffices for civil liability, but excludes defences based on mere possibilities or theoretical doubts that might allow an individual to escape conviction.

There is no doubt that deportation orders which were known to inflict conditions of life calculated to bring about the destruction of a substantial part of the Armenian people were given by *de jure* organs of the state such as ministers and government officials, and that massacres involved both *de jure* and *de facto* agents of the Ottoman Empire. Moreover that state was, through the agency of its ministers and officials, well aware of historical animosities prone to break out in mass murder of the Armenian minorities (as had happened with the Hamidian massacres in 1894–6 and 1909) and had stirred up that animosity through its Turkification programme: the officials who ordered the deportations must have known of the likely consequences yet took no effective steps to avoid them or to put safeguards in place and in fact ensured that the state benefited by confiscation of 'abandoned' property. In such circumstances, where killings are being carried out by criminal gangs with the knowledge and acquiescence of authorities who could (but do not) act to prevent them, 'command responsibility' principles make the authorities themselves responsible for murders by criminal gangs which they foresee yet fail to prevent or subsequently to punish.[204]

It is important to understand the basis upon which the ICJ held the Serbian government internationally responsible for the failure to prevent the Srebrenica genocide. Milošević and his generals were 'fully aware of the climate of deep-seated hatred' between the Bosnian Serbs and the Muslims in the Srebrenica region. The evidence proved that they knew there was a serious risk of genocide. Yet they took no initiative to prevent the massacres, despite their influence over Mladić and his force. 'It does not need to be proven that the state concerned definitely had the power to prevent genocide; it is sufficient that it had the means to do so and that it manifestly refrained from using them.'[205] The Ottoman state manifestly had the power to save the Armenians, and obviously had the means to do so.

So too did the allied state of Germany, and the ICJ's ruling on Serbia's complicity in Republika Srpska's genocide in Srebrenica is particularly apposite for Germany's responsibility in international law for its connivance in the Armenian genocide. Berlin was told in no uncertain terms by its diplomats of the Ottoman intentions to exterminate the Armenians, and of the massacres and life-threatening deportations as they were happening. Moreover, it knew in May 1915 of the Entente promise to punish this 'crime against humanity' which Germany undoubtedly had the means to stop – the Ottoman Empire was heavily dependent on German money, munitions and machinery, and German generals and soldiers supported defenders on the Russian and the Dardanelles fronts. Yet the Kaiser and his Chancellor refused to use their power and influence, and Germany even assisted the main perpetrators to escape justice (it sent a destroyer to enable them to escape to Berlin and later refused to extradite them). Milošević's inaction engaged his nation's responsibility for Srebrenica, and so should Bethmann-Hollweg's decision to acquiesce in the crime against humanity he knew was being committed in Anatolia. This complicity in genocide may yet have consequences for the German state, which after the war was required to make reparations for its role in the destruction of the Armenians.

A Crime against Humanity

The indisputable facts of the Armenian deportations and massacres must on any view constitute a crime against humanity. This appellation was applied by the Allies in 1915 more as rhetoric than as a legal description, since international law had not at the time developed a criminal jurisdiction. Today, this category of crime is authoritatively defined by Article 7 of the Statute of the International Criminal Court: it covers widespread or systematic attacks on civilians, specifically including deportation or forcible transfer of population (i.e. 'forced displacement by expulsion or other coercive acts from the area in which they are lawfully present')[206] and persecution (the 'intentional and severe deprivation of fundamental rights by reason of the identity of the group' when such group or collectivity is identifiable 'on racial, national, ethnic, cultural (or) religious grounds...').[207] Thus forcible deportation or persecution amounts to a crime against humanity when part of a 'widespread or systematic attack directed against any civilian population'. It is beyond reasonable doubt that the deportations of the Armenian population of Anatolia, under conditions known to be life threatening, amounted to what would now be accurately described as a crime against humanity, all the more so when attended by the well-attested massacres. Does it therefore matter if it also answers to the description of genocide?

There is a considerable overlap between the two international crimes: in effect, all genocides are crimes against humanity, but by no means do all crimes against humanity amount to genocide. The distinction will rest upon whether the perpetrator has the necessary racist or discriminatory intention to destroy the group in whole or in part. It is this element which makes genocide so heinous, and attaches duties and penalties to perpetrator states under the Genocide Convention. But duties and penalties attach to all crimes against humanity at international law. They cannot be the subject of amnesty, or of time limits on prosecution. They impose duties to extradite suspects and to prosecute perpetrators under what is termed a 'universal jurisdiction', which any state may invoke to punish nationals of other countries who have been responsible for massacres in their own nation. There is a developing right for 'victims' – widely defined – of such crimes to obtain reparations from states which bear responsibility for these crimes. What is most shocking about Armenian genocide denial is that its exponents, so obsessed with legalistic arguments over the elements of the crime of genocide, rarely show any awareness that the 1915 deportations in any event clearly constitute a crime against humanity, for which Turkey, as the successor state of the Ottoman Empire, should be prepared to apologise and to make appropriate reparation (and for which Germany too, ever so silent over the past century, should admit some international responsibility). Were Turkey prepared to admit on this basis the guilt of the Ottomans – in effect, if it were prepared to offer a plea bargain – there would be some hope that both Armenia and Turkey could move on.

Those running the Ottoman Empire in 1915 knew what was apparent to unbiased foreign observers, and their racist intention may be inferred, not only from their reported statements, but also from their knowledge of racial and religious pogroms in 1894–6 and 1909; their deliberate fanning of racial superiority theories in the Turkification programme; the deportation orders and their foresight of the consequences; and their failure to protect the deportees and their laws that effected the expropriation of their homes and property. They instigated and approved the extermination of a significant part of the Armenian race – over half of those who were alive in eastern Turkey at the beginning of 1915. Put another way – if these same events occurred today, there can be no doubt that prosecutions before the International Criminal Court of Talaat and other CUP officials for genocide, for persecution and for other crimes against humanity would succeed. Turkey would be held responsible by the International Court of Justice for genocide and for persecution and would be required to make reparation. That court would also hold Germany responsible for complicity with the genocide and persecution, since it had full knowledge of the massacres and deportations and decided not to use its power and influence over the Ottomans to stop them. But to the overarching legal question that troubles the international community today, namely whether the killings of Armenians in 1915 can properly be described as a genocide, the analysis in this chapter returns a resoundingly affirmative answer.

© HULTON ARCHIVE/GETTY IMAGES

Talaat Pasha (*centre*) in Brest-Litovsk with his chosen allies, Austro-Hungarian (*left*) and German (*right*) foreign ministers.

Enver Pasha – young Turk war minister.

The Sheikh-ul-Islam, appointed by the CUP as spiritual leader of Sunni Muslims, declaring *jihad* (holy war) against infidels (Germans excepted). Constantinople, 14 November 1914.

© THE ARMENIAN GENOCIDE MUSEUM-INSTITUTE

Armenian civilians being led out of the city of Kharput, May 1915.

© THE ARMENIAN GENOCIDE MUSEUM-INSTITUTE

Unarmed Armenian conscripts, drafted into labour battalions, 1915.

On a death march: Armenian
mother with her remaining
possessions – and her child –
photographed by Armin Wegner.

Dr Johannes Lepsius (1858–1926) – German
theologian and missionary who published details of
the Hamidian massacres in 1896 and defied German
censorship to denounce his government's complicity
in the annihilation of Armenians in Turkey in 1915.

Armenian refugees approaching Aleppo, photographed by Armin Wegner.

ARMIN T. WEGNER © WALLSTEIN VERLAG

The end of the road: deportees photographed by Armin Wegner in typhoid-ridden 'relocation', Aleppo/Zor, 1915.

© THE ARMENIAN GENOCIDE MUSEUM-INSTITUTE

'Piles of corpses, among which still living children crawled.' Photograph taken by German consul from Dr Martin Niepage's school in Aleppo to illustrate his protest to German Parliament, 15 October 1915.

Armenian orphans taken in by Near East Relief.

Russian soldiers contemplating the remains of a massacre of Armenian villagers in the Muş province.

Sultan Abdul Hamid II, Gladstone's 'Great Assassin', with blood on his hands.

© ARMENIAN NATIONAL COMMITTEE OF AMERICA

Henry Morgenthau Senior – American
ambassador to the Sublime Porte.

Raphael Lemkin – progenitor of the
Genocide Convention.

© FRANK SCHERSCHEL/THE LIFE PICTURE COLLECTION/GETTY IMAGES

Professor Arnold
Toynbee – compiler and
editor of the Blue Book.

An international lie?
Atatürk contemplates
Perinçek.

Further Background

6. Supporters of the "genocide" claim have argued that Turkey's accession to the EU should be conditional on Turkey's acceptance of the events as "genocide". We disagree. But parliaments in nine of our EU partners have passed resolutions recognising the "genocide" (France; Italy; Poland; Greece; Cyprus; Belgium; Slovakia; the Netherlands; and Sweden). The French, in particular, have a large Armenian diaspora. They have recognised the "genocide" in French law and, ▓▓▓▓▓▓▓▓▓▓▓▓▓▓▓▓▓▓▓▓ *SECTION 22* .

7. Turkey is neuralgic and defensive about the charge of genocide, despite the fact that the events occurred at the time of the Ottoman Empire as opposed to modern day Turkey. There were many Turks who lost their lives in the war and there may also be an element of concern over compensation claims should they accept the charge of genocide. This ▓▓ recognised it. HMG's position, as set out in answers to PQs and replies to letters – for example Ms Quin's letter to Julia Drown MP of 11 February, attached – is that we are aware of no evidence of intent on the part of the Ottoman administration in the of the day to destroy the Armenians (a key element in the crime of genocide) and that it is for historians, not Governments, to determine what happened. HMG is open to criticism in terms of the ethical dimension. But given the importance of our relations (political, strategic and commercial) with Turkey, and that recognising the genocide

1

Reductio ad absurdum:
Foreign Office memos.

In memoriam.

HRANT DINK
1954-2007

CHAPTER 5

JUSTIFYING
GENOCIDE

Justification or Excuse?

TURKEY HAS, SINCE and initially as a result of the leadership of Atatürk, turned into a stable and reasonably progressive democracy and a steadfast NATO ally. But it has had fitful periods of repression under military rule, and its legal system has repeatedly been held to infringe the European Convention on Human Rights, in particular by oppression of Kurdish separatists and through censorship of social media and prosecutions for 'insulting Turkishness'. Its massive commitment to denying genocide is something of a mystery, especially since the crime was committed by the Ottoman Empire, and not the republic under Atatürk, who in 1921 condemned the deportations as 'a shameful act' and later spoke out against 'these residues from the former Young Turk party, who should be held accountable for the massive and brutal expulsion of millions of our Christians from their homes, and for the massacres'.[208] Yet Turkey, especially under Prime Minister (now President) Erdoğan, has gone on the offensive: it evinces no shame at all about the massacres. And its arguments reduce to the proposition that this kind of treatment of minorities is acceptable, even today. That is why its denialist arguments are more than just deplorable – they are dangerous, unless powerfully refuted.

The government of Turkey defends the deportation policy (as the CUP did at the time) as having been necessary for the country's self-defence: it was justified in removing 'fifth columnists' at the moment of the Gallipoli invasion, as well as threats on its eastern border where the Armenian population posed a real risk of welcoming a Russian invasion – a risk that was demonstrated by an uprising of Armenians in Van on 20 April. However, despite acknowledging the existence of pockets of armed Armenian resistance, few historians think this was a justification for ordering the deportation of an entire population. As Donald Bloxham concludes:

> Overall, there is little evidence of a general Armenian threat in the eastern region ... Armenian religious and political leaders in 1914–15 were actually preaching loyalty and placidity as well as encouraging young men to fulfil their Ottoman army obligations. Moreover, the vast majority of Armenians remained unpoliticised. What Armenian resistance there was

appears to have been localised, desperate and *reactive* in the face of liquidation.[209]

The cautious Christopher de Bellaigue, sympathetic to the Turks and an advocate for 'avoiding the G word' (whether or not genocide occurred) nonetheless observes:

> Relentlessly monitored, intermittently terrorised, the vast majority of Armenians, even in the politically literate towns, were in no state to launch a rebellion. For most poor farmers, deportation was a death sentence, and there is no doubt that deportation orders came, for village after village, from central government, implemented by local officials who knew that the hastily assembled convoys would be subjected to pillage, rape and massacre from local paramilitaries, robbers and police. Many killings were motivated by opportunistic greed or lust, but they would not have taken place without a rooted ethnic hatred towards Armenians, or the religious hatred encapsulated in the cry of 'God is Great' which accompanied many of the killings.[210]

These are accurate summaries of the evidence. Nonetheless, it would be wrong to discount the perception of the Ottoman leaders that the Armenian population was a threat – a fifth column that could ally itself with Russia in the event of an invasion. When the Tsarist forces advanced into eastern Anatolia later in 1915, some Armenian soldiers in their ranks treated local Kurds and Turks with brutality. And towards the war's end, after the tide had turned in 1917, there were some atrocities committed by vengeful Armenians, and in due course, after the Turkish nationalists had regrouped, they too committed reprisal massacres – making Auden's weary point:

> I and the public know
> What all schoolchildren learn,
> Those to whom evil is done
> Do evil in return.

These clashes – they continued until the tiny new state of Armenia was established and then absorbed into the USSR – cannot alter the characterisation of Ottoman actions in 1915 as genocide. They do not excuse or extenuate, much less justify, a policy that aimed to rid eastern Anatolia of a race that accounted for 30 per cent of its population. The crime of genocide was introduced by the Convention precisely to deter the formation of a policy to persecute minorities in times of threat and national emergency, when minorities which have been discriminated against are for that very reason tempted to welcome an invader. This danger may justify their temporary removal from the front line, or the internment of revolutionary leaders, but it cannot begin to excuse what the Harbord Report to the US government in 1919 described as 'this wholesale attempt on the race'.[211]

The Denialists

Denialist historians (and 'denialist' is used in a descriptive, not a pejorative, sense) have been concerned to explain the circumstances under which the deportations came to be ordered. They highlight the tensions arising from the collapse of the Ottoman Empire and the Allied landing in the Dardanelles. They emphasise the provocation caused by armed Armenian resistance to Turkish rule, and the 'revolutionary' aims of the Dashnaks which contributed in 1915 to a serious uprising in the province of Van. They point out that a number of Armenians defected to fight with the Russian forces against the Turks after their incursion in July, albeit after the deportations had started, and these forces included recruits from the 1.7 million Armenians who lived in Russia. They claim that some massacres were the work of marauding Kurdish gangs, not obviously connected with central government, and that many deaths came from starvation and disease. All this is true up to a point, but it serves only to explain some of the motives behind the genocide and to identify the Kurds as an opportunist perpetrator group: it cannot serve to excuse an inexcusable crime, committed by CUP leaders and local officials who should have known – and obviously did know – that the *chetti* massacres and conditions of life they were inflicting upon Armenians *because* they were Armenians would inevitably result in the death of a substantial proportion of that people.

Justin McCarthy, a professor at Louisville University in the US, is the Western historian whose work is particularly relied upon by the Turkish government. It sometimes illuminates an important truth (he has, for example, confirmed the 'brutal and unlawful' murder of an Armenian leader by the governor of the province of Van,[212] which others say sparked the uprising). His analysis does not succeed because it is not legally correct and does not factually exclude a finding of genocide. He sees the 1915 events as a civil war, and describes it as 'a war of extermination. If you were caught by the other side you were killed. Neither side spared women or children.' This description does not seem to accord with the facts found by most other historians, but in any event can still fit the definition of genocide, if one side's killing has been directed or permitted by its government or government officials with the object of destroying a race.

McCarthy admits that the Ottoman government

ordered the deportation of the Armenians of Anatolia to Syria

> ... on the ensuing forced marches great numbers of Armeni-
> ans died from hunger and attacks, many of them killed by the
> tribesmen who were involved in a war to the death with
> the Armenians. There is no question but that the convoys
> were not well protected by the Ottomans. However more than
> 200,000 Armenian deportees arrived safely in greater Syria.[213]

This too is entirely consistent with a finding of genocide: that some victims survived (as they did in Nazi Germany and Rwanda and Bangladesh) is nothing to the point. The Ottoman government bears command responsibility for ordering the forced marches and deciding not to protect the convoys adequately, in the knowledge that many on the 'death marches' would be killed or die from starvation and disease in the absence of food or medical supplies. (Talaat himself had only the previous year rejected the idea of resettling Muslim refugees in Syrian desert areas, because they would starve). McCarthy has made the fatuous remark, 'If this was genocide, it was a very strange genocide indeed in which many more killers than victims perished.'[214] Numbers do not actually matter: it is the question of genocidal intent which counts. Besides, in 1915, the victims were predominantly Armenian, unless McCarthy is referring, like the Turkish Foreign Office website, on which his work prominently features, to the Turkish losses in the Dardanelles and on the Russian front between 1914 and 1922, which would make an entirely false point since most of those Turks were killed by the Entente allies and not by Armenians. Even assuming those skewed figures, a much higher proportion of Armenians than Turks were killed – 55 per cent on McCarthy's own calculus (600,000 out of 1.1 million) or 75 per cent (1.5 million out of 2 million). And the figures are skewed, if the comparison is with the Turks who were killed by Armenian brigades and brigands when the Russian army invaded later in

1916–17. There were massacres in war then, certainly, and one Turkish historian puts Turkish casualties at Armenian hands as high as 40,000,[215] whilst Armenian historians suggest that their own peoples' losses in reprisals during this later period were even higher. McCarthy is loudly sympathetic to the Turkish cause and has addressed the Turkish parliament to advance in passionate terms his theories exonerating their forebears, but his work does not refute the charge of genocide. The truth that his research does not refute is that a substantial proportion of the Armenians of the Ottoman Empire perished in 1915, as a foreseeable and foreseen consequence of a policy decision by the Ottoman government.

McCarthy is the historian upon whom the British government relied for its stance, until 2010, that the genocide could not be proven (see later, Chapter 7). He admits that over half a million Armenians perished. He adds 'as a result of their armed rebellion against the Ottoman state', although since most of the victims on the marches were women, children and old men this seems a propagandist rather than an accurate comment and flies in the face of evidence that most Armenian community leaders remained loyal to the central government. He goes on to admit that the causes of death were 'sickness, exhaustion following long marches, immediate change of climate and the attacks of marauders upon rich convoys'[216] – all life-threatening conditions of which those who ordered the deportations must have known (and anyone who has examined the contemporaneous photographs of the huddled masses carrying their few possessions may find his description of 'rich convoys' both misleading and distasteful). He adds that 'the Turks are estimated to have lost over 1 million people owing to similar causes' – but estimated by whom, in relation to what period? There were no deportations of Muslims ordered by the Ottoman government, and there were comparatively few Turkish casualties of the uprisings in four Armenian cities (only one of which – in Van – was successful and then only for two months). Of course, tens of thousands of Muslims were displaced (from homes that in some cases they had taken over from deportees) by the subsequent advance in parts of Anatolia by the Russian army (which had several brigades of Armenian volunteers, mostly Armenians living in Russia) and over a million Turks lost their lives in the course of a war the Ottoman government cynically chose to enter on the side of Germany, but to suggest that this in any way detracts from the genocide would be disingenuous: the comparison is not of like with like. (The heinousness of the Holocaust cannot be diminished, let alone excused, by claiming that more Germans than Jews died in World War II.)

Turkey's Position Today

The authoritative source of genocide denial by the Republic of Turkey is the website of its Foreign Ministry.[217] Under the heading 'Controversy between Turkey and Armenia about the Events of 1915' it contains a carefully honed 'overview of historical facts' which are said to refute the claim of genocide or indeed any allegation of serious wrongdoing by the Ottomans or their forces. This is followed by a selection of supportive speeches from Justin McCarthy, and more nuanced articles by Turkish historians. The website is at first blush most notable for what it does not mention – the 'Turkification' campaign of the CUP, for example, its changing of Christian place names and its laws that expropriated Armenian property without consideration or compensation. These, the very indicia of genocide, are nowhere mentioned. Nor, despite desperate attempts on every page to refute the 'G' word, is there any mention of the alternative, the commission of a crime against humanity. As we have seen, the crime of genocide is the worst example of a crime against humanity, and mass murder of a race that does not amount to genocide comes within the definition of other crimes against humanity – persecution, forcible deportation, extermination and the like – all defined authoritatively in Article 7 of the Rome Treaty (1998), which established the International Criminal Court (see Appendix 2). The Turkish government does not accept, or seem to understand, or even deign to mention, the only position logically open after it denies that the 'Young Turks' bore genocidal intent, namely to accept that their orders for widespread and systematic deportation, in deadly circumstances, of those of the Armenian race were a crime against humanity – beyond doubt, the crime of persecution. Instead, the website denies all wrongdoing, other than by using the '*tu quoque*' argument, rejected at Nuremberg, namely 'you (or others) did it too'. It was civil war, the website says: the Armenians killed Muslims and would have allied with Russia, so it was not only excusable but justifiable to 'relocate' them from the front line.

There are many things wrong with this picture, apart from the facts that have been omitted from it. It begins by lamenting the 'tragic period' for all those who 'suffered immensely' – Turks as well as Armenians, and others in the empire. Labelling a crime a 'tragedy' is a routine public relations tactic by those who defend the indefensible and has been repeatedly used by the British government to avoid alienating Turkey. The website insists that more Turks than Armenians suffered in this 'tragedy': 'Greater numbers of Turks died or were killed in years leading to and during the War.'[218] This playground calculation ('my loss is bigger than your loss') is nothing to the point: they were not killed in greater numbers by Armenians, but by Russians and British and French. Nor is it relevant that there were a number of massacres of Turks, by Armenians, after the tide of battle turned in 1917 – this has nothing to do with whether there was genocide in 1915. Nor does

Armenian terrorism in the 1970s and early 1980s, blamed for the assassination of some thirty Turkish diplomats and airline officials, which features repeatedly on the website. This was indeed a wicked form of reprisal, because it sought to extinguish the lives of diplomats and airline passengers because of their race – and was itself (as the distinguished Turkish lawyer Mümtaz Soysal pointed out) a genocidal campaign. But rather than refuting the charge of genocide in 1915, the comparison actually illuminates it.

After exuding sympathy for all in the Ottoman Empire, the 'Overview' waxes lyrical about 'eight centuries of Turkish Armenian relationship, which was predominantly about friendship, tolerance and peaceful coexistence'[219] between Turks and Armenians. But it was, of course, peace at the price of second-class citizenship, and tolerance so long as Armenians were prepared to accept that status. By 1914, indeed by the light of Article 61 of the Treaty of Berlin in 1878, this was unacceptable, and Turkey today should have the integrity to acknowledge it. After all, the Republic of Turkey is a different country, with people who should be proud of the fact that under Atatürk, they emerged as a modern nation from the authoritarian Ottomans and the vicious CUP. Instead, they have chosen to remain mired in the hypersensitive nationalism that holds every honest criticism of their history as an insult to 'Turkishness'. (In this respect, the comparison with modern Germany's rigorous refusal to defend any aspect of the Holocaust could not be more striking).

Then we are told that it all happened in 'an Empire at the verge of collapse fighting for survival on various fronts'.[220] True, up to a point, although this would not excuse a crime against humanity and there is no admission that 'the Empire' did not deserve to survive, or that its fate was due to the CUP's choice to throw its army behind Germany, notwithstanding the illegality and brutality of the German invasion of Belgium. Neutrality was the moral option, which most people in the empire favoured, but the Young Turks calculated that Germany was likely to win and by allying with it they might grab some land from Russia and win back some crumbs of their crumbled empire.

Then comes the main contention – that in response to 'politically motivated missionary activities and a radicalisation and militarisation of nationalistic Armenian groups, some of which joined forces with the invading Russian army',[221] the government 'ordered in 1915 the Armenian population residing in or near the war-zone to be *relocated* to the southern provinces away from the supply routes and army transport lines.'(Emphasis added.)[222]

This is the big euphemism – the use of the pallid word 'relocation' to describe forcible expropriation of land and home, mass executions of menfolk, followed by marching women and children at gunpoint for hundreds of miles unprotected from climate or disease or pillaging brigands, and ending in a typhoid-ridden swamp in a desert, without food or housing. As for the 'relocatees' living 'in or near the war zone', the map shows just how far most of them lived from that zone. In Ankara, very far from the conflict, some 60,000 Armenians were deported out of a population of 62,000. The notion that military emergency required the 'relocations', other perhaps than from Van when it was recaptured, must be rejected.

How to justify, even on the underestimated Turkish assumption that 'only' 600,000 out of 1.1 million died (which deliberately ignores the many thousands who were sold into slavery or who were forced to convert to Islam to save their lives), the carnage wreaked on the convoys and the government's indifference to the death toll over the months that it was mounting? The website claims that the government 'took a number of measures for safe transfer' but 'war-time conditions' were responsible for the deaths – banditry, famine, epidemics, but never the central government.

This is not credible: it was the central government that promoted and passed 'The Temporary Law of Deportation' and soon knew (and must have foreseen) the consequence. The website admits the existence of some 'unruly officials' – an apparent reference to provincial governors who ordered the murder of Armenian men, in which case 'unruly' is an even more disgraceful euphemism than 'relocation'. It claims that they were punished in 1916 after courts martial and some were, but usually for corruption and for making personal gain from seizure of Armenian property. There is no mention of the confiscation laws that permitted these seizures of 'abandoned' property and allowed Armenian homes to be sold and used for rehousing of Muslim refugees – proof positive that the central government did not intend the return of the 'relocatees'.

The website claims that 'no authentic evidence exists' for a 'pre-meditated plan to kill off Armenians'. Criminal law works authentically by inference from all the evidence: quite apart from confessions by Turkish leaders and the verdicts of the Constantinople trials, the deportations were certainly pre-planned, as were the laws providing for asset and home seizure by the state. Sending Armenians (and only Armenians) on long marches in the knowledge that most would be killed en route, by brigands and local vengeful Muslims, or by disease and starvation, necessarily entails pre-meditation, and government responsibility for the foreseeable consequences.

'The Ottoman socio-cultural fabric did not harbour racist attitudes that would facilitate such a horrific crime,'[223] the website blandly maintains, although that fabric facilitated horrific crimes at Urfa Cathedral in 1895 and at Adana in 1909. The 'Turkification' campaign after 1908 was designed to educate Turks in their socio-cultural superiority, to demonise Armenians as diseases on the body politic and to remove non-Islamic names from their towns and streets. The CUP's tame ayatollah even pronounced a *fatwa* on infidels when the war started, offering a pathway to paradise to any killers of Christians (Germans excepted).

The website moves on to set out in more detail what it terms 'The Events of 1915 and the Turkish/Armenian Controversy over History',[224] although this controversy is over law, and its application to history. It repeats that the only actual guilt, for loss of hundreds of thousands of Armenian lives, attaches to 'some unruly Ottoman officials'. It goes on to develop the 'military necessity' defence – the Armenian population was in cahoots with the Russians in order to obtain their own autonomous homeland: this meant that Armenians 'residing in and near the war-zone should be relocated to the southern Ottoman provinces away from the supply routes and army transport lines.'[225] This does not begin to justify deportation of old men, women and children, who constituted no threat at all, let alone deporting them from places hundreds of miles from 'supply routes and army transport lines'. The website, like denialists in general, ignores the well-attested fact that conscription for able-bodied Armenian men, aged twenty to forty-five, was introduced on 3 August 1914, the day after the secret agreement with Germany, and later extended to those in the 18–20 and 45–60 categories. In February 1915, these conscripts were disarmed and moved into labour battalions in the Ottoman army. The result was to denude the villages of eastern Anatolia of most able-bodied men. There were still men in exempt categories, and draft dodgers and males awaiting call-up, but the obvious point is that there were not many fighting men available: the picture of a seething province of murderous insurgents must be a distortion.

The website is bereft of reference to the independent observers who refute the 'civil war' argument. Vice-Marshal Pomiankowski, the Austro-Hungarian military plenipotentiary attached to

Ottoman Army Headquarters, said that the able-bodied Armenian men were conscripted and liquidated 'in order to render defenceless the rest of the population'. He had investigated the uprising in Van, and characterised it as an 'act of despair' and a defensive action because the Armenians 'recognised that the general butchery had begun in the environs of Van and that they would be the next victims'. Morgenthau, too, noted that able-bodied men were removed 'for the purpose of rendering the weaker part of the population an easy prey'. The German consular despatches to Berlin in 1915 consider and refute the suggestion that there was any kind of civil war or that Armenians had any intention or capacity to mount a general uprising – 'the vast majority are not in any way involved in uprisings,' said the vice-consul at Samsun, and Ambassador Wangenheim himself, chief architect of the Turkish military alliance with Germany, told Berlin emphatically on 15 April 1915 that since the overthrow of the Sultan, 'the Armenians have relinquished the idea of a revolution, and presently there is no organisation for such a revolution'.[226]

So-Called 'Facts'

The next section of the website seeks to refute 'The Armenian Allegation of Genocide' with a number of what it terms 'facts':[227]

> Fact 1: Fewer than 1.5 million Armenians lived in the Ottoman Empire, so fewer than 1.5 million would have died.

The suggestion is made that 1.05 million Armenians lived there (the Ottoman estimate) and 600,000 died. These propagandists do not seem to realise the legal significance of what they are admitting. 'Genocide' involves the extinction of a race or *any part* of a race. The extinction of over 60 per cent of a race is a very substantial part. Besides which, of course, the Armenian Church (which should have known) estimated 2.1 million Armenians; at the time it was widely said that 1.5 million had died; other reasonable calculations by impartial historians range from 800,000 to 1.2 million. Does it matter? Not for genocide, and not for crimes against humanity. That it matters so much to the Turkish Foreign Ministry (only 600,000 died!) suggests a cynical refusal to take on board the iniquity of any mass killing.

> Fact 2: Armenian losses were few in comparison to the 2.5 million Muslims dead from the same period.

Armenian losses, of 60 per cent of their people, 'few'? In any event, the 2.5 million turns out *not* to be in 'the same period', but from 1912–22, over which time Muslims were in Turkish armies that lost the Balkans (1912), lost the war, and then (1919–22) fought against each other, the Russians, the Greeks, the Assyrians and the Armenians. This is a hopeless and hapless argument. Everyone suffers in wars, especially of their state's making – there was no necessity at all for the Young Turks to enter the World War but they did so out of greed for spoils and they committed the initial aggression against Russia in 1914. They sacrificed two million of their men over the next four years for no legitimate purpose. But the question here is whether it can ever be right for a government, when fighting a war, to take action to wipe out a large part of a race, for the most part innocent civilians, in order to destroy a small terrorist (aka independence) faction within that race. The decision to do so was taken by the Young Turks, and has since been taken by other rulers – most recently by President Rajapaksa of Sri Lanka, whose army in 2009 killed

40,000–70,000 civilians in order to destroy the Tamil Tigers. It is a decision which is wrong, both morally and legally, and one problem with denying the Armenian genocide on this ground is that it can assist rulers like Rajapaksa to defend genocidal mass murder as a legitimate tactic to drain a terrorist swamp.

Fact 3: Certain oft-cited Armenian evidence is derived from dubious and prejudiced sources.

So is oft-cited Turkish evidence, which is why impartial scholars place weight on German and Austrian diplomats and missionaries, and on the Harbord Report, and American consular cables. The website only identifies one allegedly 'dubious source', namely the American ambassador Morgenthau, on the grounds that he maligned the Turks in order to persuade President Wilson to enter the war (this contradicts another denialist criticism of Morgenthau, namely that some of his incriminating quotes from conversations with Talaat were published after the war was over and do not appear in his cables). Brazenly, 'Fact 3' is bolstered with a quote from the US ambassador in Turkey in 1921 – six years later – complaining about false reports at that time of Turks massacring Armenians. The quote is deceptive: it has no relevance to events six years previously. Whatever Morgenthau's motives, there is no doubt that he had many conversations with Talaat and reported the latter's most self-incriminating remarks in his cables to Washington. Morgenthau is, of course, just one of many sources. As ambassador, he was vouchsafed information from a large number of his own sources, notably American consuls and missionaries in eastern Anatolia, where the deportations began, and Aleppo, where they ended. Their reports and cables leave no doubt of the CUP's genocidal intent.

Fact 4: Armenian deaths do not constitute genocide.

This proposition – which is one of law and not fact – relies primarily on the claim that the Armenians as a group took up arms against their own government, rushed to join the Russian forces and were fighting a civil war led by Dashnaks and Hunchaks. This does not tally with objective accounts, which suggest that the liberation fighters (or terrorists, as Turkey invariably describes them) had little support from community leaders such as churchmen and merchants. The only evidence here presented consists of quotes from Dashnak leaders, who naturally exaggerate their own influence in articles written for Dashnak newspapers. Whilst it is true that the Russian army had several Armenian brigades, they were mostly made up from Armenians living in Russia. The website makes the interesting legal argument that 'Ottoman Armenians' violent political alliance with the Russian forces' means that it was their politics and not their race that caused them to be dispossessed and deported, i.e. that the killings (like Stalin's extermination of the Kulaks) amounted to 'politicide' but not genocide. This is an admission of a crime against humanity, but the website does not notice the logic of its own argument. That argument in any event muddles motive with intention: however much the Young Turks may have believed that the Armenians would welcome a Russian army, they intended to destroy them because they were Armenians. Besides which, the convoys comprised old men, women and children who were in no sense violent political revolutionaries or of any potential assistance to the Russian army. Most of the able-bodied men had been conscripted into labour battalions: those left were in many towns massacred by order of provincial governors before the march.

Then reliance is placed on the fact that the 'relocation' orders make no mention of any direction to kill the relocatees – a 'fact' that is neither here nor there, since genocide rarely comes with an explicit order to kill. The Wannsee Meeting minutes, for example, record only a decision that Jewish women and children should be 'evacuated to the East' whilst older men should be put in 'care homes'. One Talaat directive certainly exudes concern for the deportees and gives instructions about food and medicine for the marches, but even denialists accept that any such instructions, if they were given, were not carried out, and this was obvious to all observers and must have been known to the central government.

There is a brief passage below 'Fact 4' which amounts to an admission, namely that 'columns of hundreds of Armenians [were] guarded by as few as two Ottoman Gendarmes. When local Muslims attacked the columns, Armenians were robbed and killed.' But the admission is quickly followed by an excuse – 'These Muslims had themselves suffered greatly at the hands of the Armenians and Russians.' Does this mean that the 'local Muslims' (in fact, normally gangs of *chettis* – prisoners released in order to kill) could be excused for inflicting criminal vengeance on unguarded columns of women and children? Murderous revenge can never be acceptable, whether from suffering Muslims or from the suffering Armenians who later killed old 'Young Turks' as part of Operation Nemesis. Raphael Lemkin was inspired to devise a genocide law precisely because he realised, after the acquittal of Talaat's killer, that there should be no excuse for the vengeful vigilante.

Then there are some invidious comparisons with the Holocaust – the worst of genocides certainly, but not for that reason the only example of the crime. 'The Jews of Berlin were killed, their synagogues defiled. The Armenians of Istanbul lived through World War I, their churches open', the website relates. This is an intellectually dishonest point. Firstly, the Armenian leaders of Istanbul were rounded up on 24 April, and most were never seen again, and there is evidence from Lepsius that 10,000 Armenians were discreetly deported from Constantinople (others estimate 30,000). Secondly, over 1,600 Armenian churches in Anatolia were destroyed, or turned into Mosques. Thirdly, Istanbul (i.e. Constantinople) was the capital, where the foreign embassies and press agencies kept watch and where the government could not therefore allow any destruction of Christian churches, to which their allies, the Germans, went to worship.

Fact 5: The Malta trials exonerated Turkey.

This 'fact' advances the preposterous argument that there were no crimes committed against the Armenians, because those Turks taken to Malta for trial were 'acquitted' and 'exonerated'. This is a lie, because they were never charged, let alone tried, so they could not have been acquitted, let alone exonerated. The reality is that the British, as they admitted, faced jurisdictional difficulties: in those days, states could not put on trial officials of foreign governments for crimes against their own people. The main perpetrators had escaped to Germany; there was a lack of evidence to show that some detainees were involved in the massacres; and in any event the British, in the absence of any support from France, Russia and Italy and the failure of the Sèvres Treaty, were forced to release the men in exchange for British soldiers held as hostages for this purpose in Ankara.

It is a sorry comment on the present state of Turkish denialism that no mention at all is made of the court proceedings in 1919 and 1920 which *did* result in convictions, albeit *in absentia*, of the main CUP perpetrators. These proceedings arose from genuine shame and anger felt by the Liberal party which dominated the post-war Constantinople parliament, and from evidence gathered by two inquiry commissions and considered by five judges of a military tribunal under procedures which were acceptable at the time and which did (contrary to denialists' claims) involve active participation by sixteen defence lawyers, led by the president of the Turkish Bar Association, who 'frequently and vigorously challenged the prosecutors, their witnesses, and often the panel of judges, at the same time raising many hostile trial questions'.[228]Turkey should take some pride, or at least some heart, from the fact that Ottoman war criminals were put on trial so soon after losing the war, but the dictates of denialism require this fact to be suppressed, and replaced by a false claim to British 'exoneration'.

> Fact 6: Despite the verdicts of the Malta Tribunal, Armenian
> terrorists have engaged in a vigilante war that continues today.

It is dishonest to refer to the 'verdicts' of a tribunal that never came into existence. As for a 'vigilante war', there certainly were some Armenian terrorist shootings and bombings of Turkish consulates and airline offices from the 1970s until the mid-1980s. They resulted in over thirty deaths and they are unforgivable – morally wrong as well as counter-productive. But they are obviously irrelevant to the characterisation of what happened in 1915. There is mention of 'Operation Nemesis' in 1921, in which Soghomon Tehlirian assassinated Talaat, but this fact sheet fails to report the fact that the Berlin court heard from Pastor Johannes Lepsius, General Otto Liman von Sanders and other German eyewitnesses and decided that the atrocities were so abhorrent that the assassin (who had lost his entire family in them) should not be convicted: his mind had been overborne by trauma.

> Fact 7: The archives of many nations ought to be carefully
> and thoroughly examined before concluding whether geno-
> cide occurred.

Historical research is always a good thing, and all the Ottoman and Armenian archives should be open to all scholars, and Turkey should repeal Article 301 of its Criminal Code, which has been used to punish 'genocide affirmation'. But as the centenary of the genocide approached, the so-called 'fact' that any finding of genocide must await further historical research was increasingly stressed, and featured prominently in President Erdoğan's 2014 statement, which argued that it is too early to decide whether genocide occurred because archives are yet to be opened to historians.[229] This is absurd – we all know what happened to the Armenians in 1915, and why it happened. We have all the eye-witness reports and diplomatic statements and memoirs that will ever be published. There may be a few more incriminating cables to be unearthed in the Ottoman archives (Taner Akçam found some for his 2012 book)[230] and some more bloodthirsty notes from the Dashnak underground. If there is exonerating evidence still lurking in Ottoman archives, it would be astonishing if the Turks had not by now released it. Justin McCarthy and other researchers have been examining Turkish army cables in order to suggest that the uprisings were more widespread and dangerous than other sources indicate, but the perceptions of army officers cannot alter what impartial (and partial but honest) witnesses saw in 1915, as it happened, and would have labelled genocide had the word then been in the lexicon. The argument that any decision about genocide should be postponed until all archives are open is just a delaying tactic.

Fact 8: The Holocaust bears no meaningful relation to the Ottoman experience.

The Holocaust bears no very close similarity to any other genocide, either in its mechanised gas chambers or in its targeting of

a race that was not demanding liberation or engaging in resistance. But these differences (and there were others) obviously do
not disentitle attacks on other races at other times from satisfying
the definition of genocide. In any event, there is a clear relationship (as most Jewish organisations accept) between these two
attempts by a state to destroy a people. In most cases, the target
racial group has been a 'people' with organisations demanding
independence or autonomy. The same 'pattern of purposeful
action' proves the genocidal intent: dehumanisation, ethnic hatred
fuelled by nationalistic fervour, preparation, persecution in peace
and then deportation and extermination under the cover of a
world war, expropriation of property, followed by denial (which
in the case of Germany did not last for long after the fall of Hitler). The whole point of a genocide law is to stop governments
from killing or deporting citizens who come from the same race
because they come from the same race. In that sense, and in
many of the corresponding indicia, there is a clear similarity
between the two genocides, and an unsettling question – one of
the great hypotheticals of history – as to whether the Holocaust
would have happened had the International Criminal Courts
promised at Versailles and Sèvres for the Kaiser and his generals
and for Talaat and his accomplices come into being in 1921. At
least Hitler would not in 1939 have said, 'Who now remembers
the Armenians?'

*   *   *

IN SUM, THE present Turkish government does not deny that
the deportations and the massacres took place, but endeavours to
categorise them either as a justifiable response to civil insurgency
or alternatively as a justifiable response to a foreign threat to break
up the Ottoman Empire, which threat had become drastic with

the Allied landings in the Dardanelles in April 1915 and advances by Russian forces in the east. The Unionist government and its 'Young Turk' leaders undoubtedly feared that these events might lead to an independent Armenia, and those officials who were defendants in person at the 1919 trials spoke in dramatic terms of the seven-month siege at Gallipoli as a direct threat to Constantinople,[231] which undoubtedly it was, although the invaders were quickly bogged down and showed no signs of advancing before their eventual withdrawal. Their arrival on 24 April had been the trigger for the round-up and murder of Armenian intellectuals, and in subsequent months for the deportations. But there is no threat – even to the existence of the state itself – that can justify genocide, the deliberate extinction of a substantial part of a race of people living in that state. An official note from Talaat's interior ministry to the grand vizierate on 26 May 1915 recited both that some Armenians in the war zones had been helping the enemy and that foreign powers were supportive of Armenian autonomy, and explained that 'deliberations were underway [i.e. over the deportation policy] for eliminating this trouble ... in a manner that is both comprehensive and absolute'.[232] There could hardly be better evidence of an intention to eliminate 'trouble' – i.e. the Armenians – in an 'absolute' way. This is a genocidal intention: difficulties though the Ottoman Empire had at the time, nothing can excuse its choice of this final (i.e. 'comprehensive and absolute') solution. It goes unmentioned, of course, on the website, as do the confiscation laws and the 'liquidation commissions' seizing all Armenian homes and property, dishonestly describing them as 'abandoned'. This palpable evidence of genocidal intent is not a 'fact' with which denialists can deal.

CHAPTER 6

THE POLITICS
OF GENOCIDE
RECOGNITION

Parliamentary Declarations

B Y THE CENTENARY of the Armenian genocide, the parliaments of many countries (and, in federal nations like the
US and Australia, state parliaments as well) had declared
that the 1915 massacres and deportations amount to genocide.
The authority of such declarations is doubtful, in so far as politicians are no better equipped than historians to deliver a legal

verdict, although as statements of the people's representatives they do have some symbolic force. Political recognition reassures the local Armenian community that it now lives in a state that acknowledges the reality of their suffering and serves as a talismanic promise that it will not happen to them again. This always has the diplomatic downside of infuriating Turkey, but in practical terms it will help the genocide to become noticed and notable – in school courses and textbooks, in war memorials and museums, and in the discourse of heads of state – when, for example, they meet Turkish leaders and mention it. This last consequence became pronounced as the centennial neared. In the spring of 2014, for example,

- German Chancellor Angela Merkel told the visiting Turkish Prime Minister Recep Erdoğan, 'Turkey must come to terms with its history.'[233]
- French President François Hollande visited Turkey and told its leaders to reassess: 'Memory work is always painful … but must be done. By recognising the historical events you will be elevated not only in your own eyes, but also in the eyes of the world.'[234]
- The President of the Czech Republic told the visiting Armenian President, 'Next year marks the 100th anniversary of the Armenian genocide. In 1915, 1.5 million Armenians were killed.'[235]

The leaders who made these statements were fortified by recognition of the Armenian genocide by their parliaments. Other leaders have been more reluctant: Swedish Foreign Minister Carl Bildt refused to adhere to the Riksdag decision to recognise the genocide, on the pretext that the current Turkish government could not be blamed for the crimes of its predecessor – an argument that was wrong in law but convenient for his foreign policy.[236] In any event, Turkey reacted in such a neuralgic way to Swedish parliamentary recognition – by recalling its ambassador – that it simply proved how much it still identifies with its Ottoman predecessor. When in the same year (2010) the US House of Representatives voted to recognise the Armenian genocide,[237] Turkey withdrew its ambassador to the US and proclaimed, 'This resolution accuses the Turkish nation of a crime it has not committed.'[238] When France in the same year passed a law recognising the Armenian genocide and criminalising its denial, Turkey in reprisal banned the French air force from its air space[239] (the ban was lifted after the law was struck down as unconstitutional by the Conseil d'Etat). In Canada, recognition was followed by a decision by the school board in Toronto that children should be educated about the Armenian, Jewish and Rwandan genocides. Canadian Turks, funded by the Turkish government, are contesting the decision, claiming that the textbooks upset Turkish students – as they always will, until the government accepts that its predecessor was responsible for a crime against humanity, and moves on.

Statements in school textbooks, and in history or politics courses, may be the most important consequence of national or state recognition of the genocide – local education authorities will have a duty to recognise it as well. There is no reason why Turkish students should feel more anguished about it than German students inured to reading about Nazi guilt for the Holocaust: these crimes were, after all, committed by past governments, with an atavistic brutality inconceivable in progressive democracies today. German students might well think – as many international lawyers think they should – that the Holocaust might not have happened had the Young Turk and German leaders been punished by the international courts which would have been set up by the Treaty of Sèvres and of Versailles. Failure to deliver on all the promises to try the authors of the Armenian genocide 'made the Nazis more brazen and the Holocaust more likely'.[240] It still remains unrecognised in Turkey, where textbooks are censored and it is a crime to speak of what happened to the Armenians – even though many thousands reside there. State recognition may also assist in resisting the inevitable complaints by Turkish embassies whenever it is suggested that a monument or memorial should be erected to the victims of the genocide, or that Armenia should be included in commemorations of the Holocaust. Jewish organisations have generally avoided claims to victim exclusivity in horror (although in Britain, regrettably, they have not objected to the exclusion of Armenia from Holocaust Memorial Day). Elsewhere, Jewish Holocaust museums have not hesitated to include the Armenians – the museum run by the Simon Wiesenthal Center in Los Angeles, for example, has a room devoted to them (although the tribulations of the Palestinians go unmentioned). Turkish organisations are likely to fail in their attempt to censor learning in Toronto, but Armenian diasporians might take a leaf out of their book by taking legal action to ensure that the genocide is relevantly mentioned in every war museum, school history course and university legal study.

The Turkish government, however, still insists on justifying the massacres as strategically necessary in a civil war, and pays millions to lobbyists and PR agencies in the West to promote this excuse. It can also threaten mean-minded reprisals against genocide-recognising states – against Australia, for example, with which Turkey has had exceptionally good relations. The Anzac landing at Gallipoli on 25 April 1915 now marks Australia's National Day, and its centenary, in 2015, brought many Australians and their politicians to a dawn service in the Dardanelles, where thousands of Anzacs are buried. But members of the New South Wales parliament had been threatened with a ban from entering

Turkey for the memorial service because they passed a genocide recognition law in 2013.[241] This spiteful reprisal seems to have frightened the Australian Foreign Minister, Julie Bishop, who in June 2014 succumbed to pressure from local Turks and actually denied the genocide.

Local Turks complained about New South Wales and other states recognising the genocide, and Ms Julie Bishop wrote back:

> The Australian government acknowledges the devastating effects which the tragic events at the end of the Ottoman Empire have had on later generations, and on their identity, heritage and culture. We do not, however, recognise these events as 'genocide' … the long-standing and clear approach for the Australian government has been not to become involved in this sensitive debate.[242]

The foolish Foreign Minister (or, more likely, her foolish departmental advisors) did not seem to appreciate that a sure way of becoming involved in this 'sensitive debate' is to declare that 'the Australian government does not recognise these events as genocide'. This sounds as though the government was denying the genocide, and the statement was immediately reported in this sense by Turkish newspapers: 'Australian Foreign Minister: Armenian case not genocide' their headlines screamed. This aroused the fury of Armenians in Australia, who joined with the Executive Council of Australian Jewry and the Australian Hellenic Council (there are more Greeks in Australia than there are in Athens) to condemn Ms Bishop, whose mistake had been to say 'we do not recognise these events as "genocide"' instead of saying 'we have expressed no opinion as a government on whether these events are genocide or not'. No Australian government or official has ever issued a denial and the Prime Minister, Tony Abbott, when in opposition issued an annual statement condemning 'the Armenian Genocide'.

As the Obama example of double-speak (*Meds Yeghern*) shows, however, entering government means developing a capacity for artful deceit, in the assumed commercial and strategic interests of the nation. Australia had no such interests, but rather a bizarre emotional investment through Anzac Day, commemorating all who have died in its wars, anchored to the date of this first disastrous defeat when 6,000 of its troops, commanded by blimpish British generals, were cut down on the beaches of the Dardanelles by Turkish machine-gunners.

Today, friendship with Turkey serves to symbolise the hope for peace and reconciliation that is devoutly wished on such commemorative occasions, and Ms Bishop's letter went on to explain that 'Australia attaches great importance to its relationships with Turkey, which is underpinned by our shared history at Gallipoli...' But any camaraderie existed only in nostalgic retrospect: 'diggers' who were taken prisoner and treated with a grudging humanity were shocked to witness their captor's race-based hatred of Armenians. Mr Abbott was welcomed in Turkey for the Anzac Day ceremony on 25 April 2015, but did not dare, in his long speech commemorating the Gallipoli landings, mention that they triggered the Armenian genocide. Nor did any of the speakers refer by name to the victorious leader of the Ottoman forces at the Dardanelles, General Liman von Sanders, the commander of the Turkish 5th Army whose military genius in fortifying the landing beaches and directing the battle ensured that the invasion was a failure. He had to be written out of history, because he later saved some Armenians from death marches and because he testified on behalf of the defence at the trial of Soghomon Tehlirian, who assassinated Talaat Pasha after the war. Von Sanders's excision from the centenary was tantamount to remembering the Battle of Waterloo without any reference to the Duke of Wellington. Perhaps the most pronounced irony of the juxtaposed centenaries was that Australia (unlike the UK) yielded to Turkish pressure and refused to send any official representative to the Armenian genocide commemoration at Yerevan on 24 April. A government that exuded pride at how its soldiers braved Turkish bullets capitulated, a century later, to Turkish threats. In every country where political recognition is mooted, there is the question of a trade-off: is it worth alienating a powerful, important and otherwise civilised Western ally? Politicians may wish to display humanitarian credentials, but knee-jerk declarations that the massacres were genocide, without any formal inquiry or evidence from experts, can be seen as provocations. It must be said that in several countries the promoters of such declarations have not only been local Armenians, but groups with a decidedly anti-Muslim or pro-Christian agenda. This was the case in the Netherlands, where Geert Wilders and his Islamophobes were active in support, whilst in New South Wales the politician who led the movement had been a long-time opponent of human rights for homosexuals and placed undue emphasis on 'the Muslim genocide against Christian Armenians'.[243] Political motives behind recognition declarations may be mixed, which is why diaspora supporters must be wary of Islamophobe allies, and parliaments which pass well-intentioned recognition motions should only do so after some examination of the evidence by a committee or inquiry which is unaffected by religious or political bias.

This message was brought home in 2014 when a few Armenians actually welcomed the latest convert to recognition of the genocide, none other than President Assad of Syria – after his troops had butchered and gassed tens of thousands of his own people. Assad had previously supported Turkish denialist policies, banning books on the genocide and preventing examination of evidence about the cruel end of the convoys in Syria. But after foreign fighters against his regime were harboured by Turkey, he turned against his former ally and denounced 'the massacres perpetrated by the Ottomans against the Armenians when they killed a million and a half' and the Syrian ambassador to the UN condemned the 'Armenian genocide'.[244] With friends like Syria...

Nonetheless, genocide recognition has been impressive. The otiose comment in the *Perinçek* decision (see later, p 204) that only twenty countries had recognised whilst 170 had not ignores not only the fact that the great majority of those 170 had not been asked, but also the quality, as exponents of international law, of those which had nailed their colours to the mast. They include Canada (three times), France (twice), Russia (twice) and Germany (twice, but without admitting its own complicity), along with Italy, the Netherlands, Sweden, Switzerland, Poland, Greece, Lithuania, Slovakia, Belgium and three regions of Spain, together with Argentina (a record five times), Chile, Uruguay, Venezuela and three state assemblies of Brazil. Closer to Turkey we find Cyprus (three times), Armenia (of course), Lebanon and the cities of Aleppo (what is left of it) and Tehran. There has been silence from the vast majority of Asia, but not from two states of Australia – New South Wales and South Australia. The UK and the US remain equivocal in order to keep Turkey on side, but that has not stopped state legislatures from recognition – Wales, Scotland, Northern Ireland and the London borough of Ealing have declared in favour of the Armenian genocide, as have forty-three of the fifty American states.

The US Backtracks

The national governments of the US and UK, however, are not prepared to alienate a crucial ally in the war against terror – and in the proxy war against Syria – by taking this step. President

Reagan was prepared to call the great crime genocide,[245] but Turkey was then a 'third world' country mainly known in the West for carpets and hippie drug trails. Although it had NSA spy bases, valuable to the US in the Cold War, its military government did not overreact. But in 2007, when resolutions condemning the genocide were introduced in Congress, Turkey spent millions of dollars on a successful lobbying campaign. President George W. Bush announced that passage of the resolutions 'would do great harm to relations with a key NATO ally and to the war on terror … we all deeply regret the tragic suffering of the Armenian people that began in 1915, but…'[246] And so the formula was established: history as tragedy, but never to be accurately described in a word to which a close ally would take grave offence. The White House was not prepared to risk the air bases and monitoring stations that had been so useful for its war in Iraq. Nancy Pelosi, the Californian Democrat, persevered with the resolution, describing it as a measure of restorative justice which would provide closure to victims' descendants and correct the historical record, but the assumed need to avoid antagonising Turkey prevailed.[247] Even President Obama, who as a senator had promised to acknowledge the genocide once he became President, chose instead to refer to it in code. His message on Commemoration Day 2012 was a masterpiece of equivocation:

> Today we commemorate *Meds Yeghern*, one of the worst atrocities of the twentieth century and we honour the memory of 1.5 million Armenians who were brutally massacred or driven to death … I've always said what my opinion is on what happened in 1915. It has not changed.[248]

To find out what his opinion really was (the opinion that it was *Meds Yeghern* – the great massacre – meaning nothing to

Americans who did not speak Armenian), the President's audience had to Google his speech on the subject when he was running for the office in 2008. 'It is imperative that we recognise that the horrors inflicted on the Armenian people was a genocide.'[249] Not imperative enough, however, once he became President, to recognise it other than elliptically, lest the Turks take offence. President Obama might at the very least try to get his tongue around *ts'yeghaspanut'yun* – the word that actually means 'genocide' in Armenian. The question came back to haunt the White House in April 2014, when the Senate Foreign Relations Committee voted 12–5 for recognition in Resolution 410.[250]

Turkey is now a more important NATO ally than ever, taking the strain of refugees from the civil war in Syria as well as serving as a conduit for Western aid. This presents a problem for the UK, which shares US concerns but instinctively deals with them in a more devious way – a feature of the diplomatic tradition of its Foreign & Commonwealth Office (FCO). Britain was, of course, the first to denounce the massacres as 'crimes against humanity', to publish comprehensive eyewitness accounts of the atrocities in the Blue Book and to promise to punish the perpetrators: it made a serious attempt at Malta to do so, and its statesmen (Churchill, Lloyd George and Balfour) denounced the extirpation programme in the strongest language. But from the early 1990s until 2010, the UK adopted a public stance which gave great comfort to Turkish denialism – the claim that the evidence was 'not sufficiently unequivocal' to amount to genocide. Those who devised this formula privately admitted that it was unethical, but nonetheless believed it necessary to safeguard British commercial and strategic interests. The machinations behind what was, in effect, a deception of Parliament and the public were revealed when FCO policy documents came to light through Freedom of Information Act requests, as the next chapter explains.

CHAPTER 7

GENOCIDE
EQUIVOCATION:
A CASE STUDY

MORE INFLUENTIAL THAN genocide deniers are genocide equivocators – those officials and policy makers
in the West who do not know, and do not really care,
whether genocide took place, but whose overriding consideration is to avoid alienating Turkey. For that reason, the internal
strategy devised by mandarins at the UK's Foreign and Commonwealth Office (FCO) for deceiving their political masters
(and, through them, the British public) into thinking that the
issue of whether there was ever an Armenian genocide was open

to serious dispute, is worth careful study. In 2009, through Freedom of Information Act 2000 requests, I obtained internal policy memoranda prepared within the FCO during the period of the Blair and Brown Labour governments, 1997–2009, although the strategy had commenced under the Thatcher regime, when Turkey became important to British business and to its geopolitical strategy.

UK Policy Documents – Two Basic Errors

The secret documentation relating to the policy of the UK government begins with the Eastern Department of the FCO formulation on 8 March 1999 of a ministerial response to Lord Avebury, who had provided a bibliography of 400 scholarly works which described the Armenian massacres as genocide,[251] and had asked the minister why the government had failed to recognise it. The department privately admits that it has neither the resources nor the inclination to study these references and anyway they would not impact on present policy. The memorandum says 'the argument is not about what happened or what to call it' – although that is precisely what the argument was about (i.e. whether to call it 'genocide'). The Eastern Department considers that it is not the work of Her Majesty's Government (HMG) to decide what constitutes genocide: 'Investigating, analysing and interpreting history is a matter for historians.' At the outset, this basic error can be detected, namely the FCO's belief that historians are qualified to decide a legal issue. Deciding what amounts to genocide is a matter for judgment according to law. Historians establish facts: lawyers must judge whether those facts amount to a breach of international law.

It further appears from this memorandum that the Eastern

Department is simply not interested, and does not want HMG to be interested, in the question of whether the massacres and deportations amount to genocide. The memorandum estimates that 600,000 Armenians were killed and 'hundreds of thousands more died in flight' (in fact, they were killed in the course of being deported) and 'some historians say there is evidence that the deaths were part of a deliberate state policy, or that the Ottoman government must have given at least tacit approval to the killings. But we know of no documentary evidence to prove this.'[252] Here we have another canard that appears routinely and repeatedly from the Eastern Department memoranda of the FCO: the notion that there must be some written document that records a government or leadership decision to exterminate the Armenian people. No such document, of course, exists in relation to the Rwandan genocide (as the International Criminal Tribunal in Rwanda has pointed out).[253] It is obviously wrong to suggest that there must be documentary evidence of a policy decision to commit genocide before it is possible to make a finding of genocide.

The memorandum goes on to consider the clout of the campaign to recognise the genocide and notes that 'the campaign does not appear at this stage to have enough support or direction to seriously embarrass HMG'.[254] With this cynical message to ministers, the recommendation is to follow the longstanding 'line' that

> HMG has long recognised the massacres of 1915, and they were condemned by Parliament in the strongest terms, but a) there is no evidence to show the Ottoman government took a specific decision to eliminate the Armenians under their control at that time and b) it is for historians, not governments, to interpret the past.

This formulation embodies the two basic errors: a) the failure to recognise that there is no requirement for evidence of a 'specific government decision' or indeed any documented decision to destroy all Armenians, as an element of the crime of genocide, and b) the failure to understand that it is a matter for legal judgment, and not a matter for historians, as to whether past events amount to a crime of genocide. The latter error was compounded by the Eastern Department in a draft of the letter responding to Lord Avebury which the minister (Joyce Quin) was asked to endorse: 'I continue to believe that it is not the business of the British or any government to pronounce on matters more properly addressed by historians. We must leave it to the experts.'[255]

Historians, of course, as has become all too clear, are not experts on genocide. This was the Eastern Department draft, which the minister did not send. She did, however, write to Lord Avebury on 9 February 1999 stating, 'It is for historians to interpret the past and society learns and benefits from their assessment of events. Generally speaking, I do not think it is the job of today's government to review past events with a view to pronouncing on them according to today's values and attitudes.'[256] That the values and attitudes in respect of genocide are timeless does not seem to have occurred to this minister.

The 1999 House of Lords Debate

The matter came to a head a few months later, with a full-scale debate in the House of Lords initiated by Baroness Cox. A note from the Eastern Department put the matter exactly in perspective. It said, with an honesty that British diplomats only allow themselves in private,

HMG is open to criticism in terms of the ethical dimension.

> But given the importance of our relations (political, strate-
> gic and commercial) with Turkey, and that recognising the
> genocide would provide no practical benefit to the UK or
> the few survivors of the killings still alive today, nor would
> it help a rapprochement between Armenia and Turkey, the
> current line is the only feasible option.[257]

This reveals the cynical truth behind the position urged by the FCO on Labour government ministers over the next decade, and almost invariably accepted by them without demur, namely that the position they were taking was open to ethical question, but that the economic, strategic and political importance of maintaining good relations with Turkey meant that the ethical dimension should be ignored. There was no countervailing profit in making any truthful answer that might displease the Turks. In other words, this particular genocide could no longer be recognised – not because it had not taken place, but because it was politically and commercially inconvenient to do so.

In this note, dated 12 April 1999, the FCO repeated the familiar, and doubly mistaken, mantra that 'we are aware of no evidence of intent on the part of the Ottoman administration of the day to destroy the Armenians (a key element in the crime of genocide) and that it is for historians, not governments, to determine what happened'.[258] 'We' of the Eastern department were apparently ignorant of evidence that the deportations which killed more than half the race were ordered by the Ottoman government, which passed laws confiscating the property of those who were intended not to return. The FCO even sounded a note of caution about the Secretary of State's use of the word 'genocide' to describe the actions of Milošević and his Serb forces in 'ethnically cleansing' Kosovo: there was concern that this would provoke calls for the same label to be attached to the massacres of the

Armenians, whose 'ethnic cleansing' by way of deportation was, in fact, of a much higher level of gravity to the sufferings of the Kosovars, who were not starved and attacked and killed in their hundreds of thousands.

Attached to this note was a draft speech, which Baroness Ramsey, for the government, delivered virtually verbatim on 14 April.[259] (So many of the self-regarding politicians who strut the despatch box in Parliament do no more than recite speeches prepared by manipulative officials: this is the thesis of the popular BBC comedy *Yes Minister*, which the FCO's memoranda show to be all too true to British political life.) As well as claiming that there was no evidence of 'a specific decision to eliminate the Armenians', the speech considered whether a tribunal like the ICTY or ICTR should be set up to resolve the issue, but pointed out that potential defendants were long since dead and that it 'had not been established … if the genocide convention can be applied retrospectively'. This is a bad point, because nobody was suggesting that criminal charges should be brought now against long-dead individuals. The question was whether the massacre of the Armenians is correctly described as 'genocide', according to the definition adopted by the UN Convention in 1948.

The Eastern Department brief was at least read by the minister, Joyce Quin. She took exception to its extreme 'genocide denial' position, which included lines such as 'We are aware of no firm evidence of intent on the part of the Ottoman administration of the day to destroy the Armenians' and 'HMG has no first-hand evidence of why the atrocities took place'. Quin privately and correctly pointed out, the day before the debate, that the question of intent had never been examined by the government or by anyone else in the FCO.[260] These passages were duly deleted, but it is remarkable that that the FCO could inform a minister of state that there was 'no firm evidence of intent': were they unaware of Ambassador Morgenthau's conversations with Talaat, or of the Harbord Report, or of the Treaty of Sèvres, or of the Constantinople trial verdicts? It was even more remarkable to claim that there was no first-hand evidence of why the atrocities took place – ignoring the hundreds of witness statements from victims, missionaries, consular officials etc., not to mention the Blue Book, HMG's own publication. This ministerial briefing does show the extent to which genocide denial had entrenched itself in the Eastern Department by this time, to such an extent that it was briefing ministers with a bare-faced disregard for readily ascertainable facts. Perhaps this is in part explained by how easily British government ministers allow themselves to be manipulated – in all the secret policy memoranda, over twelve years, this is the only time when a minister declined to repeat verbatim in Parliament an answer written by FCO officials, all too willing to turn a blind eye to genocide in the interest of political and commercial relations with Turkey.

Three 'Denial' Historians

A few days after this debate, the Turkish ambassador initiated a correspondence, which continued over the following years, with several FCO ministers: Joyce Quin, Keith Vaz and Baroness Scotland. He sent them extracts from work by Justin McCarthy, and sought to portray the 1915 killings as having been provoked by 'Armenian terrorists' who continue to murder Turkish diplomats to this very day. He claimed that more Turks than Armenians died, the latter not from government action but from 'starvation, disease and attacks by guerrillas which the authorities at the time were powerless to prevent'.[261] The Turkish embassy was pleased with the FCO's formula for refusing to acknowledge genocide ('in the absence of unequivocal evidence to show the Ottoman administration took a specific decision to eliminate the Armenians…'). This, said the embassy, was 'the correct view and we hope it would be maintained'.[262]

This hope was well founded. Keith Vaz MP boasted to the Turkish ambassador[263] that the government had refused to include the Armenian massacres as part of Holocaust Memorial Day. This decision, Mr Vaz made clear, reflected 'wide inter-departmental consultation, including with the FCO'. The unprincipled decision to exclude the Armenian massacres from Holocaust Memorial Day was, regrettably, greeted with no Jewish protest. There may have been objection had it been known how Vaz was influenced by the flawed perspective of the Eastern Department, overly concerned with maintaining good relations with Turkey.[264]

There was further pro-Turkish advice from the Eastern Department in 2001 as it prepared answers to questions put down by Lord Biffen arising from the Holocaust Day exclusion. One favoured approach was to say that 'interpretation of events is still the subject of genuine debate among historians'. There is a background note that says, 'Research analysts looked again at the balance of views in the academic community last year: they confirmed that disagreements remained.'[265] However, this background note seems to be incorrect, because no such analysis was disclosed, and the FCO covering letter responding to the Freedom of Information request denies that anything of the kind exists. In any event there was no 'balance' of views in the academic community – overwhelmingly, impartial British historians come down on the side of genocide affirmation. There is still no understanding by FCO officials that academics establish facts but the question of genocide is for legal judgment. It never occurred to the FCO that the great majority of historians of the period record facts that are only consistent with genocide, and even the work of Justin McCarthy, relied upon by the Turkish government, by no means excludes this legal characterisation.

An FCO draft answer for Baroness Scotland to give to Lord Biffen in 2001 stated:

> Additionally, the government's legal advisors have said that the 1948 UN Convention on genocide, which is in any event not retrospective in application, was drafted in response to the holocaust and whilst the term can be applied to tragedies that occurred subsequent to the holocaust, such as Rwanda, it cannot be applied retrospectively.[266]

This seems to be a dubious attempt to blind Parliament with bogus legal science, and if the government legal advisors ever said that the term cannot be applied to 'tragedies' before the Holocaust (there is no suggestion in the disclosed documents that they ever did), they were palpably mistaken. Of course the term 'genocide' can be applied retrospectively, and frequently is – to the attempted extermination of the Tasmanian Aborigines in the 1830s, for example, when British soldiers and convicts and settlers killed almost all of them: the forty-seven survivors were exiled to an offshore island. A parliamentary committee reported in 1838, endorsing Sir Gilbert Murray, that this was 'an indelible stain': an apt description of the crime of genocide, a century before Lemkin coined the word. Moreover, the 1948 Convention was not drafted solely in response to the Holocaust: Raphael Lemkin had the Armenian genocide very much in mind.

The UK policy was next considered in 2004, after the Armenian government had taken offence when the British ambassador to Armenia undiplomatically emphasised, in Armenia, the view that there was 'no unequivocal evidence' that genocide had ever been committed. But a memorandum to Under-Secretary of State

Bill Rammell (written by FCO official Simon Butt) warned that Turkey 'devotes major diplomatic resources to heading off any possible recognition. Turkey would react very strongly indeed to any suggestion of recognition by the UK.'[267] This seems to have been the reason why Butt recommended that the policy of genocide equivocation should be maintained.

At some point, either in 2004 or in 2005 (the disclosed memoranda are undated), the FCO supplied the usual mantra to ministers for answers in the House but suggested that 'if pressed' they might add:

> There is genuine debate amongst historians as to whether or not the events of 1915–16 would constitute genocide as defined by the 1948 UN Convention. Prominent historians who dispute the genocide label include Professor Bernard Lewis, formerly of Princeton, Dr Heath Lowry of Princeton and Professor Justin McCarthy of the University of Louisville.[268]

The Turkish ambassador, as we have seen, provided text from Justin McCarthy back in 2001. The three names appear first in March 2001 in a letter written by Keith Vaz to an MP who asked on what sources the FCO were relying.[269] Vaz wrote: 'Professor Bernard Lewis formerly of Princeton … said in 1993 that it was "extremely doubtful" that the Turks had carried out a policy of systematic annihilation.' This was not the full truth.

Bernard Lewis is a well-known professor of Middle Eastern studies. What Vaz (or whoever at the FCO drafted his letter) did not reveal was that his remark, in an interview with *Le Monde* in 1993, caused him to be prosecuted in France and fined (if only one franc) for denying the Armenian genocide.[270] In a later interview he said that 'no one has any doubts that terrible events took place' and that hundreds of thousands of

Armenians died.[271] He explained that he had only been seeking in *Le Monde* to deny the claim that there was a close parallel between the sufferings of the Armenians and the sufferings of the Jews in Nazi Germany: some of the former were active in fighting against the state whilst the latter were not in any kind of armed opposition to Hitler. He accepted that 'the Turks certainly resorted to very ferocious methods' in repelling Armenian freedom fighters but naively insisted, 'There is clear evidence of a decision by the Turkish government to deport the Armenian population … there is no evidence of a decision to massacre…'[272] Lewis does not understand that a finding of genocide may be inferred from a government's deliberate failure to protect those it is deporting, the majority of whom – women and children – were certainly not active in fighting against the state. He also overlooked all the evidence about massacres of Armenian men prior to the deportations, and by *chettis* under direction of the Special Organisation. Lewis complains that 'nowadays the word "genocide" is used very loosely even in cases where no bloodshed is involved at all'[273] – which is not a complaint that could be made against labelling as 'genocide' events in which over half the members of a particular race were brutally killed or died from typhus or starvation as a result of brutal state policies. The Vaz letter suggests that Lewis is an FCO 'source', but there is no evidence in the documents that he was ever consulted. It is probable that the FCO was only alerted to his view as a result of the publicity about his prosecution, and then did not understand his position.

Dr Heath Lowry is a controversial figure who provoked the 'Heath Lowry affair' after Princeton University accepted a large sum of money from the Turkish government and appointed him to the 'Atatürk Chair', which that government sponsored. Controversy erupted when he was discovered to have acted as a propagandist, drafting letters for the Turkish ambassador denying the genocide.[274] Both Dr Lowry and the university were condemned by a petition of over 100 leading writers and scholars, including Arthur Miller, Harold Pinter, Susan Sontag, William Styron, John Updike, Kurt Vonnegut, Norman Mailer, Seamus Heaney, Deborah Lipstadt and Allen Ginsberg.[275] It is only fair to point out that writers may have no greater insight into the law of genocide than historians, and it does not appear that Dr Lowry in his personal capacity has actually denied the genocide, but has merely said that he is reluctant to apply this label to the massacres until he has fully studied the Ottoman archives. He maintains that he 'cannot accept the characterisation of this human tragedy as a pre-planned, state perpetrated genocide … unless and until the historical records of the Ottoman state … are studied and evaluated by competent scholars'.[276] According to a website that supports him, his privileged access to the Ottoman archives has enabled him to find one document which he says 'strongly suggests that there was government involvement in the killing of Armenians'.[277] In any case, historians who take a pro-Turkish position after taking Turkish government money and have been proffered special access to documents have a conflict of interest. Given the controversy surrounding Dr Lowry, his comparatively modest scholarly standing and his financial relationship with the Turkish government, he was a strange choice for the British government to rely upon against the views of so many eminent British historians and genocide scholars.

Further Inquiries

In the 2004/5 memoranda there is a 'background memo' attached, which makes some attempt to be fair:

> The extent to which the killings were official government pol-
> icy is a long standing dispute. But the Young Turk movement
> which ruled the Ottoman Empire from 1908 undoubtedly
> had come to believe that the Armenians posed a threat to
> the unity and security of the empire ... non-partisan non-
> specialist European historians would seem to agree that there
> was some official collusion. But how far did it go? One such
> historian, A. L. Macfie in *The End of the Ottoman Empire
> 1908–23* (Longman 1998), draws the following balance, 'It
> is difficult if not impossible, to escape the conclusion that,
> once the deportations were instituted the Ottoman leader-
> ship, or at least elements in it were not averse to exploiting
> the opportunity to resolve a problem that had for decades
> caused the empire much difficulty.'[278]

This cautious conclusion is the only approximation to historical
truth to be found in the many hundreds of pages of legally obtuse
FCO briefings to British ministers about the state of the evidence.

Nonetheless, in mid-2005, HMG's pro-Turkish position was
revisited and confirmed. Pressed about Article 301 of the Turkish Penal Code, under which writers and intellectuals were being
threatened with prosecution for mentioning the Armenian genocide, the FCO claimed that alleging genocide was not prohibited by
the Code but only by the 'explanatory note' about what it should
cover.[279] This was a pettifogging response to the persecution by
Turkey of citizens for speaking the truth, or at least for publishing
honest and well-sourced opinion, and Turkey's obvious contravention of Article 10 of the European Convention on Human Rights
was in due course condemned by the European Court in the Hrant
Dink case (See Chapter 8).[280] But the FCO, reluctant as always to
take up free speech issues against repressive regimes who are political allies, advised its minister to weasel out of giving any answer.

There has been one credible international inquiry into the Armenian genocide, and it is extraordinary that among the hundreds of pages of policy documents there is only one obscure and dismissive reference to it. It was directed by the UN's Economic and Social Council (at the request of the Commission on Human Rights) and conducted by its Special Rapporteur on Genocide, Mr Ben Whitaker – a British barrister and formerly Labour MP for Hampstead. He reported in 1985 and had no hesitation in concluding that the 1915 atrocities amounted to genocide.[281] This was a key issue: the previous rapporteur had initially concluded that Turkey was guilty of genocide, but had removed this finding after Turkish protests in order to 'maintain unity within the international community'.[282] Whitaker's conclusion should have weighed with any British government, yet the FCO makes no reference to Whitaker or his distinguished qualifications, and suggests that ministers should speak dismissively of the '1985 Report'.[283]

2006 Parliamentary Proceedings

In 2006 Steven Pound MP initiated an adjournment debate on the issue. The FCO briefed its minister, Geoff Hoon, that 'HMG has long argued that there is an absence of unequivocal evidence to prove that the top level of the Ottoman Administration took a specific decision to eliminate all Armenians under their rule. There has been no reason to change that position.'[284]

There was reason: by this stage eight EU parliaments had passed resolutions recognising the genocide: France, Italy, Poland, Greece, Cyprus, Belgium, Slovakia and the Netherlands, not to mention the Holy See, Uruguay, Argentina, Russia, Lebanon and Canada. Various parliaments, including the German Bundestag and the US House of Representatives Foreign Affairs Committee, were debating the issue.[285] This time the briefing went on, accurately for a change:

> Turkey is neuralgic[286] and defensive about the charge of genocide despite the fact that the events occurred at the time of the Ottoman Empire as opposed to modern day Turkey. There were many Turks who lost their lives in the war and there may also be an element of concern over compensation claims should they accept the charge of genocide. This defensiveness has meant that Turkey has historically stifled debate at home and devoted considerable diplomatic effort to dissuading any further recognition.[287]

The debate initiated by Steven Pound went ahead on 7 June 2006. Geoff Hoon, for the government, repeated that 'the evidence is not sufficiently unequivocal', and flagged up the pettifogging point about retrospective characterisation of genocide:

> The fact is that the legal offence of genocide had not been named or defined at the time that the actual atrocities were committed. The UN Convention on Genocide came into force in 1948 so it was not possible at the time of the events that we are considering legally to label the massacres as genocide within the terms of the convention. I recognise that it is perfectly possible intellectually to try to apply the definitions of genocide from the Convention to appalling tragedies that occurred in this case some thirty years before. The common practice in law is not to apply such judgment retrospectively…[288]

This is nonsense. There is no 'common practice in law' not to apply the definitions of genocide 'intellectually' to tragedies that occurred before the Convention was ratified. The 'common practice in law' applies to the rule against prosecuting for a crime that did not exist at the time it was committed, but nobody is talking about prosecution: there is no one left to prosecute. It is common practice to apply modern definitions to historical events which satisfy them – and this practice is exemplified by the US submission to the International Court of Justice in 1951 in the case about the interpretation of the Genocide Convention:

> The practice of genocide has occurred throughout human history. The Roman persecution of the Christians, the Turkish massacres of the Armenians, the extermination of millions of Jews and Poles by the Nazis are outstanding examples of the crime of genocide. This was the background when the General Assembly of the United Nations considered the problem of genocide.[289]

It was preposterous to suggest that there is some legal inhibition in characterising pre-Convention events as genocide. As the International Centre for Transitional Justice pointed out in its 2003 opinion,

> The term genocide as used in the Convention to describe the international crime of that name, may be applied to many and various events that occurred prior to the entry into force of the Convention. References to genocide as a historical fact are contained in the text of the Convention and its *travaux préparatoires*.[290]

In October 2006 Mr Hoon visited Armenia: the brief he took with him (which had been heavily redacted before release to me for fear of 'damaging international relations' – i.e. with Turkey) does end with the unredacted sentence, 'Turkey would react very strongly indeed to any suggestion of recognition of the genocide by the UK.'[291] This undoubtedly explains the real reason for the FCO advice and for the UK position from about 1990 – by which time American presidents changed their tune and ceased to use the 'G' word. Both nations feared alienating an ally whose geo-political importance had become apparent during the first Gulf War against Saddam Hussein.

In March 2007 Lord Avebury returned to the fray, by asking for the names of the British historians on whom HMG relied for its refusal to describe the treatment of Armenians in 1915–16 as genocide. The response was to claim that the FCO had 'input from a variety of historical sources and works'.[292] This was seriously misleading. The only sources mentioned were the Blue Book (which contains witness statements irreconcilable with genocide denial) and a British historian named Malcolm Yapp, who was said to 'question' other accounts. This again was misleading. Professor Yapp is a member of the Editorial Advisory Board of the *Middle Eastern Studies Journal*, who has indeed questioned Vahakn Dadrian's *The History of the Armenian Genocide*, but not in a way that refutes his allegation of genocide.[293] Yapp accepts that the massacres took place and that 'there was some connivance and even participation by local Ottoman officials'. He accepts that the Ottoman government ordered the deportations 'without adequate arrangements for the transport, food or security'. He says that 'although Dadrian produces many reports seeming to suggest that members of the Ottoman government wanted to destroy the Armenians, he fails to find any document which constitutes a definite order for massacre'. This failure is not crucial nor even important: no such documents are to be found in Rwandan government papers, either, although the circumstantial evidence is overwhelming. Yapp does not purport to apply the law, and his book review provides no basis at all for the UK government to resist the characterisation of genocide.

In the same note, the FCO states with a distasteful satisfaction that none of the ministers invited to Armenian Genocide Memorial Day on 24 April (Mrs Beckett, Mr Hoon and Mr Howells) will be attending.[294] No doubt as a result of advice from the FCO, as in the case of the Conservative minister Mr Hogg in 1995. It was a sad reflection on the British government and on the FCO that ministers deliberately became unavailable so they would not be seen by the Turks to be paying respects to Armenian dead.

On 2 July 2007 a memorandum on HMG's position on Armenian genocide restated the position that 'there is an absence of unequivocal evidence to prove that at the top level the Ottoman administration took a specific decision to eliminate all Armenians under their rule'.[295] It has been pointed out (repeatedly, because it is a repeated legal howler) that a 'specific decision' is unnecessary. The FCO further added the misleading claim that 'it is not common practice in law to apply judgments retrospectively'. This was still nonsense: judgments usually relate to past events, and the so-called 'common practice' would prevent HMG describing the Holocaust, 1941–5, 'retrospectively' as genocide, because the Convention against Genocide came later in 1948. There can be no logical or legal objection to an authoritative judgment which decides whether the events of 1915 satisfy the 1948 definition. As Professor William Schabas put it, the use by Mr Hoon and FCO officials of the argument that 'it is not common practice in law' was 'no more than the mealy-mouthed efforts of bureaucrats and politicians to avoid tension with Turkish diplomats'.[296]

Throughout this voluminous material there is never any mention that Britain denounced the massacres in 1915 as 'a crime against humanity'. Indeed some memos read as if the government had denounced both sides and had not blamed the Turks. The FCO again reveals its manipulative hand in a briefing to a minister about to receive a delegation of Armenian Solidarity members, telling the minister that 'this is an emotive subject and we do not anticipate an easy meeting – ultimately there is no positive message that HMG can give to this audience on this issue. But it is important to demonstrate that we are listening.'[297] (In other words, 'we' have a closed mind on the subject but will pretend that it is at least partly open.) Since the delegation comprised not only Armenia Solidarity members but the vice-chairman of the International Association of Genocide Scholars and the respected historian Professor Donald Bloxham, the FCO's advice was, in effect, to string them along, despite the fact that 'the genocide scholar in the group is likely to take issue' with the British position.[298] (There is no sign that anyone at the FCO had read Bloxham's book *The Great Game of Genocide*, published by Oxford University Press in 2005, which powerfully refutes its 'genocide equivocation' stance.) Genocide scholarship is one thing that the FCO have never been interested in applying to an issue they wish would go away. There is no reference in the papers to the 2007 resolution of the International Association of Genocide Scholars, which resolved that 'the Ottoman campaign against Christian minorities of the empire between 1914–23 constituted a genocide against Armenians and the Assyrians and Pontian and Anatolian Greeks'. The FCO merely evinces concern that the US House Foreign Affairs Committee had resolved to recognise the events as genocide: as a result, 'we can also expect the Armenian Diaspora worldwide lobbying machine to go into overdrive'. This is hardly the language of an impartial inquirer: the FCO had become a rather cynical adversary of the truth, or at least of a Foreign Minister ever uttering it.

Although the FCO accepts that Article 301 of the Turkish Penal

Code can result in charges of 'insulting Turkishness' made against those who allege genocide (such as Orhan Pamuk and Hrant Dink), this was not a reason for lobbying Turkey in support of free speech. The British position in 2007 hardened behind the Bush administration's renewed support for Turkey. Fearing that a negative reaction would harm US interests, particularly its NSA surveillance bases and its oil interests, President Bush took the unusual step of speaking out before the House Foreign Affairs Committee passed Resolution 106, which called upon him to 'reflect appropriate understanding of the Armenian genocide in US foreign policy'.[299] Bush said, 'This resolution is not the right response to these historic mass killings … its passage would do great harm to our relations with a key ally in NATO and in the global war on terror.' On 23 October 2007 Prime Minister Blair met Prime Minister Erdoğan of Turkey, who said 'that his view remained that the "genocide" was an issue for historians'. This is the position that, as we have seen, the FCO had long promoted. There is no suggestion in the heavily redacted minutes that Mr Blair pointed out the importance of nations coming to terms with their own past. Once again, the deceptive device of 'leave it to the historians' was used as the excuse to avoid legal judgment.

The Downing Street Website Incident

In 2008 the FCO was caught out when its stock response about historians being unable to agree about genocide was placed on the Downing Street website in answer to an e-petition, and its inaccuracy was pointed out by many members of the public. FCO draftsperson Sofka Brown was warned by a colleague, Matthew Extance, about high-level dissatisfaction with this 'line'. Apparently the minister (Jim Murphy) had at last demanded to know exactly what evidence had been deemed 'not sufficiently unequivocal'. His demand 'very specifically requests a detailed list of all the evidence looked at which leads us to believe that the evidence is not sufficiently unequivocal'. This request may have proved difficult, because there had been no evidence ever looked at within the FCO, at least since 1997. She urgently requested someone called Craig Oliphant to provide some names:

> We do not propose to provide a list in reply but would like
> to point to a few instances of debate among historians. We'd
> like to cite historians on each 'side' – I think you may have
> quoted names to us before but I'm afraid I don't have a record
> of them. Would you be able to please email them to me?[300]

Mr Oliphant replied, just three hours later, with the denialist trio put forward in 2001 and 2005: Bernard Lewis, Justin McCarthy and Heath Lowry. Oliphant finds an 'intermediate view' in Macfie (see above) and in Dr Eric Zürcher, whose view is not 'intermediate' at all:

> There are indications that, whilst the Ottoman government
> as such were not involved in genocide, an inner circle within
> the Committee of Union and Progress under the direction
> of Talaat wanted to solve the eastern question by the exter-
> mination of the Armenians and that it used the relocation
> as a cloak for this policy.[301]

Then Oliphant cites six historians who have written 'authorita-tive' accounts of what they firmly describe as genocide.

The FCO ploy of citing historians on either side, which can give the misleading impression that the historians are *equally* divided (and that those on the Turkish side understand the legal definition of genocide or are unbiased and independent) did not, on this occasion, pass muster. The draft answer made no mention of historians and was accompanied by a handwritten explanation to Jim Murphy, the responsible minister:

> Jim – added some more detail as requested. Not mentioned historians explicitly. We stopped referring to historians in June 2007 when this new line was deployed. We found that references to historians tended to raise further questions/ allegations.[302]

This signalled the end of the familiar FCO 'spin' about divided historians. However, Murphy appears to have been too easily pacified: his answer, given by Lord Malloch-Brown on 4 March 2008, was a brief restatement of the classic formula: 'Neither this government nor previous governments have judged that the evidence is sufficiently unequivocal to persuade us that these events should be categorised as genocide, as defined by the 1948 UN Convention on Genocide.'[303]

It is regrettable that this continued formula should be associated with this particular peer (the 'Malloch-Brown statement'), as he has some human rights credentials, but he was just another minister who read out verbatim the words put in his mouth by the FCO. The words were misleading to the point of being deceptive. The documents since 1997 now establish that neither the Blair government nor previous governments had 'judged the evidence' at all. They had neither judged, nor been provided with evidence on which to judge. The FCO had never sought such evidence, other than by asking Craig Oliphant for a few names 'on each side' so as to give the impression that there was a genuine dispute.

What was actually meant by saying that the evidence is 'not sufficiently unequivocal'? This is a standard of proof that seems to have been invented by the equivocators at the FCO, playing with words, and does not reflect the law. There are only two standards of proof in UK law: the civil standard (on the balance of probabilities; i.e. more likely than not) and the criminal standard (beyond reasonable doubt). To apply a test of whether evidence is 'not sufficiently unequivocal' therefore makes no sense. The term is an oxymoron (something is either unequivocal, or it is not: it cannot be a little bit unequivocal). The phrase seems to have been chosen by the FCO not only to beg the question but to fudge it. They invented a meaningless and novel standard, under which the bar could be set at an impossible height. The question is not whether genocide can be proved beyond reasonable doubt, because there is no question of any criminal prosecution. It is whether the Ottoman Empire was *responsible for* the genocide, a matter on which the evidence is unequivocal.

A Summing Up

The advice provided by the FCO to government ministers, and reproduced by ministers in parliamentary answers given between 1997 and 2009, was advice which reflected neither the law of genocide nor the demonstrable facts of the deportations and massacres in 1915, and was calculated to mislead Parliament into believing that there had been an assessment of evidence and an exercise of judgment on that evidence. The truth is that throughout the life of the Labour government and (so the FCO admits) during the terms of previous governments, there was no proper or candid appraisal of 1915 events condemned by HMG at the time and immediately afterwards in terms that anticipate the modern definition of genocide, and which were referred to by the drafters of the Genocide Convention as a prime example of the kind of atrocity that would be covered by this new international crime. HMG consistently and wrongly maintained, until 2010, both that the decision is one for historians and that historians are divided on the subject, ignoring the fact that the decision is one for legal judgment and that no historian worth his or her salt could possibly deny the central facts of the deportations or the racial and religious motivations behind the deaths of a significant proportion of the Armenian people.

HMG also maintained the fiction that it is somehow contrary to legal practice to apply the description 'genocide' to events that occurred prior to 1948. This and other mistaken or illogical arguments have been made, so the internal policy memoranda reveal, in an effort to avoid upsetting the 'neuralgic' Turkish government. The dubious ethics involved in this approach have been internally acknowledged (once, back in 1999) but there was until 2010 no interest in establishing the truth of the matter, or in understanding (let alone applying) the modern law of genocide as it had emerged from decisions of the ICJ, the ICTY and the ICTR. There was no recognition at all of the importance of nations acknowledging their past crimes against humanity, or of supporting the descendants of victims who still, almost a century later, have to live with the consequences.

The case study shows that the UK Parliament had been routinely misinformed, by ministers who recited FCO briefs without questioning their accuracy. HMG's real policy has been to evade accurate answers to questions about the Armenian genocide, because the truth would discomfort the Turkish government. Until 2010 HMG simply refused to come to terms with an issue on which it was once so volubly certain, namely that the Armenian massacres were a crime against humanity which demanded retribution. Times change, but as other civilised nations recognise, the universal crimes of genocide and persecution have no statute of limitations.

Carefully Treading Between Bear Traps:
FCO Genocide Avoidance, 2010–14

In March 2014 I lodged a Freedom of Information Act application for disclosure of all recent FCO memoranda on the
Armenian question since the date of my previous application in
2009. The foreign policy exemption was immediately invoked,
on the basis that disclosure would damage our foreign relations
– not only with Turkey but also, oddly enough, with Scotland
(perhaps because the Scottish Assembly had recently recognised
the genocide). After three months of stalling, on the grounds
that the exemptions were still being discussed, a cache of hitherto secret documents finally arrived. Certain lessons had clearly
been learned, the first of which was to redact all names of FCO
officials, who evidently did not enjoy seeing their names in
print. Thus most of these documents are sent by 'Redacted' to
'Redacted'. Then there was a complete removal of almost all
references to Turkey – not, as last time, by blacking out large
parts of the document (which looked sinister when reproduced)
or leaving in the occasional reference to 'neuralgia', but simply
by use of the word 'redacted', in brackets, so that the extent
of the censorship would not be appreciated. Notwithstanding
these excisions, I am grateful to Michael Fenn (who had to give
his name, as he was the person writing to me) and his staff for
releasing about sixty emails and policy memoranda, which do
show that there has been an evolution of FCO policy thinking
in the last five years, and in the right direction.

The last occasion on which the wretched and wrong phrase –
that the evidence was 'not sufficiently unequivocal' – was deployed
was in July 2009, in opposing a Private Member's Bill that sought
government support for a national day 'to learn and remember
the Armenian genocide'.[304] Later in that year, my opinion was

published, and received close scrutiny from the FCO. In December, the minister asked, 'Why do we not simply say that the Genocide Convention cannot be applied retrospectively?' This dodge was tricky, the minister was told, because it could also prevent the Holocaust being described as genocide, since that took place before the 1948 convention.[305] The search began for another 'line' that could answer the question 'Will HMG recognise the Armenian genocide?' without answering the question.

The first occasion for unveiling a new 'line' came with a debate initiated in the House of Lords by Baroness Cox on 29 March 2010. It was preceded by a 'steering briefing' from the FCO which suddenly dropped the 'not sufficiently unequivocal' language, which has never been heard again other than from the Turkish government website, which pretends it is still the current policy, and the European Court of Human Rights (in the *Perinçek* case), which was gulled into believing that it is. The new line was a little blurred at this point. ('We believe that it is not appropriate to apply the term "genocide" to events that predate the 1948 Convention and where no legal judgment can be made.') The briefing came with a private warning, headed 'BEAR TRAPS'.

> Geoffrey Robertson QC published an opinion titled 'Was there an Armenian Genocide?' He concluded that the events of 1915–16 do amount to genocide. Further, he states '[FCO] advice reflects neither the law on genocide nor the demonstrable facts of the massacres in 1915–16, and has been calculated to mislead Parliament into believing that there has been an assessment of evidence and an exercise of judgment on that evidence.'[306]

Baroness Kinnock, the hapless minister called upon to make the reply, duly repeated the new mantra, despite the fact that legal judgments *can* always be made on events prior to 1948. She read a further section of the steering brief, maintaining that the government did not accept that Parliament had been misled, which of course it had been by repeated false statements that the government had considered the evidence and had made a judgment upon it. This misrepresentation was effectively acknowledged in a full brief to the new Conservative–Liberal Democrat government after its election in June 2010:

> Following Mr Robertson's report and the publicity it attracted
> we have updated our public lines to make clear that HMG
> does not believe it is our place to make a judgment (historical
> or legal) on whether or not the Armenian massacres consti-
> tuted genocide. Instead our lines focus on the need for the
> governments of Turkey and Armenia to accept some form
> of truce and reconciliation process.[307]

The advent of a new government required an explanation about the recently 'updated' and 'evolved' public line:

> Although the UK has consistently refused to recognise the
> Armenian massacres as genocide, our public lines explaining
> why we take this position have evolved over time. For many
> years we used the line that the historical evidence was not suf-
> ficiently unequivocal to persuade us that these events should
> be categorised as genocide. However, whilst some historians
> continue to dispute the scale of the massacres and the level
> of intent behind them, outside of Turkey there is increas-
> ing agreement about the extent of the deaths and suffering
> experienced by the Armenian community. At the same time,
> jurisprudence in relation to genocide, and particularly the
> nature and type of evidence required to prove the relevant

> intent, has developed significantly in the wake of events in
> Rwanda and the Balkans in the 1990s ... [Robertson] argues
> (drawing in part on case law from the genocide trials that
> have followed events in Rwanda and the Balkans) that there
> is sufficient evidence to prove both the 'actus reus' (physical
> acts) and 'mens rea' (mental intent) required for genocide.[308]

This briefing nonetheless advised against recognising the genocide. This position had been agreed not only by the ambassadors
to Ankara and Yerevan but by the 'Parliamentary Relations Team'
and the Press Office (evidently important for deciding matters
of principle), not because it had not occurred, but because there
were 'relatively few risks' associated with not recognising it, since
'the Armenian diaspora in the UK is relatively small (less than
20,000) and there is limited wider public interest' (so much for
the principle) and 'the Armenian government will see continued
non-recognition as confirmation that the UK prioritises relations with Turkey and Azerbaijan over relations with Armenia,
but this is a view they already hold'.[309] Their view is correct, but
to avoid confirming it the FCO have redacted most of the next
paragraph, which sets out the 'risks' of reprisals from Turkey and
its viciously anti-Armenian (but very rich) ally, Azerbaijan.[310]

There was some nervousness at the FCO when, in October 2010,
Ealing Council recognised the genocide: the Turkish embassy had
been quick to protest, and 'our lines to the Turks' are that 'the
views of Ealing Council (which for background has the largest
concentration of Armenians in any London borough) do not rep-
resent the central government'.[311] There were problems as well
from the Welsh Assembly: from one of its officials (name redacted,
no doubt to shield him or her from criticism for truckling to
HMG) came information that 'our First Minister has declined
an opportunity to attend an Armenian Remembrance event in

Cardiff next Monday in view of the sensitivities involved'.[312] It requested the FCO to vet an anodyne message to be sent instead on the First Minister's behalf. The official – presumably in the office of the First Minister, Carwyn Jones – wanted to ensure that the FCO was 'comfortable' with it. Mr Jones's actions, both in dodging a remembrance ceremony for politically 'sensitive' reasons and then having his sentiments 'vetted' by the national government, may not have pleased members of the Welsh Assembly, who later voted to recognise the genocide.

Nonetheless, it is clear from the internal policy documents that by 2012 the FCO was rattled – by the US Senate resolution recognising the genocide, by the French parliament's strengthening of its genocide denial laws and particularly by Pope Francis, who had described the mass killings of Armenians during World War I as 'the first genocide of the twentieth century'. It had to remind ministers that 'Turkey is a key strategic ally in the region on a number of international issues, such as Syria, Cyprus and the EU' and that 'security of energy supply is one aspect of UK interests in the South Caucasus'.[313]

But as the centenary approached, there was a new drum-beat of what might almost be described as decency that enters into the cynical soul of FCO memoranda. It is exemplified by an exchange with the British ambassador in Beirut, who had been invited to a 'commemorative evening' at the Armenian embassy. 'I'm assuming we politely decline,' he emailed, 'but grateful for guidance.' It came by return: 'No need to decline.'[314] Given all the pressure the FCO has applied over the years, on government ministers and officials, and even on the Welsh, to decline any event commemorating Armenian deaths, this reply surely justified an exclamation mark. From now on, the FCO said, although not recognising the genocide, 'it is very important we do not give the impression that we deny what happened in 1915 … we still consider them [the massacres and deportations] to be truly dreadful and in need of remembrance.'[315]

In August 2013 the FCO went so far as to consider a really useful idea: gifting to Armenia for exhibition at the genocide museum in Yerevan some 'historical government documents'. A search in the National Archives produced files of some importance from 1915 relating to '*Punishment of Turks guilty of outrages on Armenians in Turkey; Massacres of Armenians at Urfa; Turkish massacres of Christians; Atrocities committed by Turks in Mosul Vilayet; Turkish-German outrages on Armenians and British prisoners; Investigation of Turkish massacres and atrocities; Turkish offenders; Deportation and massacre of Armenians at Merzifoun; Turkish black lists*' with '*a list of those responsible for the massacres and deportations of Armenians*', and so on.[316] Original documents detailing such evidence would have been a gift not only to Armenia but to genocide scholarship, and the copying cost was a mere £431.20. Quite incredibly, it was decided that this was too much because 'the only pot of money eligible for us to use was the WWI Commemoration Fund' and after speaking to some senior FCO mandarin (whose name was of course redacted, in this case perhaps for good reason) it was decided, incomprehensibly, that using this fund would be perceived as 'the UK downgrading the events as part of WWI – rather than a colossal stand-alone tragedy'.[317] The result was that the colossal tragedy would stand alone, because it would not be appropriately commemorated, since the British government could not muster £431.20 to pay its own national archives for photocopying its own documents! This very worthwhile and easily achievable proposal might really have been rejected for fear of Turkish reaction: there was no alternative proposal for commemorating the 'colossal stand-alone tragedy'.

Meanwhile the government's final 'line' on genocide avoidance was being honed. The problem, as we have seen, was that simply refusing to apply the term to events before the 1948 Genocide Convention would prevent the Holocaust (1941–45) from being so described. It dawned on the FCO that the answer might be to apply the term only to an event labelled 'genocide' by a competent court. There had been such a court at Nuremberg (it had not convicted anyone of genocide, because its judgment was handed down in 1946, two years before the Convention, but it had exposed the evidence) and for Rwanda (the ICTR) and for Srebrenica (the ICTY and the ICJ). This test would mean there could be no recognition of Saddam's Anfal campaign against the Kurds (7,000 gassed at Halabja) as he had not been prosecuted for genocide (and his court, in any event, had hardly been 'competent'). Nor could Rajapaksa's killing of 40,000–70,000 civilians in Sri Lanka, as he had not been called to account, or Bashir's genocidal violence in Darfur (he had not surrendered to his indictment). It begs a lot of questions about Bangladesh, where a self-styled 'international tribunal' (which bans all foreign lawyers) has in 2013–14 been unfairly convicting and indeed hanging Islamists for genocide by attacks on Bengalis and Hindus back in 1971. However, relying on court decisions (and ignoring the Constantinople Tribunal of 1919/20) seemed the best way for HMG not to answer the Armenian question. The new policy formula, now the current response to questions about Armenian genocide recognition, follows a stock reference to British empathy towards the 'suffering' of Armenian people in the 'tragedy' of 1915:

> Our view remains, however, that it is not for governments to decide whether genocide has been committed as this is a complex legal question. Where an international legal body finds a crime to have been genocide, this will often play an important part in whether we will recognise one as such.[318]

Despite this policy of genocide avoidance, there is a more upbeat tone in the FCO memoranda as the centenary approaches. In September 2013, the UK ambassador to Armenia was told, 'We appreciate the sensitivities that the centenary has for Armenia and understand the need to tread very carefully'[319] – not on Turkish toes, presumably, but never again as a genocide denialist. 'We believe a more forward-leaning stance that makes clear our understanding of 1915 and desire to commemorate the memory of the victims is appropriate for the centenary years,'[320] says the most recent background paper, and it is endorsed by a ministerial comment (by William Hague or David Lidington) to the effect that 'we should ensure that [our approach] is not misread as a lack of recognition (in the wider sense) of the appalling events of 1915–16. It would be right to participate more actively in 2015 centenary events.'[321]

That participation will not go as far as the gifting of historical documents (for want of £431.20) but UK policy has undoubtedly moved beyond the obeisance to Turkish neuralgia that characterised it in the Blair/Brown years (and before). That movement is recognised in the 2013 background paper:

> Geoffrey Robertson's Opinion raised important questions about the basis on which the FCO and HMG had justified publicly the position of non-recognition (in particular suggestions that we had reached our position because of lack of sufficient evidence that the events constituted genocide) and highlighted the recent ICJ, ICTY and ICTR judgments in the aftermath of massacres in former Yugoslavia and Rwanda which had further clarified our modern understanding of genocide. This led to a change in public line which now focuses on making clear our understanding of the scale of the tragedy and affirming the role of HMG in supporting these two countries in addressing their common history.[322]

Well, it has led to a change in public line that now focuses on avoiding the question, but at least it has abandoned the damaging and untrue statement that the evidence is 'not sufficiently unequivocal'. It must now go further. It should stop talking about the events of 1915 as a tragedy. It must use the correct word: it was not a tragedy, it was a crime. A crime against humanity – as Britain said in 1915, and should, in 2015, repeat.

CHAPTER 8

SHOULD
GENOCIDE
DENIAL BE
A CRIME?

The Free Speech Problem

....

THE CONVENTION ON the Prevention and Punishment
of the Crime of Genocide binds contracting states to
punish not only the crime itself, but attempts to commit it and all forms of complicity, including 'direct and public

incitement to commit genocide'.[323] But the undertaking to 'prevent' genocide, by which states are bound under Article I, is not elaborated further. This lacuna in the Convention, reflecting both the infancy of international criminal law in 1948 and the reluctance of states to allow intervention in their domestic affairs, has been filled, perhaps to overflowing, by later conventions requiring prohibition and punishment of hate speech.[324] The International Convention of the Elimination of All Forms of Racial Discrimination, for example, demands that states shall 'condemn all propaganda ... based on ideas or theories of superiority of one race ... or which attempt to justify or promote racial hatred and discrimination in any form' and 'shall declare an offence punishable by law all discrimination of ideas based on racial superiority or hatred'.[325] Article 20 of the International Covenant on Civil and Political Rights calls on states to forbid by law advocacy of 'national, racial or religious hatred that constitute an incitement to discrimination, hostility or to violence'.[326]

Many countries now have provisions against stirring up racial or religious hatred, although this has been a step too far for the United States, bound by the First Amendment to reject laws that fetter freedom of speech (even, as the Supreme Court famously held, speech as crude as 'Fuck the Draft')[327] other than utterances that equate to the shouting of 'fire!' in a crowded theatre.[328] Most genocide deniers shout in empty theatres their crazed conjectures about the absence of gas chambers at Auschwitz or the gentleness of 'relocation' to Syrian deserts. Should these people be arrested, brought to trial and fined or jailed after conviction for their perverse opinions? Or should they simply be ignored, or else derided and made liable to civil rather than criminal penalties? Criminal laws against genocide denial, which include expressly or by implication any denial of the Armenian genocide, are widely approved by diaspora groups. It provides some solace to know that their state empathises sufficiently with their historical sorrow that it is prepared to imprison those who deny there is anything to feel sorry about.

This is understandable, but misguided in principle and likely to prove counter-productive in practice. Whilst racial and religious antagonism, especially when promoted or countenanced by the state, can be a harbinger of genocide, something more than mere denial is required before it can be criminalised by laws against racial hatred, lest such dragnets catch robust criticisms of cruel and irrational religions or political criticisms of immigration policies or condemnations of corrupt and dishonest ethnic leaders. No matter how shocking or disgusting an idea or theory, its proponents must in a democracy be safe from arrest unless their proven objective is to stir up violence or to arouse racial conflict, the kind of deliberate and socially dangerous incitement that Article 20 envisages as necessary for prohibition. This may, of course, be the intention of some genocide deniers, but absent that intention their often honest (if ignorant and perverse) opinions a free society must suffer to be expressed unless the circumstances of the expression pose a real danger to public order or social harmony.

This is not, however, the position taken by some European states, which have made denial of the Nazi Holocaust a crime, either because they were once responsible for it (Austria and Germany) or suffered it through Nazi occupation (e.g. Belgium and France). There is no evidence that occasional enforcement of these laws has stemmed neo-Nazism in European countries, which in 2014 was on the rise. Holocaust-denying historian David Irving was jailed for three years in Austria,[329] although it was Irving's obsessive knowledge of Hitler that had helped him expose the fraud perpetrated on (and by) the Murdoch press over the 'Hitler Diaries'. He was disgraced much more effectively when forced to bring a libel action in Britain, which he lost when his racist motivations were proved in court.[330] In another case, an Australian who came to the UK was held at Heathrow under a German arrest warrant accusing him of Holocaust denial: he had to be released because of inadequate details of the offence in the arrest warrant[331] and the overarching fact that the UK does not criminalise genocide denial *per se*. Nonetheless, the European Court of Human Rights has lacked the gumption to strike down Holocaust denial laws as incompatible with free speech – which they are unless confined to situations of social danger.[332] Its failure has caused some to think that, if they are not, why not also make it a crime to deny the Rwandan genocide, and the Armenian?

Although no European state has yet expressly incriminated the denial of the Armenian genocide, some have passed 'denial' laws that are not confined to the Holocaust. Spain bans justification of any genocide, Luxembourg bans denial of the Holocaust 'and other genocides' whilst Malta, Liechtenstein and Switzerland prohibit denial of 'genocides and other crimes against humanity'.[333] Since the 1915 massacres were a genocide 'other than' the Holocaust, it would follow that any denial of the fact that they occurred would amount to a crime in these countries. So, it would seem from the drafting of these vague laws, would be an opinion that although the massacres took place, they did not have the legal character of 'genocide'. Logically, this would follow: 'genocide denial' may cover not only historians who ignore or distort the facts of the past, but historians and others, including lawyers, who venture to suggest – mistakenly – that the real facts do not amount to genocide. Thus interpreted, these laws cannot withstand free speech scrutiny, because they purport to punish an honest opinion about the analysis of historical facts, whenever or wherever that opinion is uttered and irrespective of any intention to vilify Armenians or to cause social disruption.

However, principle aside, since Holocaust denial laws have been upheld in several cases in the European Court, why not punish deniers of the Armenian genocide?

Why not indeed – unless laws against deniers of the Holocaust contravene the right to freedom of expression and the European Court has failed in its duty to apply free speech principles to strike them down. This, regrettably, is the case, because the court has held that the free speech guarantee in Article 10 of the Convention is trumped by Article 17, which does not allow other articles to be interpreted as implying that anyone has a right 'to engage in any activity or perform any act aimed at the destruction of any of the rights and freedoms set forth herein or at their limitation to a greater extent than is provided for in the Convention'. Hence the court held that a French author convicted for Holocaust denial could not complain to Strasbourg because his book aimed to 'rehabilitate the Nazi regime and, as a consequence, accuse the victims themselves of falsifying history'. But this is wrong, in logic and in law. Victims of a crime have no right to silence a suspected perpetrator who proclaims his innocence, nor are the descendants of victims 'defamed' in any meaningful sense by an argument, however threadbare, that their grandparents died e.g. as 'collateral damage' rather than in a genocide. Banning a book because it attempts to excuse conduct the victims of which rightly proclaim (along with everyone else) is inexcusable, is still a breach of free speech guarantees. Holocaust denial does not defame everybody who accepts the truth of the Holocaust, or accuse the children of its victims of lying, and the judgment in this case – *Garaudy v France* – is plainly mistaken.[334] However, it has been used in Strasbourg to prevent consideration of other cases where Holocaust deniers have sought to complain about their convictions.[335]

The free speech principle in respect to Holocaust (and other) denial has now been recognised by the French Conseil d'Etat, which in 2012[336] ruled unconstitutional a new law against 'denying or grossly trivialising crimes of genocide, crimes against humanity and war crimes' on the basis that it contravened the 1789 Declaration of the Rights of Man and the philosophy of Voltaire, not to mention Article 19 of both the Universal Declaration of Human Rights and the International Covenant on Civil and Political Rights, which proclaims, 'Everyone has the right to freedom of opinion and expression; this right includes freedom to hold opinions without interference and to seek, receive and impart information and ideas throughout any media…'

Article 20 of the ICCPR permits the punishment of race hate advocacy 'that constitutes incitement to discrimination, hostility or violence' but that, in the view of the French constitutional body, did not allow punishment for 'trivialising' a genocide 'recognised by French law', because anyone has the right to express disagreement with a decision of Parliament, no matter how offensive that disagreement may be.

Similarly, the Constitutional Court of Spain in 2007 declared that a law punishing the 'denial or justification' of genocide was only valid in relation to 'justification' which would involve approval of it or at least identification with its perpetrators: mere denial of the aptness of the legal label 'genocide' did not incite to violence and might hinder historical research.[337] These decisions correctly apply the freedom of expression principle, namely that any criminal law which bans denial of the Holocaust, or any other genocide, is incompatible with free speech unless guilt is made to turn on an intention to stir up racial hatred or to disrupt public order or uttered with some other malice aforethought. Only a genocide denial law which comes with such qualifications will satisfy the test of being 'necessary in a democratic society' to answer to a pressing social need – the only proper basis for state censorship of ideas and opinion.[338] There may be occasions when an unqualified denial law *would* answer to a pressing social need – if there were to be a recrudescence of social conflict or another terrorist campaign in a particular country that passed the law – but otherwise, genocide denial laws that come without qualifications are incompatible with freedom of expression principles.

This is why Armenians are mistaken in expecting states to punish every provocateur who proclaims Turkey's innocence. They may be naive, stupid or perverse, but so long as the opinion is honestly ventured in circumstances where the utterance presents no social danger, it is not appropriately visited with criminal sanctions. It may be made the basis for employment decisions – people who deny established genocides may not be fit to work as teachers or police officers. Their opinion may be of little or no worth, but like obscenity it qualifies for minimal free speech protection, namely the right of the free speaker not to be sent to jail.

Quite apart from the free speech principle, and the consideration of the appropriate and proportionate limit of criminal law in a democracy, there is a severely practical reason for ignoring rather than punishing most genocide deniers. Although it is offensive for victims – and 'victims' of genocide include the children and grandchildren of those deemed unfit to live because of their race – to be assailed by a claim that the cause of their family sorrow was non-existent, the damage caused by allowing that malign racism to be clothed in the favourable rhetoric of free speech is greater than any damage that this claim could do if left to dangle in hot air and then dissipate. It is for this very reason that malevolent genocide deniers thrive on the real-time publicity that prosecution brings, and embrace the alluring prospect of martyrdom to a cause that would otherwise remain despised and derided.

So it is an illusion for Armenians to think that punishing extreme Turkish nationalists who venture to the West with the object of provoking prosecutions will somehow avenge or make up for the atrocities of 1915 or give back to their people some of the dignity and respect of which they were deprived under the Ottoman Empire and lately by its apologists. On the contrary, it will only provide their enemies with the opportunity to masquerade as defenders of free speech – a massive irony in the case of Turkey, with its own disgraceful record of suppressing historical truth and legitimate opinion. This is the lesson of *Perinçek v Switzerland*,[339] a case decided by the first level of the European Court of Human Rights in 2013, and which was re-argued in the full court (the 'Grand Chamber') in January 2015, whose judgment is awaited. It had begun as a criminal action brought by Swiss Armenians against one obsessive Turkish genocide denier, but the confused decision of the preliminary judges enabled Turkey – until the re-hearing which exposed its hypocrisy – to exult in its unlikely role as the victorious defender of freedom of expression in Europe.

The Perinçek Case

Perinçek demonstrates the danger of looking to genocide denial laws to provide any kind of symbolic satisfaction. Dr Perinçek – a doctor of laws, no less – was head of an extreme Turkish nationalist political party, and so obsessed with the belief that his countrymen could never be guilty of genocide that he declared that his mind would never change, no matter what evidence might persuade an international court to declare otherwise. In 2005, determined to present himself as a martyr, he attended a conference in Lausanne commemorating the eponymous treaty, where he declared 'the Armenian genocide is an international lie'. This claim had a certain appropriateness to the occasion, because the Treaty of Lausanne overrode the Treaty of Sèvres and treated the genocide as if it had not happened (and bestowed an amnesty upon everyone, in case it had) because the great powers by this time (1923) wanted business in Turkey and were seeking an alliance with Atatürk against the Bolsheviks. The utterance was not proved to pose any danger to public order in Switzerland: Perinçek's antics were for publicity back in Turkey. He did not, apparently, deny the atrocities of 1915, but merely disputed the application to them of a legal characterisation. Nonetheless the Swiss Armenian Association filed a criminal complaint and Dr Perinçek was, presumably to his delight, convicted by the police court and fined €2,500. He challenged the genocide denial law on appeal, but the Swiss courts held it constitutional. This enabled him to take his case to the European Court of Human Rights in Strasbourg, claiming that his freedom of speech had been infringed. He was powerfully supported by the government of Turkey, which intervened (as it was entitled to do under Article 36(1) of the Convention) on behalf of its national, notwithstanding the fact that Dr Perinçek had by this time just been convicted of trying to overthrow the Turkish government and sentenced to life imprisonment in Turkey for terrorism offences.

The first thing to notice is that these preliminary proceedings in Strasbourg were procedurally unbalanced. The case for Dr Perinçek, that the characterisation of the atrocities as 'genocide' was open to legitimate dispute, was enthusiastically supported by the intervening Turkish government's legal team. The Swiss – the defendants in the case, since it was their law that was challenged – did not much care about what happened in 1915, as its main (national) parliament had not recognised the genocide. Armenia, which would have been given permission to intervene on the side of the Swiss, was not notified of the case and failed to apply. So Turkey and Dr Perinçek had little forensic opposition for their claim that the issue of 'genocide' is still open to dispute. Their prime evidence was the Malloch-Brown statement in the UK parliament on 8 March 2008, that neither the current British government nor its predecessors 'has found that the evidence is sufficiently unequivocal to convince us that these events should be classified as genocide as defined by the UN Convention on Genocide'.[340] This devious formula, devised as we have seen to avoid upsetting the Turks, had been abandoned by the UK in 2010, but nobody pointed this out: the discredited and subsequently discarded UK 2008 position clearly weighed with the court and was set out in its 2013 judgment (and remains on the Turkish Foreign Ministry website), as if it were still current.

The European Court of Human Rights has judges representing forty-seven countries that belong to the Council of Europe (not to the European Union, which is a more politically compact group of European nations) and the *Perinçek* case at the preliminary stage was heard by only seven of them (nineteen sat on the Grand Chamber hearing). European judges are chosen by governments: many are former lawyers in government departments (often, diplomats with law degrees) and some are commercial lawyers or regular judges with no qualifications in human rights. The hope is that judicial differences and deficiencies will iron themselves out – and in a 'Grand Chamber' decision involving at least seventeen judges, they usually do. A small court of seven, however, carries less authority, especially when, as in *Perinçek*, it divides three ways.[341]

The issue before the court was simple: was the infringement of Perinçek's right to freedom of expression, by punishing him for describing the Armenian genocide as 'an international lie', justifiable under Article 10 (the free speech guarantee) of the Convention – i.e. did a 'genocide denial' ban correspond to a pressing social need in a democratic society? This issue was quite apart from the question – which need not have arisen at all – as to whether the Armenian genocide was *in fact* an international lie.

The only question for the court was whether it should be a crime to say so. Sensibly, the court judgment begins: '*The court considers it important to state at the outset that it is not necessary to rule on the materiality of the massacres and deportations suffered by the Armenian people at the hands of the Ottoman empire from 1915 nor whether the characterisation of those facts amounts to genocide.*'[342]

This opening disavowal means that the decision cannot be read as any sort of legal authority on the subject of whether there is any doubt over the Armenian genocide. All that it decided – by five votes to two – was that freedom of expression should protect speech that was neither overtly racist nor directly inflammatory, and that Perinçek's utterance at an academic conference should therefore not be criminalised. But all seven judges made some comments on the subject of the genocide. The two dissenting judges found that the massacres and deportations were genocide beyond any doubt and that Perinçek's denial of a historical fact was conduct a state was entitled to outlaw. Two other judges, the court president, Judge Raimondi, and Judge Sajó, said that the 1915 conduct was definitely genocide but agreed with the three other judges, that criminal laws prohibiting the expression of any contrary opinion should not be banned. Raimondi, confusingly, also 'signed' their opinion, so that it became the decision of the court, because he agreed with their conclusion that there had been a contravention of Article 10, although apparently not with their irrelevant view that there was some doubt about the genocide. His signature was appended under the court's Rule 77, which requires the court president to sign off on a decision so as to make it the judgment of the court. This was unfortunate, because although their conclusion about a breach of Article 10 was one they were entitled to make, the three judges made a number of foolish comments in the course of reaching it.

The problem they thought they faced was that the court had

in the past – in *Garaudy v France*, for example – upheld laws requiring punishment for denial of the Nazi genocide. Instead of questioning or distinguishing those precedents, they made an invidious and distasteful comparison between the two genocides, suggesting that the Holocaust was somehow more important and more convincingly proved than the Armenian genocide.

They began by stating that 'genocide was a very narrow legal concept that was moreover difficult to substantiate'.[343] This is not correct – genocide is a very clear legal concept which is not difficult at all to substantiate in respect of mass murders intentionally directed by state forces for racial or religious reasons. Although there may be evidential difficulties in proving 'beyond reasonable doubt' that an individual has genocidal intent, the ICJ has confirmed that this is not the test for holding a state responsible for genocide. Astonishingly, the three judges went on to find that Perinçek's comment that the genocide was 'an international lie' was a speech 'of historical, legal and political nature which was part of a heated debate'.[344] His speech had no historical, legal or political value, other than as a crude expression of a discredited and discreditable opinion, and to describe this three-word provocation as a contribution to a 'heated debate' was fanciful: as the International Association of Genocide Scholars pointed out, in its acidic comment on the decision:

> Scholars who deny the facts of genocide in the face of overwhelming scholarly evidence are not engaging in historical debate but have another agenda – to absolve Turkey of responsibility for the planned extermination of the Armenians – an agenda consistent with every Turkish ruling party since the time of the genocide in 1915.[345]

The court then decided that there was no 'general consensus' because 'only about twenty states out of the 190 in the world had officially recognised the Armenian Genocide'[346] – a silly point, since the great majority of the non-recognising states had never been asked to recognise it, and the most important European states – with the exception of the UK – do recognise it. Then, astonishingly, the court decision said there could be no consensus 'given that historical research was by definition open to discussion and a matter of debate, without necessarily giving rise to final conclusions or to the assertion of objective and absolute truths'.[347] This is incoherent: historical research establishes facts, and it is their causes or their significance which later research may illuminate. But this view that 'historical research' may be incapable of locating objective truth applied only to the Armenian genocide and not to the Holocaust, for three reasons:[348]

1) The Holocaust facts were 'very concrete such as the existence of gas chambers'. Almost as concrete, one might say, as the laws passed by the CUP government for the deportations and expropriations, the photographs of the Armenians on their death marches to and through the desert, and the endless eyewitness accounts of barbaric, racially fuelled killings in Anatolia. The idea that these facts are not 'very concrete' is absurd.

2) Holocaust deniers 'denied the crimes perpetrated by the Nazi regime for which there had been a clear legal basis, namely Article 6(c) of the Statute of the Nuremberg Tribunal'. This is a legal howler, because this statute was agreed in 1945, *after* the Holocaust, and made no mention of genocide (it referred only to crimes against humanity). Both the Armenian genocide and the genocide of the German Jews took place before the Genocide Convention of 1948 or the Nuremberg Statute of 1945, and both involved mass killings by a state of its citizens on the ground of their race. The judges were demonstrably wrong, both on law and on fact.

3) The historical facts challenged by Holocaust deniers were 'clearly established by an international court'. But it is wrong to suggest that a fact is not a 'fact' unless and until it is established by an international court. That would preclude characterisation of Halabja, Darfur, Sri Lanka, Bangladesh etc. as genocides because although the facts are clear, international courts have not considered them. The Nuremberg Tribunal decision certainly put the facts of the Holocaust beyond dispute, although it would not pass muster as an international court today (all the judges were drawn from victor powers, for a start) and such courts are not infallible – the ICTY, for example, has had a number of trial chamber convictions, and a few acquittals, overturned by the Appeal Court because of erroneous assessments of the facts proved in evidence. In any event, as the two dissenting judges pointed out in *Perinçek*, the main authors of the genocide were all convicted of mass murder of Armenians by a court in their own country, applying (in their case) international military law. So long as the facts are clear in relation to the Armenian genocide – and they are – it cannot matter that because of the negation of the Treaty of Sèvres they were never considered by an international court.

The European Court came to the conclusion, by five votes to two, that Perinçek's conviction breached his right of free speech. For this decision the three judges did not need to consider whether the genocide was an 'international lie' and should not have done so. They announced this disavowal at the outset of their judgment, and then unaccountably (in fact, irresponsibly) proceeded to do exactly that, with invidious and illogical comparisons with the Holocaust and a reference to the UK government's 'not sufficiently unequivocal' formula, ignorant of the fact that that the UK government had, for good reason, abandoned this position in 2010.

The president of the court, Judge Raimondi, was required under Rule 77 to add his signature to the three-judge decision which expressed doubts about the genocide, although he had concurred in or jointly written a judgment expressing no doubt that the atrocities did amount to genocide:

> If we look at the period in question in this case in light of the Hamidian massacres that preceded it, sufficient evidence is available to prove that Armenian citizens of the Ottoman Empire underwent a state policy that caused the death and suffering of hundreds and thousands of people (estimates range from 600,000 to 1.5 million) and nearly caused the extermination of the Armenians as a separate community.[349]

This conclusion is irreconcilable with that part of the court's official decision that cast doubt on the characterisation of genocide. Judges Sajó and Raimondi go on to point out that Lemkin had the Armenian massacres squarely in mind when he coined the word 'genocide' and they refer to 'an extermination plan hatched by Talaat Pasha and his acolytes'. The two dissenting judges, who actually had the best qualifications in international criminal law and in human rights, delivered a powerful and compelling analysis of why the massacres and deportations amounted to genocide – their dissent was because they thought Switzerland was entitled to punish Perinçek's denial. So the misbegotten three-judge 'court' decision is only a decision on the free speech point, and will in any event be consigned to the dustbin of lower court decisions once it is superseded by the Grand Chamber judgment at the end of 2015 or in 2016. On the question of the fact of the genocide, four of the judges had no doubt about it. The minority view was that of three judges out of seven, who happened to be the judges on the court with least experience of and qualifications in international criminal law and human rights. The decision itself, of course, is fact-sensitive: the majority of judges assumed that Perinçek's statement had not impacted on Armenians in Switzerland. They failed to realise that it was intended for publication in Turkey and did not consider its effect on the tens of thousands of Armenians who are resident there. In January 2015, the Grand Chamber hearing took place in Strasbourg attended by hundreds of Perinçek supporters chanting nationalist slogans and waving Turkish flags. Although he had been jailed for terrorist offences, Turkey allowed him to attend the court in order to promote genocide denialism, and supported his case with its own lawyers. Their public relations exercise backfired when he was upstaged by the new Mrs Clooney, making the case for Armenia, which had been permitted to intervene to refute the points of the three first instance judges. It did not buy into the question of whether Perinçek was guilty – this depended on whether his words were intended and likely to rouse hatred against Armenians, in Turkey as well as in Switzerland. Armenia urged the court to adopt a modified free speech approach, so that Article 10 could protect Armenians in Turkey against being prosecuted for affirming the genocide.

Although the massacres of 1915 amounted to genocide, denial of this characterisation cannot, consistently with free speech, be criminalised unless there is an additionally proven intention to stir up race hatred or else a threat to public order or social cohesion. This should be an essential condition for conformity with Article 10 of the European Convention in the case of genocide denial laws, including those applied to or specifically targeting Holocaust denial. It may be, of course, that the Grand Chamber, in reviewing the Swiss proceedings, will find that the condition was in fact satisfied, and there was a 'pressing social need' in Switzerland in 2007 to punish Armenian genocide denial, if only because the 'crime' was staged for the benefit of nationalists in Turkey who seek to justify the massacres and so to whip up hatred against the Armenians who live in Turkey today.

Better Not

In the absence of inflammatory circumstances, however, Armenians and their supporters might be best advised to let Perinçek-style provocation pass. There are a number of reasons:

- Criminalising honest opinion is the sort of thing the Turks do, and were condemned by the European Court for doing in the case of Hrant Dink (namely prosecuting him for 'insulting Turkishness' by insinuating that the Ottomans committed genocide).[350] Armenians should not go down this path, in memory of the courage of Dink and the fact that the Turkish prosecution of him fanned flames that led to his assassination. It is worth remembering that shortly before his death, Dink said that he was as opposed to criminalising genocide denial as he was to criminalising genocide affirmation. ('Turkey and France can race to see who can jail me first.')[351]

- Criminalisation of speech is anathema to American values, which many in the diaspora share because they live in California, and is unacceptable in the UK and Ireland. Holocaust denial laws also conflict with free speech principles, although their continued existence in Europe reflects historical guilt in countries that collaborated or suffered under Nazi occupation, or had voted Hitler into power, as well as an understandable wish to combat racism.

- A genocide denial law extending to the Armenian atrocities can give no lasting relief for family suffering: the controversy over the law itself will attract liberal support for the deniers and give their perverse opinions more publicity and perhaps more credibility.

- The very existence of criminal laws against genocide denial is a gift to zealots, anxious to clothe their zealotry in the attractive garb of free speech martyrdom. As exemplified by *Perinçek*, genocide denial laws cause confusion when the defendant is acquitted in the interests of freedom of expression: this gives the impression that there is real doubt over state responsibility for the crime they have denied.

The purpose of the crime of genocide is to identify the most execrable of all crimes against humanity – namely the promotion by the state of extermination of members of a group solely for reasons of their racial type or religious upbringing, factors over which they could have no control. This presents an evil of a different kind to liquidation for their politics (or lack of them) even of the many millions who died during Mao's 'great leap forward' or Stalin's war on the Kulaks. This distinction between genocide and 'politicide' is justified in terms of practical deterrence: communal blood hatreds are more easily fostered, and more likely to turn into brutal violence against neighbours from different tribes and creeds, than political differences. For this reason, human rights treaties allow exceptions to the free speech principle in order to punish those who fan racial hatred, whilst the fanning of political hatred must be tolerated so long as it does not incite or spill over into violence. Genocide is for this reason regarded as the worst kind of crime against humanity, with its own convention and rules that aim to prevent it being fostered or forgotten. The very fact that it is the worst of crimes makes the freedom to deny it essential.

Turkey – A Champion of Free Speech?

The idea, promoted by genocide deniers after the lower court decision in *Perinçek*, that Turkey's intervention made it a free speech champion, would come as a surprise to anyone familiar with the Article 10 casebook of the European Court. Turkey has been the most egregious violator, with two thirds of its adverse rulings relating to freedom of expression, in particular by using Article 301 of its criminal code to jail and to harass those who 'insult Turkishness' by affirming the Armenian genocide. The worst case was that of Turkish/Armenian newspaper editor Hrant Dink, who wrote a series of highly intelligent and probing articles about the effect of Turkish genocide denial on Armenians. Extreme nationalists, who did not understand the point (somewhat critical of Armenians) that he was making, had him prosecuted under Article 301, and judges who did not understand it either convicted him and an appeal court upheld the guilty verdict. The court prosecutor, of all people, brought an appeal on the grounds that Dink's article had been misconstrued, but the ignorant judges refused to change their verdict. The publicity-fuelled extremist hatred of Dink including hatred within his local police force, which withdrew protection. He was assassinated, probably with police connivance, and on his family's complaint to Strasbourg it was held that both his right to life and his right to freedom of expression had been violated. Biased judges at every level had in reality decided to punish him for what they took to be an affirmation of the 1915 genocide.[352] Between 2003 and 2007, no fewer than 1,894 Article 301 proceedings had been initiated, 744 resulting in convictions.[353]

Turkey is well aware that the terms of Article 301 breach human rights law. In 2005 the offence was amended, from the crime of 'publicly insulting or deriding the moral character of Turkishness, the Republic, its government, ministers, army and judiciary' to the crime of 'publicly denigrating Turkishness, the government, the judges etc.'. This was virtually the same offence, albeit with lower penalties (up to three years, nonetheless) and a filter that made prosecution subject to the approval of the Minister of Justice. The Strasbourg court has held that giving a government minister this discretion cannot bring the law into conformity with the Convention, and between 2008 and the end of 2012 the ministry had allowed 105 cases to come to trial. A law that punishes 'the denigration of Turkishness' is too vague to satisfy the Convention requirement for certainty in criminal prohibitions.[354]

There have been other notorious attempts to prosecute for genocide affirmation – Nobel Prize winner Orhan Pamuk was charged for saying 'a million Armenians were killed', although his case did not go ahead. The leading historian of the genocide, Taner Akçam, was prosecuted by court order in 2006 merely for expressing solidarity with Dink. The European Court ruled that the 'stress, apprehension and fear of prosecution' as a result of starting an Article 301 investigation had been intended to chill his freedom of speech and that the law was so vague that the crime could not be said to be 'prescribed by law'. The Minister of Justice, on hearing that a friend had claimed Dink was killed for talking publicly about the Armenian massacres, declared, 'I will not allow the state to be called a murderer' – presumably by using his discretion to prosecute anyone who suggests it once was.

Although Amnesty International reported in 2013 that critical references to the 1915 massacres 'are no longer certain to be prosecuted' there is no shortage of complaints from extremists about them, and charges depend on government discretion.[355] This is a frail protection; Amnesty concludes: 'Freedom of expression is under attack in Turkey. Hundreds of abusive criminal prosecutions are brought every year ... against individuals who criticize the state or express opinions contrary to official positions on sensitive issues.'[356]

Article 301 is not the only problem – Article 125 criminalises defamation, threatening up to two years in prison for statements devaluing a person's 'honour, dignity or prestige'. This law is routinely used by politicians – especially by Prime Minister (now President) Erdoğan – to prosecute critics and fines can be high. In 2012 a cartoonist who depicted Erdoğan chained to a US flag was sentenced to eleven months in prison – as the result of a complaint by Erdoğan. In the three months before he won the 2014 presidential election, no less than thirty-eight people were jailed or fined (or both) for 'insulting and attacking the personal rights of Prime Minister Erdoğan'.[357] The election monitor, OCSE, commented on the timidity of the Turkish media and it was noted that, over three crucial days before the election, state television accorded 533 minutes to Erdoğan, compared with three minutes to one opponent and 45 seconds to the other.[358] This is a Prime Minister who was once a victim of his country's contempt for free speech (he was jailed for reciting a poem that the secularist government claimed would incite religious hatred) but he now has no hesitation in putting editors and journalists in prison, along with hundreds of those who peacefully protest about the treatment of the Kurds or write about it without supporting violent resistance.

It is internet censorship which has more recently made Turkey a laughing stock. The government has a special law allowing it to block websites – the suggestion on one that Atatürk was gay led to the blocking of them all. In December 2013, a corruption investigation into several government ministers, largely ignored by mainstream media, was widely reported on the internet, so the government assumed further power to block websites without a court order.[359] A few months later Erdoğan vowed to 'eradicate' Twitter, and then blocked YouTube when it carried audio recordings purporting to be of Erdoğan himself arranging a corrupt deal with a developer.[360] Eventually, after sixty-seven days of blank screens, the Constitutional Court struck down the ban, saving Turkey from further international ridicule.

Turkey is now ranked 154 of 180 in the World Press Freedom Index: it was downgraded from 'partially free' to 'not free' in 2014.[361] This was not only because of its laws (forty journalists were in jail by the end of 2013)[362] but because of the manner in which companies that have newspaper interests are punished by the government (usually by a tax investigation) if those papers criticise the government. This understandably makes newspapers nervous enough to sack journalists who arouse government ire – there are numerous examples of journalists being fired or forced to resign after being singled out for criticism by the then Prime Minister and fifty-nine reporters were dismissed after he took umbrage at their coverage of the Gezi Park environmental protests.[363] The problem of a nation that is 'neuralgic' about criticism begins with its constitution, which guarantees free speech subject not only to the usual exceptions, but to a highly unusual one: the freedom 'may be restricted for the purposes of … safeguarding the basic characteristics of the Republic and the indivisible integrity of the state'. This goes far beyond what is permissible under human rights conventions, which have exceptions for national security, public order, privacy and so forth, but not for criticisms of the state and its 'indivisible integrity'.

If Turkey is to be admitted to the European Union, a new commitment to freedom of expression will be required, which must remove any threat of criminal prosecution for affirming the Armenian genocide. It is fair to say that, partly as a result of the courage of Hrant Dink and Taner Akçam, the taboo over such discussion has, since 2007, been lifted, although the laws remain a threat should extreme nationalists prevail on prosecutors and judges to activate them. It may be the most beneficial result of the *Perinçek* case will be to persuade Turkey to live up to its ill-found reputation for free speech – it is logically absurd to champion the right to hear Perinçek's opinion whilst prosecuting the views of Dink and Akçam. Whether this will ever be appreciated is open to question: in one triumphalist analysis of *Perinçek* the decision was hailed not only as a victory for freedom of speech, 'but also as an additional legal basis for defamation cases against Armenian nationalists who attempt to portray their opponents as no better than Holocaust deniers'.[364] The notion that a victory for free speech can be the foundation for criminal defamation actions may be paradoxical, but given funding by the Turkish government and the capacity, even of hopeless libel actions, to harass and bankrupt their defendants, this is another reason for overturning the *Perinçek* decision.

CHAPTER 9

REPARATIONS

They have no cemetery; we are their cemetery.

Elie Wiesel[365]

'R EPARATIONS' IS A legalistic word, damaged by association with the over-punitive and counter-productive impositions on Germany at Versailles, for responsibility for Allied losses in the First World War but not for complicity in the Armenian genocide. Genocide scholar Colin Tatz prefers the German word '*Wiedergutmachung*', which means 'making good again', but then asks, 'How, in God's name, does one make good again the Armenian *vilayets* of Erzurum, Bitlis,

Trabzon, Sivas, Kharput, Cilicia and Anatolia? … if you can't give back the ungiveable, or restore the un-restorable, then we are left with only one thing – money.'[366] For want of any available alternative, this has been the demand of victims of the Holocaust (in 1952 the German Federal Republic agreed to pay, over some years, US $850 million to the state of Israel) and victims of recent atrocities, such as the Lockerbie bombing (US $2.7 billion was paid in compensation by Gaddafi). International law posits that there can be no international wrong without a remedy, and 'blood money' in cases where there is no alternative does not deserve a prejudicial connotation where it symbolises a measure of punishment for the perpetrator. Modern Germany should certainly pay for its complicity with the Armenian genocide and indeed for its commission of that crime (commanded, ironically enough, by Hermann Goering's grandfather) against the Herero people. There are more powerful signals that Turkey might send to express both recognition and contrition for a historic crime against humanity, the damage having been exacerbated by its attempts at justification.

What Recompense Can International Law Offer?

There is no recompense that money can make for the physical and psychological injuries inflicted by genocide, not only to survivors who witnessed family members die but to their children and grandchildren who inherit the memories and suffer the grief that is exacerbated by Turkish attempts to justify the events that caused the suffering. In April 2014 the oldest survivor of the deportations (she was four at the time) was pictured with the world's best-known Armenian (Kim Kardashian!) to remind the international community of all the families whose psychological

scars it has done nothing to heal. International law at least recognises the obligation to provide reparation for intentionally
wrongful acts, and it is often said that Turkey's obsession with
denying genocide has to do with a fear that courts will require it
to pay compensation. But money – even if paid to people who
could prove their kinship with those massacred or marched to
death – could not repair a life-long hurt. Many victims of Nazi
crimes, when entitled to up to £20,000 compensation from the
German state, said that the humiliation of claiming the money
and being forced to justify the amount added insult to original
injury.[367] Nonetheless, a payment of damages, either as a lump
sum to a memorial trust or to individuals who could prove their
direct descent as members of a second or third Armenian gen-
eration, would appropriately underline the genuineness of any
Turkish apology for the Ottoman crime.

An apology, at least for a crime against humanity, would be an
important form of reparation, as it would counteract the damage being done by the 'genocide justification' school currently
promoted by the Turkish government. Its 'on-going campaign of
denial, de-legitimisation and disinformation affects the Armenians
as a psychological continuation of persecution'.[368] The very idea
that 'military necessity' can excuse a crime against humanity that
was calculated to kill over half of a racial group – whether 600,000
of 1.1 million or 1.5 million of 2 million – is morally unconscion-
able, and in the case of the Armenians, legally mistaken. The US
government, which adopted the much less serious expedient of
internment for many Japanese Americans after Pearl Harbor, has
apologised to them – fifty years later – for its unconstitutional
action and has paid $20,000 each to the surviving internees, who
report that the apology was much more important.[369]

What then might follow from the conclusion that the treatment of the Armenians by the Ottoman Empire amounted to

genocide? There can be no help from the prosecutor of the International Criminal Court because all human perpetrators are long since deceased, the prime mover Mehmet Talaat having himself been assassinated in 1922 by Soghomon Tehlirian. Besides, the jurisdiction of that court arises only in respect of crimes committed after July 2002, when it commenced operation. There are questions, however, that remain in respect of the Turkish state's responsibility for genocide perpetrated by its predecessor, and the further question of liability by those entities – churches, companies and the state treasury – which took over property 'abandoned' by Armenians.

There has been litigation in America brought by Holocaust survivors against the Swiss banks which allowed the Nazis to withdraw funds from the accounts of relatives who died in the camps. This case resulted in a US $1.25 billion payout by the banks and by a Swiss government fearful that the case would expose their complicity with genocide: it was settled and so established no legal precedent for liability.[370] Similar settlements have been reached with German corporations which employed Jewish slave labour.[371] The US Supreme Court has allowed an action to proceed to trial against the Austrian government, over Gustav Klimt paintings hanging in its National Gallery. They had been looted by the Nazis from a Jewish family whose members sought compensation, and the court ruled that Austria could not hide behind state immunity to take the benefit of a crime against humanity.[372]

It would seem that an international law right is in the process of developing as a result of the special abhorrence of crimes against humanity, namely that any heirs of victims of such crimes whose property was seized by the perpetrators are entitled to its return or to compensation for its loss – a right that can be asserted notwithstanding immunities and time bars, and even against third parties who purchase the seized property in ignorance of its origins. It cannot confidently be said, however, that a right in such terms has crystallised, and in the case of the Armenian genocide there would be a number of problems in both sourcing and asserting it, whether by reference to the Genocide Convention or customary international law. In relation to the former, two arguments have been advanced specifically on the basis of a right to reparation for the retrospective crime of genocide, whilst the case under customary law would hinge on the emerging right of victim recompense for a crime against humanity.

Is the Genocide Convention Retrospective?

Article 1 of the 1948 Convention on the Prevention and Punishment of Genocide simply states that 'genocide, whether committed in time of peace or time of war, is a crime under international law'. This treaty has been ratified by 146 states, most importantly the United States: Turkey ratified in 1950, and Armenia in 1993 shortly after it became independent (previously, it had been part of the USSR). Neither country made any reservations, i.e. neither objected to being bound by Article IX, which provides that 'disputes between the Contracting Parties relating to the interpretation, application or fulfilment of the present Convention, *including those relating to the responsibility of a state for genocide* ... shall be submitted to the International Court of Justice at the request of any of the parties to the dispute'. (Emphasis added)

This is an important article, which gives Armenia direct right of access to the court if it wishes to make Turkey accountable under the Convention. It was under Article IX that Bosnia sued Serbia at the ICJ, and the court ruled that Article IX furnished it with the jurisdiction to assess the responsibility of a state for genocide.[373]

However, Article IX leaves unstated and open whether the consequences might be compensation or restitution ordered by the ICJ. There is no case law directly on the point of reparations for direct state responsibility for genocide, although in *Bosnia v Serbia*, the ICJ held that a declaration that the Serbian state had failed to prevent genocide in Srebrenica and an order that it must undertake to punish acts of genocide amounted to a sufficient reparation – so financial compensation for failing to satisfy earlier court orders was rejected.[374] However, a potential *Armenia v Turkey* action may establish a factual basis for financial recompense. The legal hurdle, however, for Armenia and for descendants of Armenian victims to surmount would be whether the Convention operates retrospectively, to impose any form of legal accountability for events in 1915–16.

Some scholars argue that 'genocide' has been a crime ever since the 1907 Hague Convention outlawed behaviour that flouts the rules of civilisation and humanity. But international law cannot be 'developed', however desirable the direction, without some basis in treaty or precedent.[375] The Vienna Convention on the Law of Treaties[376] sets up a presumption that treaties are not retroactive, and this presumption is all the stronger in the case of a treaty establishing a criminal offence in international law. This does not of course mean that the legal label 'genocide' cannot be affixed to pre-1951 massacres: the Preamble of the Convention, which recognises that 'at all periods of history genocide has inflicted great loss on humanity', is sufficient warrant for applying the label to pre-Convention events that satisfy its definition. Moreover, the 'responsibility' of states in respect to genocide does not depend on any successful prosecution of an agent. Does this mean that the 1948 Convention may be used as a basis for suing or legally pursuing Turkey for Ottoman atrocities in the First World War?

Some genocide scholars think so. In William Schabas's opinion, for example, there is nothing in the Genocide Convention that says it does not operate retrospectively.[377] The Genocide Convention is a treaty that must be interpreted according to its ordinary meaning and in light of its object and purpose. Its purpose was to prevent another Holocaust (or another Armenian genocide, for that matter) by requiring prosecution of the perpetrators of any future crime, and the reference to state responsibility in Article IX is explicable on the basis that imputing responsibility to a state for a past genocide is one way to deter that and other states from committing genocide in the future. It may, on this argument, be open to the Armenian government, as a contracting party, to invite the ICJ to rule that another contracting state is responsible for genocide, even prior to the Convention, and to make a declaration that the Ottoman Empire committed genocide and that the Turkish Republic, as successor state, is liable to compensate those who can show direct injury (including suffering through loss of parents and other relatives, including grandparents), and must restore seizèd property to families who can trace their right of possession. This interpretation would require the Convention to be given retroactive effect in respect of civil claims against the state of Turkey – a position that is arguable as an interpretation of Article IX, although the argument's success would be problematic.

Was Genocide a Crime before the Convention?

Another argument, this time for allowing civil claims to proceed in national courts, would be that the crime of genocide existed in customary international law in 1915, at least in the form of a prohibition on the mass murder of people because of their race or religion. The Preamble to the Genocide Convention recognises that 'at all periods of history genocide has inflicted great losses on humanity', plainly referring to events before 1948. But the Preamble describes the concept, not the crime, of genocide. It is the recitation of an established fact, but cannot be intended to mean that genocide *as a crime* has existed throughout human history – in early civilisations, for example, genocide was a mark of military and strategic success. The name itself was not coined until 1944, and the first recognition was in General Assembly Resolution 96(I), adopted on 11 December 1946, which 'affirms that genocide is a crime under international law which the civilised world condemns, and for the commission of which principals and accomplices … are punishable'.[378]

This resolution was relied upon by the American military tribunal in the *Justice Case* as authority for the existence of the crime of genocide during the Second World War,[379] although the better view was also expressed which referred to the crime of genocide in that period as 'the prime illustration of crimes against humanity'. In other words, the genocide committed by the Ottomans in the First World War fell into the most heinous category of crimes against humanity, but did not crystallise as a separate and distinct offence until (at the earliest) the UN declaration in 1946 and probably not until the Genocide Convention itself, either at the time of its introduction (1948) or entry into operation (1951). Those who argue for the existence of genocide as a separate crime by 1915 must explain why the British authorities failed to charge the Young Turk leaders with any conceptually similar offence, and indeed despaired of charging them with criminal involvement in actions authorised by their government against its own nationals.

This is a somewhat arid academic debate. The reality is that a particularly heinous crime against humanity was committed by the Ottoman Empire in 1915, a crime which thirty years later came to be called 'genocide', and the question is whether any restitution or compensation can still be due, from the successor government, to those descendants who can show family loss through death or forcible deprivation of property in the course of perpetration of that crime.

International Customary Law

The principles on reparations for state violations of international wrongs are well established: reparation is required[380] and where possible this means restitution (putting the aggrieved party in the position it would occupy had the wrong not occurred).[381] Where restitution is impossible, or would impose a disproportionate burden, compensation should be awarded.[382]

On any view, the deportations and massacres were a gross violation of human rights law, and as such would fall within the United Nations *Basic Principles and Guidelines on the Right to a Remedy and Reparations for Gross Violation of International Human Rights Law and Serious Violations of International Law*, unanimously adopted by the General Assembly in 2005.[383] Violations are 'serious' if they amount to crimes against humanity, as defined in Article 7 of the Rome Statute.[384] Injured parties may include 'indirect victims' such as 'immediate family members or dependants', which would cover next of kin, heirs and successors, children yet unborn and possibly grandchildren, if they come to share through family memory in the trauma.[385] The International Criminal Court rules give further guidance on the category of 'victim', adding to it any organisations or institutions that have sustained direct property loss, if that property is dedicated to religion, education or science, or includes historic monuments, hospitals and other places of humanitarian interest.[386]

'Reparation' does not just include monetary compensation: the Human Rights Chamber set up by the Dayton Accords, having found Republika Srpska responsible for the genocide at Srebrenica, rejected individual compensation but fashioned remedies that included orders to release all information in its possession about missing persons and the location of burial sites and to make a large lump sum contribution to a cemetery where some victims were known to have been buried. In other cases it has ordered the republic to preserve mosques damaged in the war, to protect Islamic burial sites and to reacquire homes and to restore expropriated families to them. The Serbs of Republika Srpska had passed a 'Law on Abandoned Apartments' (mimicking the Ottoman use of 'abandonment' as a euphemism for forcible deprivation) which extinguished the rights of those Muslims forced to flee and permitted them to be handed over to soldiers.[387] There is no doubt that 'reparations' may extend to restoration of churches, and restoration of homes and property owned by a particular family and 'abandoned' (i.e. expropriated) after they were given their marching orders. Imaginative forms of reparation could include reversing the street names that were Christian until the Young Turks ordered them to be changed, or indeed actually naming streets after Armenian leaders – in Van, for example, naming streets after Vramian and Ishkahn, the Dashnaks whose murder at the hands of Governor Djevdet had inflamed the uprising in the city. Most important of all, perhaps, is reparation in the form of an honest history in school textbooks.

Might reparations include the homelands from which the Armenians were unlawfully extirpated in 1915? This was promised by the Treaty of Sèvres, which was never brought into effect and was superseded by the Treaty of Lausanne, which made no mention of reparations and effectively betrayed every promise made to the Armenians by the Allies. They had – and still have – to be content with a small land-locked territory around Yerevan, carved out of Russian Armenia. It stands in the shadow of

Mount Ararat, the great Christian symbol of renewal after the flood, which is located just a few kilometres inside the domain of Turkey. Many of the old 'Armenian homelands' have been repopulated, by Turkish citizens who would not, presumably, wish to become Armenians. If the boundaries were to be redrawn, either as the result of an arbitration or, better, as a symbolic gesture of atonement by Turkey, the gifting to Armenia of Mount Ararat and its environs would go a long way towards healing the rift between the two nations.

Turkish Government Accountability

Any action for reparations brought against Turkey under international customary law would first have to establish that the Turkish Republic must shoulder the burden of responsibility for crimes committed by the Ottoman government. Two arbitral tribunals have determined the Turkish Republic is the continuation of the Ottoman Empire[388] and there is a general principle of continuation of state responsibility for international crimes. Moreover, there is a wider principle of international law that the state retains its former self notwithstanding revolution or geographical change.[389] In any event, even if the Turkish Republic constitutes a new state, it has continued and defended the wrongs of its Ottoman predecessor and so must be taken to assume that previous state's international responsibility.[390] Continuing responsibility would derive from the fact that the Ottoman Empire's immediate successor, once the Sultan and the liberal government had been forced out, was a nationalist government in Ankara, primarily formed of ex-CUP members,[391] and it continued the policy of confiscation of Armenian properties.[392] Its parliament obstructed the prosecutions of those accused of war crimes and crimes against humanity,[393] and reneged on its promise to the British that it would put the Malta detainees on trial after it had forced their repatriation in return for British soldiers held hostage for this purpose. Moreover, by denying any crime against humanity, and justifying a demonstrable crime as a legitimate military exercise, it has continued the original wrong.

It has been argued that the amnesties in the Treaty of Lausanne expunge any liability for genocide,[394] but this is misconceived. These treaty provisions are of dubious legality (amnesties cannot operate to obviate guilt for crimes against humanity) and in any event they relate to amnesties for individuals and are not directed to state responsibility. They cannot affect the principle that the Turkish Republic is responsible for the international crimes committed by the Ottoman Empire or the fact that those crimes included genocide.

Restoration of Property

Proof of the genocidal intentions of the CUP government emerges from its programme of confiscation of Armenian property, which was seized by the state without recompense and without any arrangement for compensation or provision of equivalent property in the desert places to which the deportees were being transferred. Taner Akçam argues that 'Unionist government policy was intended to completely deprive the Armenians of all possibility of continued existence',[395] which seems true in respect of their continued existence in Anatolia, if not in respect of its capital, Constantinople (albeit without their leaders, most of whom were abducted on 24 April 1915 and later murdered, and some 10,000 who were deported). Confiscatory legislation was passed in June 1915, empowering state seizure and registration of property they were forced to leave behind and forbidding them from taking legal action to reclaim it. Dishonestly titled 'Commissions for the Administration of Abandoned Property' were set up in different regions and empowered to sell 'abandoned' possessions and keep the money as payment for bogus costs incurred in their owners' deportations, and to use their homes to resettle Muslim refugees or dispose of them to the Turkish army. This confiscation legislation was analysed at the time by lawyers at the German embassy as 'a legalisation of pillaging', and many documents relating to these obnoxious transfers remain in the Ottoman archives.[396]

There would, therefore, be a possibility today that descendants of a dispossessed family, or a company or organisation which is still in existence a century after its property was expropriated, could sue the Turkish state for compensation, if not for restitution. Although certain to fail in Turkish courts, there would be an appeal to the European Court of Human Rights, which has shown, in rulings against Turkey in relation to expropriation of property in Northern Cyprus, which it invaded and illegally occupied in 1974, a robust determination to award belated compensation for arbitrary expropriation of property without recompense.[397] Normally an action must first be launched in the courts of the allegedly responsible state, in order to 'exhaust domestic remedies' as required by Article 26 of the European Convention. However, the very bringing of an action in Turkey for restitution of homes, land or churches expropriated in the course of a Turkish genocide might be treated as an insult to Turkishness under Article 301 of the Penal Code. In this case the victims could go direct to the European Court complaining not only of confiscation without compensation but also a denial of access to justice. They would not need to 'exhaust domestic remedies' in Turkish courts, if bringing an action would risk criminal prosecution.[398] An action in German courts based on a 'complicity with genocide' theory might also be contemplated, particularly if assets were confiscated from accounts in Deutsche Bank, which actively traded in Constantinople in 1915, and whose executives were well aware of the extermination and did have a number of Armenian clients.

Descendants of Armenians who can identify their expropriated property may be able to bring actions in other national courts, if they can overcome the problems of time bars and state immunities. The Nazi expropriation cases in the US show that these obstacles are not insurmountable where the expropriation is part of a crime against humanity. In California, where an active diaspora had persuaded the state legislature to remove time bars in respect of claims arising from the Armenian genocide, descendants initially had some success in relation to insurance policies which genocide victims had had the foresight to take out with American insurers. In 2004, these companies settled claims brought by descendant beneficiaries for US $20 million.[399] Of course, the case did not involve the Turkish government and did not require proof of genocide – the companies had declined to pay out at the time because the insured men had simply gone missing – and the proceedings were contested on the ground that the statute of limitations barred the claim. The insurance companies were under pressure to settle because their position was perceived in America as historically unfair to victims of genocide, but one insurance company held out, and the Federal Appeals Court invalidated the Californian statute removing the time bar on the basis that it was an unconstitutional fetter on the federal government's power to determine foreign policy.[400] The Supreme Court refused leave to appeal, although interestingly the US Solicitor General in written submissions claimed that the Treaty of Lausanne had resolved all claims for compensation.[401] This argument is wrong both in history and in law, and overlooks the fact that America, thanks to diaspora pressure, refused to sign the treaty. The Supreme Court did not rule on the point, but merely refused leave to appeal the decision that the Californian statute was unconstitutional.

Cultural Property

There is an increasing jurisprudential recognition, aided by UNESCO conventions and state practice, of the critical value of cultural treasures or symbols to national identity and dignity. Case law is beginning to recognise a right to the return of looted or expropriated art or monuments or churches of cultural significance. As Lord Phillips put it in *Republic of Iran v Barakat Galleries*, 'It was essential for every state to become alive to the moral obligations to respect the cultural heritage of all nations.'[402] Courts in America have permitted states to reclaim cultural artefacts looted from churches and it follows that any cultural property, now in Turkey or abroad, seized from Armenian churches or art galleries during the genocide, might be the subject of restoration proceedings brought by the church itself or by descendants of the original owner. In 1915–16 it was estimated that well over 1,000 Armenian churches and monasteries had been seized or destroyed, whilst many others were converted to mosques.[403] These can be made the subject of an action for restitution and/or compensation brought by the Armenian patriarchy, which finally announced during the centenary that it would commence a test-case action in Turkey's Constitutional Court. This is a necessary step to force the Turkish government to agree to a programme of restoration.

There are now a number of international instruments requiring the return of cultural property. Whilst not binding law, the draft declaration on the illegality of forced population transfers requires that victims of forced transfers be accorded the right to 'restoration of properties of which they were deprived in connection with or as a result of population transfers, compensation for any property that cannot be restored to them, and any other reparations provided for in international law'.[404] The UN General Assembly's *Basic Principles and Guidelines on the Right to a Remedy and Reparation for Victims of Gross Violations of International Human Rights Law and Serious Violations of International Humanitarian Law* requires that 'a state shall provide reparation to victims for acts or omissions which can be attributed to the state and constitute gross violations of international humanitarian law'.[405] There is also an argument that the combination of Articles 1 and 27 of the International Covenant on Civil and Political Rights (ICCPR) requires return of cultural heritage in order to rectify a 'historical inequality'.[406]

The force of these conventions has already had some political effect. In 2007 the Turkish government restored a church on Lake Van, and the first Catholic Mass took place there in 2010.[407] Turkey has been disinclined to go beyond this symbolic gesture, and has crassly insisted that Lake Van Church should be used only as a museum not for worship. On 13 December 2011 a bi-partisan resolution was adopted by the US House of Representatives calling upon Turkey to return confiscated churches and secure freedom for Christian religious worship (a similar resolution was also put to the Senate, and was referred to the Senate Foreign Relations Committee).[408] On 24 April 2013, the Catholicoses (the heads of the Armenian Church) called upon Turkey to return the 'Armenian churches, monasteries, church properties, and spiritual and cultural treasures to the Armenian people as their rightful owner'.[409] That call went unheeded, and in April 2015 the Church finally stopped pleading for Turkey to do the right thing and began legal action, in the Turkish courts, as a pathway to the European Court of Human Rights. Only with the force of international law will there be any prospect that the restoration of the church at Lake Van will provide a precedent for restitution of property of cultural or religious significance to Armenians – the largest and most significant of which would be Mount Ararat.

German Complicity

This issue has been given a special relevance by the decision of the International Court of Justice in the *Bosnia v Serbia* case, which held Serbia complicit in, and therefore responsible in international law for, the genocide at Srebrenica committed by the army of its ally, the Republika Srpska. Milošević knew of the danger, and did not use his influence over Mladić to stop it. By the same token, Germany was closely allied with Turkey and was made fully aware that the Turks were bent on exterminating the Armenian race, by explicit cables from its ambassadors and consuls and by German businessmen and missionaries. They constantly warned Berlin of the danger of Germany being held complicit in the deportations: as the consul Scheubner-Richter reported from eastern Turkey, 'The word is deliberately being spread here that the expulsion is taking place at the instigation of the German government.'[410] Moreover it had a powerful military mission in Turkey throughout the war, and its officers were commanders in the Turkish army. Indeed General Otto Liman von Sanders took charge in December 1913, and it was his strategic genius that directed the fortification of the Dardanelles, which contributed crucially to the successful resistance against the Gallipoli landing. He was so morally appalled by the behaviour of his local allies towards the Armenians, especially by the *chetti* brigades, that in 1923 he gave evidence on behalf of Talaat's assassin. He exercised his power on a number of occasions, when not countermanded by Berlin, to stop the deportations (notably from Adrianopole and Smyrna).[411] There is therefore no doubt that the German government could have intervened: the Ottoman army was heavily dependent on it for munitions and machinery, and initially for strategy, certainly after the army's disastrous defeat at Sarikamish at the end of 1914. The Germans were put in charge of the army's technical departments: as the diplomats joked at their club in Constantinople, this was a case of 'Deutschland über Allah'.[412] Yet the Kaiser turned a blind eye to the horrors portrayed by his consuls and the government imposed strict censorship to prevent publication in Germany of any exposure of the massacres by missionaries or newspaper reporters. The Chancellor, Bethmann-Hollweg, spelled out the reason to those who urged him to condemn the Ottomans:

> The suggested public condemnation of an ally during the present war would be a measure unlike any in history. Our sole object is to keep Turkey on our side until the end of the war, no matter if Armenians perish over that or not. In the face of a longer continuing war we will still need the Turks very much.[413]

'Military necessity', once again, was cynically and unnecessarily invoked to justify indifference to a humanitarian disaster. But it was not merely indifference. An American agent on the ground in Constantinople reported that the German military mission had been actively advising the government over the deportations (recommending, for example, that its Christian soldiers be disarmed and consigned to labour battalions) and that

> under the pretence of not wishing to interfere in the internal affairs of Turkey, the Germans have sanctioned in silence every crime ... in the beginning, when it lay in their power to stop these iniquities, they did nothing, and allowed free rein to be given to all the barbarous offences at work here without raising their voice in restraint. The Germans to their eternal disgrace, will not lift a finger to save the Armenians.[414]

When they did, belatedly, through Ambassador Wolff-Metternich, the German response to Turkey's complaint was to remove him rather than to stand firm and insist that the Ottomans behave with a minimum of humanity. Eyewitness accounts by British internees and prisoners of war accuse German officers of permitting attacks on the Armenians because they profited from the spoils: 'Hundreds of boxes of carpets were sent to Germany – seven bags of jewellery were shared between three high officials, large amounts of valuables left for safe-keeping with German soldiers were packed off to Germany.'[415]

The German position is epitomised in the story of its General Colmar von der Goltz, commanding Ottoman troops in Iraq, who in November 1915 motored past one of the death camps near Aleppo where Armenian deportees were dying from starvation and typhus. German missionaries had begged his help, so he stopped to survey the camp through his field glasses at two kilometres distant. When he reached Aleppo he is said to have given orders to evacuate the camp so as to prevent the typhus from spreading: those who could not walk were to be shot, which he said would put them out of their misery.

Armenian leaders have been strangely reticent about criticising Germany, perhaps because so many of its diplomats and missionaries protested about their travails and left indelible eyewitness evidence of the barbarities they attributed to the CUP and its officials. But this compassion does not relieve their government of the responsibility which comes from knowledge of and complicity in genocide. If there is any doubt about German consciousness of guilt, it was emphasised when the Reich sent a gunboat to rescue the main perpetrators – Talaat, Enver, Cemal and Dr Niman (the top 'Turkification' ideologue) – so they could avoid the trial that awaited them in Constantinople. Germany sheltered them and refused to give them up for trial anywhere else, despite requests from the Turkish and the British governments. Deutsche Bank, too, was complicit, both in allowing the *Ittihadist* leaders to hold accounts in Berlin and asking no questions about whether the deposits were the proceeds from confiscated Armenian property, and in funding the railway that was used for deportations from the West (its directors were sent photographs of the horrors they were financing). On the principles set out above, Germany as well as Turkey would be liable to an action brought by Armenia under Article IX of the Genocide Convention. Its complicity derives from its detailed knowledge of the massacres and deportations, from its refusal to use its power and influence to stop them, and subsequently, its protection of the criminals. Unlike Turkey it has recognised the genocide, but has failed to recognise its own responsibility for failing to stop it.

CHAPTER 10

CONCLUSION

THE TREATMENT OF the Armenian people by the Ottoman government in 1915 amounted to genocide. The present government of Turkey bears state responsibility for that crime as a matter of morality, and there may be ways of holding it liable in law. There would be difficulties in terms of time bars and state immunities, but where crimes against humanity are concerned, these are not insurmountable. It is surprising that there has been so little activity on the legal front, although the Prosecutor General of Armenia recently advocated legal action of this kind to recover historic territory lost in the genocide.[416] But delay in bringing an available claim would aid a defence argument that the claimant had waived or abandoned any right to recovery.

It would appear that Armenians, their state and their supporters, have pinned their hopes on various political initiatives. Many parliaments have recognised the genocide, but these resolutions are of little more than symbolic significance. Several European countries have gone further and made it a criminal offence to deny the fact of any genocide, although this is of questionable consistency with the right (under Article 10 of the European Convention of Human Rights) to freedom of expression, and presents as the other side of the coin to Article 301 of Turkey's Penal Code, which makes it a potential offence to proclaim the genocide as fact. The problem with such laws is that they invite constitutional challenge and, as the *Perinçek* case indicates, may be struck down under free speech principles. They attract self-styled 'martyrs' and offer no sensible way of imposing liability on the Turkish state for a historic wrong.

Other political initiatives have failed. There was hope of improvement in Turkish–Armenian relations in 2008, where some rapprochement between the two countries was achieved over a football match.[417] In October 2009, amid great fanfare, the two nations signed a protocol for normalisation of diplomatic relations by opening their common borders and developing cooperation and trade. There were two pre-conditions to the accord: that the Nagorno-Karabakh issue[418] would not form part of the protocol, and that Armenia would not demand Turkey's recognition of the genocide.[419] However, the protocol did agree to 'implement a dialogue on the historical dimension with the aim to restore mutual confidence between the two nations, including an impartial scientific examination of the historical records'. There is no point in a dialogue with the deaf on the historic dimension if it is between historians who have already taken sides. Only unbiased international judges, making a finding on the question of genocide, would resolve the issue although each side is so locked into its position that neither would accept an adverse decision.

In January 2010 the Armenian Constitutional Court upheld the 2009 protocol, but only on the proviso that it was read consistently with the constitution and Paragraph 11 of the Declaration of Independence, which reads: 'The Republic of Armenia stands in support of the task of achieving international recognition of the 1915 Genocide in Ottoman Turkey and Western Armenia.' Ankara instructed Yerevan to 'correct' the insult occasioned by this Constitutional Court decision,[420] and President Erdoğan threatened to expel 100,000 workers illegally resident in Turkey, stating, 'Unfortunately, the Constitutional Court of Armenia made a decision to tell these 100,000 to go back to their country if it becomes necessary.'[421] At the same time, in response to the US House of Representatives decision to recognise the Armenian genocide,[422] Turkey withdrew its ambassador and stated that 'this resolution accuses the Turkish nation of a crime it has not committed'.[423] The same reaction took place when Sweden recognised the Armenian genocide. After France initially passed a law prohibiting genocide denial, before it was struck down by the Conseil d'Etat, Turkey banned French air force flights over its air space.[424]

Turkey has not ratified the 2009 protocol, and in April 2010 President Sargsyan announced Armenian suspension of the 'normalisation process'. There have been no significant developments since, other than Prime Minister Erdoğan's statement on 23 April 2014, which called on bygones to be bygones but expressed no contrition or apology and offered no reparation. The 2015 centenary passed without reference to the genocide – Turkey was too busy celebrating its victory over the Allied invasion of the Dardanelles to mention the inconvenient genocide that it committed at the same time. The question of Turkey's application for membership of the European Union is pending: although its recognition of the genocide is not a formal condition for membership, the European Parliament has stated that it is 'indispensable for a country on the road to membership to come to terms with and recognise its past'.[425] This means that Turkey will have to do away with Article 301 of its criminal code, and find some way – satisfactory to Europe, if not to Armenia – of acknowledging the international crime committed by its Ottoman predecessor in 1915.

What has not been suggested – no doubt because Turkey has feared any sort of legal solution, although there is also a curious reticence on the Armenian side – is submission of the issue to adjudication at the International Court of Justice pursuant to Article IX of the Genocide Convention. The closest the two sides have ever come to an arbitral solution was in 2003, when a group of Armenian and Turkish officials in America convened a Reconciliation Commission and asked the International Centre for Transitional Justice to apply the definition of genocide to the admitted events of 1915. The verdict – that the massacres amounted to genocide under international law – was of course not binding and will never be placed on the website of the Turkish government.[426] But it was, nonetheless, a compelling statement of the legal position.

The UN Secretary General could be asked to establish an *ad hoc* court to try the issue (there are judges at the International Criminal Court with time on their hands) or the parties to the protocol might choose to submit the issue to an arbitral panel of distinguished jurists (as with contested arbitrations, the parties would select one or two judges each, and those judges would agree on the selection of an impartial tribunal chair). Armenia, for its part, should bring an action before the International Court of Justice under Article IX of the Genocide Convention, and encourage individuals and organisations that can claim and trace property expropriated by the Ottoman government in 1915 to seek legal redress. It should include Germany as a defendant, which has already admitted the genocide, although it may be less willing to confess its own complicity.

The law stated in Chapter 4 of this book, when applied to the evidence in Chapters 2 and 3, produces the inevitable conclusion that the treatment of the Armenians in 1915 answers to the description of genocide. The genocide deniers dealt with in Chapter 5, and the Turkish Foreign Ministry website on which its genocide denial policy is explained, do not raise any reasonable doubt over the verdict, and the case study in Chapter 7 demonstrates how one important government, that of the United Kingdom, has had to abandon a misinterpretation of the law that until 2010 it had adopted in order to appease Turkey. That government should, if asked again in April 2015, summon up the resolution to state the truth:

> In 1915 the Ottoman government of the Congress and Union Party, then in league with Germany, faced an Allied attack in the Dardanelles and a prospective incursion by Russian forces on its eastern front. These difficult circumstances do not, however, justify its orders to deport up to 1.5 million Armenians from Eastern Turkey and its infliction upon them of conditions of life which were calculated to, and did in fact, bring about the destruction of a substantial part of that racial group. Britain, France and Russia condemned this action at the time as 'a crime against humanity' and promised that its perpetrators would be punished, but that promise was betrayed and no reparations deserved for such a crime have ever been ordered or offered. Should the same events occur today, in any country in the circumstances of the Ottoman Empire in 1915, there can be no doubt that the Genocide Convention would be engaged and would require prosecutions for that crime as well as for other crimes against humanity.

The responsibility of the present Turkish government is a responsibility engaged both by the international law rules of state succession and by the fact that the nationalist government that succeeded the Ottomans contained many of the CUP politicians who had approved the genocide. Most significant, of course, has been Turkey's obsessive denial of the truth of the genocide, a political stratagem of its successive governments ever since the issue was revived by the human rights movement in the 1960s. This has taken the form of a massively funded international propaganda campaign, especially in the US, attempting to justify genocide. In Turkey itself, any reference to the truth has been removed from school textbooks and scholars and journalists have been threatened with prosecution under Article 301. Somewhat puerile reprisals have been taken against countries whose parliaments have recognised the genocide. It has been the very prominence that Turkey has given, not so much to genocide denial as to genocide justification, that aligns it with its Ottoman predecessor and which requires both reckoning and recompense. This can only come by shifting the debate from the history seminar to the law court, by Armenia taking action under Article IX of the Genocide Convention, by requests for the UN to establish an *ad hoc* court to try the issue or by contemplating reparations of the kind broached in Chapter 9. Germany, complicit in this crime against humanity, should acknowledge the fact and offer an apology and compensation.

Genocide is a matter for judges, not historians. This is not meant to diminish the work, often brilliant and ground-breaking, that historians have produced on the subject since the 1960s. But their concentration on *whether* there was genocide – itself a malign result of Turkish denial – has taken precedence over the question of *why* genocide happened – as the conclusions of an important workshop for Armenian–Turkish studies reported in 2011:

> Our view was that the causes of the genocide have not been
> adequately analysed, that there are a variety of explanations,
> ranging from Turkish racism, religious hatred, economic and
> social jealousy of the Armenians, the fall-out from revolu-
> tionary politics, Pan-Turanism and the making of empire,
> and clashing nationalisms...[427]

If the question of 'genocide or not' need no longer be asked,
then the exploration of its causes – so important to genocide
studies generally, and to genocide prevention – can proceed without obstruction. The present controversy is diverting even this
estimable group of historians from their professional role. They
report that 'the problem of the "G" word is both definitional and
political. Some participants hold that public acceptance of the
term "genocide" would render them ineffective with the Turkish
public. Others disagree with the standard United Nations definition of genocide.'[428]

The 'standard UN definition' is the legal definition in the Convention and it is hubristic for historians to quarrel with it or
seek to replace it, just as it is cowardly to pull history's punches
for fear of a brainwashed Turkish public or of Turkish reprisals.
The best way to enlighten them is to speak the simple truth –
that what was done to the Armenians by the Ottoman state in
1915 amounts precisely to what the UN Convention defines as
genocide. Equivocation in order to save Turkish sensitivities, as
practised by the US and the UK, has only encouraged that government to become even more defensive about its past. Stating
the truth, notwithstanding the soul-searching it will require of
the Turkish people, may produce in time the catharsis that is necessary for rapprochement between the two nations.

There is another way – a compromise, but given the deep-
seated passions of both parties, it may be the only realistic

solution if both Turkey and Armenia are to move beyond the deadlock over the 'G' word. Genocide is the worst example of a crime against humanity, but by no means the only example. The most obsessive genocide denier cannot with honesty deny that a crime against humanity – the crime of persecution, to take an obvious example – was committed by the Ottoman government against the Armenians, by its laws ordering their deportation, by its failure to provide security, by its knowledge that they were dying in their hundreds of thousands, by its laws expropriating their 'abandoned' property so they could not come back, and so on. The government of Turkey should acknowledge this crime against humanity, at the very least (Atatürk himself evinced shame) and make a historic apology. This should be accompanied by a set of genuine reconciliatory gestures: restoration of ruined churches (like the church at Lake Van), monuments to the victims of the forced marches, admission of the facts in school textbooks and official histories, the offer as a gift of the iconic Mount Ararat. That would be the kind of dignified and decent response that is now expected of civilised states which have in the past treated ethnic or religious minorities inhumanely.

As for Armenia, its response to a Turkish apology for a crime against humanity, even one that does not mention the 'G' word, should be to express regret for the vigilante killings of Turkish officials in the 1970s and 1980s: these were terrorist offences which rightly rankle and deserve more condemnation than they have yet received. In return for opening all Ottoman archives, it should make public whatever material it holds about the Dashnaks and other revolutionary groups, and show a willingness to participate in joint projects with Turkey – a Persecution Museum in Istanbul, perhaps – where the reprisal massacres by Armenians at the end of the war, as well as the Turkish attacks on Greeks and Assyrians, can be studied in a spirit of scholarship and an atmosphere of reconciliation.

There are too many modern massacres provoked by racial or religious hatreds for two civilised nations to expend so much time and money and political energy in squabbling over a word. If there is an alternative term which is neither a fudge nor a euphemism – and 'a crime against humanity' is neither – then it should be deployed by Turkey as a description of the atrocities which its predecessor state visited upon the Armenians in 1915 and Armenia should accept an apology for it, certainly if the sincerity of that apology were accompanied by some measures of restitution.

As for the crime of genocide, no amount of denial will ever persuade the descendants of its victims that it was not committed by the leaders of the Ottoman Empire and its agents, aided and abetted by Germany, in Anatolia in the spring and summer of 1915. Nor should it: no claim of military or any other kind of 'necessity' can justify the despatching of a racial group to their statistically likely deaths, irrespective of whether the perpetrators looked on with satisfaction or with perturbation. They knew, and the knowledge fixes their nation with responsibility, that their policy was destroying a significant part of the Armenian race. The importance of acknowledging guilt of a crime against humanity, even as long as a century later, is that denialism emboldens others to think they can get away with mass murder of civilians whenever it is expedient in wartime. International law sets a bottom line: whether Sunni or Shia, Hindu or Christian, whether Chechen or Tamil or Bengali or an indigenous people striving for independence, the deliberate destruction of any part of that race or religion by those in control of a state cannot be countenanced, and will encumber that state and its successors, along with aiders and abetters, with responsibility in international law that will last unless and until it makes amends, for longer than a century.

NOTE ON THE AUTHOR

GEOFFREY ROBERTSON QC is founder and head of Doughty Street Chambers, the UK's largest human rights practice. He has appeared as counsel in many leading cases in constitutional, criminal and international law, and served as first president of the UN War Crimes Court in Sierra Leone, where he authored landmark decisions on the limits of amnesties, the illegality of recruiting child soldiers and other critical issues in the development of international criminal law. In 2008 he was appointed by the Secretary General as one of three distinguished jurist members of the UN Justice Council and in 2011 received the New York Bar Association award for achievement in international affairs and law. His books include *Crimes against Humanity: The Struggle for Global Justice*; *The Justice Game* (a memoir); *Mullahs without Mercy: Human Rights and Nuclear Weapons*; *The Case of the Pope*; *Stephen Ward Was Innocent, OK* and *The Tyrannicide Brief* – the story of how Cromwell's lawyers put Charles I on trial. He is a Master of the Middle Temple and a visiting professor at London University and at the New College of the Humanities, and served as a recorder (part-time judge) in London from 1993 until 2011. He is the author of thematic papers published by the International Bar Association on *Ethics in Human Rights Fact-Finding* (2010) and *The Independence of the Judiciary* (2014).

ACKNOWLEDGEMENTS

MY INTEREST IN the study of events in Anatolia in 1915 was initially piqued by the Armenian Centre in London and subsequently by the Armenian National Committee UK, which retained me to provide opinions on whether the British government's policy statements questioning the Armenian genocide were in conformity with international law. Ms Kate Annand assisted me in making the Freedom of Information Act requests in 2009 which elicited the documents analysed in Chapter 7. I am grateful for the further research for this book undertaken by Toby Collis, Simona Tutianu and Katie O'Byrne, for work on the manuscript by Judy Rollinson and for the editing at Biteback by Olivia Beattie and at Random House (Australia) by Nikki Christer and Catherine Hill. My agent Caroline Michel has been as ever a source of comfort and encouragement. I would like to dedicate this book to the memory of my old friend Ben Whitaker, who died shortly before it was published. As UN rapporteur on genocide, he determined that the events of 1915 amounted to that crime. His life's work, both for the protection of minority rights and for freedom of information, has been an inspiration.

APPENDIX I

Convention on the Prevention and Punishment of the Crime of Genocide

Adopted by Resolution 260 (III) A of the United Nations General Assembly on 9 December 1948.

Article I

The Contracting Parties confirm that genocide, whether committed in time of peace or in time of war, is a crime under international law which they undertake to prevent and to punish.

Article II

In the present Convention, genocide means any of the following acts committed with intent to destroy, in whole or in part, a national, ethnical, racial or religious group, as such:
(a) Killing members of the group;
(b) Causing serious bodily or mental harm to members of the group;
(c) Deliberately inflicting on the group conditions of life calculated to bring about its physical destruction in whole or in part;
(d) Imposing measures intended to prevent births within the group;
(e) Forcibly transferring children of the group to another group.

Article III

The following acts shall be punishable:
(a) Genocide;
(b) Conspiracy to commit genocide;
(c) Direct and public incitement to commit genocide;
(d) Attempt to commit genocide;
(e) Complicity in genocide.

Article IV

Persons committing genocide or any of the other acts enumerated in Article III shall be punished, whether they are constitutionally responsible rulers, public officials or private individuals.

Article V

The Contracting Parties undertake to enact, in accordance with their respective Constitutions, the necessary legislation to give effect to the provisions of the present Convention and, in particular, to provide effective penalties for persons guilty of genocide or any of the other acts enumerated in Article III.

Article VI

Persons charged with genocide or any of the other acts enumerated in Article III shall be tried by a competent tribunal of the state in the territory of which the act was committed, or by such international penal tribunal as may have jurisdiction with respect to those Contracting Parties which shall have accepted its jurisdiction.

Article VII

Genocide and the other acts enumerated in Article III shall not be considered as political crimes for the purpose of extradition.

The Contracting Parties pledge themselves in such cases to grant extradition in accordance with their laws and treaties in force.

Article VIII

Any Contracting Party may call upon the competent organs of the United Nations to take such action under the Charter of the United Nations as they consider appropriate for the prevention and suppression of acts of genocide or any of the other acts enumerated in Article III.

Article IX

Disputes between the Contracting Parties relating to the interpretation, application or fulfilment of the present Convention, including those relating to the responsibility of a state for genocide or any of the other acts enumerated in Article III, shall be submitted to the International Court of Justice at the request of any of the parties to the dispute.

APPENDIX 2

Rome Statute of the International Criminal Court 17 July 1998

Article 6

Genocide

For the purpose of this Statute, 'genocide' means any of the following acts committed with intent to destroy, in whole or in part, a national, ethnical, racial or religious group, as such:

(a) Killing members of the group;

(b) Causing serious bodily or mental harm to members of the group;

(c) Deliberately inflicting on the group conditions of life calculated to bring about its physical destruction in whole or in part;

(d) Imposing measures intended to prevent births within the group;

(e) Forcibly transferring children of the group to another group.

Article 7

Crimes against humanity

1. For the purpose of this Statute, 'crime against humanity' means any of the following acts when committed as part of a widespread or systematic attack directed against any civilian population, with knowledge of the attack:

(a) Murder;

(b) Extermination;

(c) Enslavement;

(d) Deportation or forcible transfer of population;

(e) Imprisonment or other severe deprivation of physical liberty in violation of fundamental rules of international law;

(f) Torture;

(g) Rape, sexual slavery, enforced prostitution, forced pregnancy, enforced sterilization, or any other form of sexual violence of comparable gravity;

(h) Persecution against any identifiable group or collectivity on political, racial, national, ethnic, cultural, religious, gender as defined in paragraph 3, or other grounds that are universally recognized as impermissible under international law, in connection with any act referred to in this paragraph or any crime within the jurisdiction of the court;

(i) Enforced disappearance of persons;

(j) The crime of apartheid;

(k) Other inhumane acts of a similar character intentionally causing great suffering, or serious injury to body or to mental or physical health.

2. For the purpose of paragraph 1:

(a) 'Attack directed against any civilian population' means a course of conduct involving the multiple commission of acts referred to in paragraph 1 against any civilian population, pursuant to or in furtherance of a state or organizational policy to commit such attack;

(b) 'Extermination' includes the intentional infliction of conditions of life, *inter alia* the deprivation of access to food and medicine, calculated to bring about the destruction of part of a population;

(c) 'Enslavement' means the exercise of any or all of the powers attaching to the right of ownership over a person and includes the exercise of such power in the course of trafficking in persons, in particular women and children;

(d) 'Deportation or forcible transfer of population' means forced displacement of the persons concerned by expulsion or other coercive acts from the area in which they are lawfully present, without grounds permitted under international law;

(e) 'Torture' means the intentional infliction of severe pain or suffering, whether physical or mental, upon a person in the custody or under the control of the accused; except that torture shall not include pain or suffering arising only from, inherent in or incidental to, lawful sanctions;

(f) 'Forced pregnancy' means the unlawful confinement of a woman forcibly made pregnant, with the intent of affecting the ethnic composition of any population or carrying out other grave violations of international law. This definition shall not in any way be interpreted as affecting national laws relating to pregnancy;

(g) 'Persecution' means the intentional and severe deprivation of fundamental rights contrary to international law by reason of the identity of the group or collectivity;

(h) 'The crime of apartheid' means inhumane acts of a character similar to

those referred to in paragraph 1, committed in the context of an institution-
alized regime of systematic oppression and domination by one racial group
over any other racial group or groups and committed with the intention of
maintaining that regime;

(i) 'Enforced disappearance of persons' means the arrest, detention or abduction of persons by, or with the authorization, support or acquiescence of, a
state or a political organization, followed by a refusal to acknowledge that
deprivation of freedom or to give information on the fate or whereabouts of
those persons, with the intention of removing them from the protection of
the law for a prolonged period of time.

3. For the purpose of this Statute, it is understood that the term 'gender' refers
to the two sexes, male and female, within the context of society. The term
'gender' does not indicate any meaning different from the above.

ENDNOTES

INTRODUCTION

1. Letter to Cleveland Dodge, 11 May 1918, Letters of Theodore
    Roosevelt, Vol 8, 1316.

2. This translation, from the notes taken on 22 August 1939 by Wilhelm
    Canaris at Hitler's villa at Obersalzburg, appeared in Louis Lochner,
    What about Germany (Dodd Mead, 1942). A more ponderous
    translation is reproduced in *Documents on British Foreign Policy 1919–
    1939*, 3rd Series, 9 vols (HMSO 1949–1955), Vol 7 p 258, published
    by the UK Foreign Office, and can be found in 'German Foreign
    Policy Documents (Ser D, Vol 7 p 193)', published in 1961. There
    is no doubt that Hitler delivered a shocking and brutal speech on
    this day to his commanders, urging them to show no mercy during
    the impending invasion of Poland, and that he had made a similar
    remark about the success of the 'extermination' of the Armenians in
    a newspaper interview in 1931: see Edouard Calic, *Unmasked: Two
    Confidential Interviews with Hitler* (Chatto & Windus 1971), p 81.
    Canaris, head of German Military Intelligence, loathed Hitler (who
    had him executed in 1945) and is thought to have passed his notes
    to another anti-Hitler general (also later executed for treason) who
    sent them to Lochner via a trusted intermediary whom Lochner
    later identified as Hermann Maas (also executed), and Lochner
    passed them to the British embassy in Berlin a few days before
    the outbreak of war. Other notes of the speech exist which do not
    mention the comment about the Armenian genocide, but convey
    similar sentiments. Heath Lowry disputes the authenticity of the
    quote (http://www.ataa.org/reference/hitler-lowry.html), suggesting
    that it was an embellishment by the anti-Hitler faction so that,
    when published in a 'doctored' version in the West, it 'would have
    portrayed Hitler in an extremely negative light to his allies (or
    potential allies) to the neutrals and to the rest of the world'. This is
    a poor argument – the speech in any version was brutal (Goering,

who was there when it was delivered, admitted at Nuremberg that it was 'severe') and the comment about the Armenians would have added nothing to its distaste, other than to Armenians. Their fate was not yet a 'genocide' (the word had not been invented) and they were just a powerless Soviet state. (Ironically, the main 'potential ally' at the time was Turkey, which would, if anything, have been pleased by Hitler's comment.) Lowry relies mainly on the fact that the prosecution did not produce the Lochner version at Nuremberg, but he does not seem to understand the rules of evidence with which the prosecution had to comply. It could only introduce documents that were 'admissible' because it could show their origin and providence. Two other versions had been discovered at a German army base, and so they were admissible and were admitted. The chain leading to Lochner could not be proven (they had all been executed) so the version he received was 'marked for identification' – i.e. was available to the court if it became relevant (it did not – Hitler's incitement to brutality was all too clear). So the notion peddled by some denialists, that it was *rejected* by the court, is false. Lochner had no doubt at all about its authenticity, and the German government never challenged it after his book was published in 1942 and he was permitted to return to Berlin as a neutral US correspondent. The British embassy reported to London in 1939 that the Lochner version 'tallies in several details with information from other sources'. Further analysis of the quote as authentic is provided by Hannibal Travis ('Did the Armenian Genocide Inspire Hitler?', *Middle East Quarterly*, Winter 2013, pp 27–35); and see K. B. Bardakjian, *Hitler and the Armenian Genocide* (Zorayan Institute, 1985).

3.   Koran, Surah 9, *At-Tauba* (The Repentance), Verse 5.

4.   Deuteronomy 7:2.

5.   For the minutes of the Wannsee Conference, see http://prorev.com/ wannsee.htm, accessed 20 June 2014.

6.   Memorandum from the FCO Eastern Department to Minister Joyce Quin and others, 12 April 1999, Subject title: House of Lords un-starred question 14 April: Baroness Cox, Armenian Genocide.

7. William Shakespeare, *Macbeth*, Act 5, Scene 2, Line 20.

8. Geoffrey Robertson QC, 'Was There an Armenian Genocide?', University of St. Thomas, *Journal of Law and Public Policy*, Vol 4, No 2 (Spring 2010), p 83.

9. See report tabled by Baroness Cox, House of Lords, Hansard, 29 March 2010, CG 497.

10. Hansard (Lords) text for 16 June 2011, Col 873.

11. 'Turkish threat to Armenians: Prime Minister says 100,000 may be expelled'; 'Turkey threatens mass expulsions to punish Armenians for genocide ruling', *The Times*, 18 March 2010, pp 1, 4.

12. *Reservations to the Convention on the Preservation and Punishment of the Crime of Genocide*, Part C. Written Statements, Written statement of United States, pp 23, 25.

13. Statement of President Barack Obama on Armenian Remembrance Day, 24 April 2009.

14. Interview by Charlie Rose – see Harut Sassounian, 'Erdoğan claims it's not Genocide because not all Armenians were killed', *Californian Courier*, 6 May 2014.

CHAPTER I: THE ARMENIAN QUESTION

15. Joint Declaration of France, Great Britain and Russia, 28 May 1915. United Nations War Crimes Commission, London HMSO 1948, p 35.

16. Gary Bass, *Stay the Hand of Vengeance* (Princeton University Press, 2000), p 128.

17. Baroness Ramsey, House of Lords, Hansard, 14 April 1999, Col 826.

18. See Samantha Power, *A Problem from Hell* (Penguin, 2002), p 19. And see George R. Montgomery, 'Why Talaat's Assassin Was Acquitted', *Current History*, July 1921, pp 551–5.

19. See Power, above n18, pp 54–5.

20. See Steven L. Jacobs, 'Indicting Henry Kissinger: The Response of

Raphael Lemkin' in Adam Jones, *Genocide, War Crimes and the West: History and Complicity* (Zed Books, 2004), p 214.

21. Raphael Lemkin, *Axis Rule in Occupied Europe: Laws of Occupation – Analysis of Government – Proposals for Redress* (Lawbook Exchange, 2008), p 79.

22. He made this link clear in a CBS interview in 1949 on the then newly ratified Genocide Convention; for the transcript of the interview, see http://www.armeniapedia.org/wiki/Lemkin_Discusses_Armenian_Genocide_In_Newly-Found_1949_CBS_Interview.

23. William A. Schabas, *Genocide in International Law* (2nd ed., Cambridge University Press, 2009), p 19.

24. Joint Declaration of France, Great Britain and Russia, 28 May 1915. United Nations War Crimes Commission, London HMSO 1948, p 35.

25. Taner Akçam, *A Shameful Act: The Armenian Genocide and the Question of Turkish Responsibility* (Constable, 2007), p 234.

26. FO 371/2488/172811, 17 November 1915, Lord Williams.

27. FO 371/2488/148483, 6 October 1915.

28. Lloyd George, *Memoirs of the Peace Conference* (Yale University Press, 1939), Vol 2, pp 811–12.

29. Winston Churchill, *The World Crisis: The Aftermath* (Thornton Butterworth, 1929) p 405.

30. Akçam, above n25, p xxii.

31. Bass, above n16, p 118.

32. CAB 28/5 IC-99, InterAllied Conference, London, 2 December 1918, quoted by Bass, above n16, p 131.

33. See Akçam, above n25, pp 408–10, where the available and most damning evidence against nine of the detainees is outlined.

34. Vahakn N. Dadrian, *The History of the Armenian Genocide* (Berghahn Books, 2004), p 310.

35. Ibid.

36. Ibid., p 311.

37. Ibid., p 408.

38. Office of the UN High Commission for Human Rights, 'Rule of Law Tools for Post-Conflict States – Amnesties' (New York and Geneva, 2009), p 29. See also *Prosecutor v Kondewa*, SCSL-2004–14AR72 (E), Decision on lack of jurisdiction/abuse of process: amnesty provided by the Lomé Accord (25 May 2004), and Geoffrey Robertson, *Crimes against Humanity: The Struggle for Global Justice* (4th ed., Penguin 2012), pp 372–84.

39. See Hrayr S. Karagveuzian and Yair Avron, *A Perfect Injustice: Genocide and Theft of Armenian Wealth* (Transaction, 2009), p 78.

40. See Ben Kiernan, *Blood and Soil: A World History of Genocide and Extermination from Sparta to Darfur* (Yale, 2007), p 385.

41. *USA v Greifeit et al* (1948) 14 LKTWC (US Military Tribunal) p 3–19.

42. *Reservations to the Convention on the Prevention and Punishment of the Crime of Genocide*, 1951, ICJ Reports 15, 23.

43. For Gourgen Mkrtich Yanikan's trial see *People v Yanikan* 1974. CA.40553; 114 Cal. Rptr. 188.

44. UN ECOSOC, *Revised and updated report on the question of the prevention and punishment of the crime of genocide prepared by Mr Ben Whitaker*, 2 July 1985, UN Doc. E/CN.4/Sub.2/1985/6.

45. *A. G. v Eichmann* (1968) 36 ILR 5 (District Court of Jerusalem), para 80.

46. Robertson, above n38, p 485.

47. *Prosecutor v Akayesu*, Case No. ICTR-96-4-T, Judgment, ICTR TC, 2 September 1998, para 505

48. 'The Applicability of the UN Genocide Convention to events which occurred during the early twentieth century', ICTJ, 2003.

CHAPTER 2: THE HISTORY

49. See Michael Oren, 'The Mass Murder They Still Deny', *New York Review of Books*, 10 May 2007.

50. Dadrian, above n34, p 4.

51. See Akçam, above n25, pp 8–9.

52. See Dadrian, above n34, pp 114–16.

53. Blue Book: Turkey. 1895, No 1 (Correspondence Relating to the Asiatic Provinces of Turkey), Part I (Events at Sassoon and the Commission of Enquiry at Mush). London: Harrison and Sons, 1895, 208pp. (Great Britain. House of Commons, Sessional Papers, v. 109, 1895.), enclosures 36–8.

54. Peter Balakian, *The Burning Tigris* (Heinemann, 2003), p 56.

55. Ibid., p 114.

56. Ibid., p 41 – on 10 September 1895.

57. Dadrian, above n34, p 156.

58. Quoted by Kiernan, above n40, p 405.

59. See Taner Akçam, 'Demographic Policy and Ethnic Cleansing', SOAS lecture, 4 March 2008, p 10.

60. Donald Bloxham, *The Great Game of Genocide* (Oxford, 2005), pp 70–71.

61. See Akçam, above n25, pp 174–9.

62. Bloxham, above n60, pp 70–71.

63. See Aram Arkun, 'Zeytun and the Commencement of the Armenian Genocide' in Ronald Grigor Suny, Fatma Müge Göçek and Norman M. Naimark, *A Question of Genocide* (Oxford, 2011), p 221.

64. Balakian, above n54, p 215.

65. See Fuat Dündar, '"Pouring a People into a Desert": The "Definitive Solution" of the Unionists to the Armenian Question' in Suny, Göçek

and Naimark, above n63, p 281.

66. See Justin McCarthy, *The Armenian Rebellion at Van* (University of Utah Press, 2006). Despite the governor's 'brutal and illegal' actions, he argues from Ottoman army documents that the rebellion was more deep seated and widespread than Armenian sources claim.

67. See Dickran Kouymjian, *Confiscation of Armenian Property* (Armenian Studies Programme, California State University).

68. Mark Levene, 'Genocide in the Age of the Nation State' (I. B. Tauris, 2008), p 73.

69. Ibid., p 280.

70. Hilmar Kaiser, *At the Crossroads of Der Zor* (Gomidas Institute, 2002), p 60.

71. Major General James Harbord, *Report of the American Military Mission to Armenia*, 5 Doc No 266 at 7 (1920).

72. See Oren, above n49; Professor Michael J. Kelly, 'Genocide – The Power of a Label', Vol 40 No 1–2 (2008), *Case Western Reserve Journal of International Law*, pp 151–2.

73. Balakian, above n54, p 180.

74. Cathie Carmichael, *Genocide before the Holocaust* (Yale University Press, 2009), pp 18–19.

75. Bloxham, above n60, p 4.

76. Rössler telegrams 93, 100, 101, 9, 14 and 18 September, to Embassy Aleppo. See Kaiser, above n70, p 24.

77. Robert Fisk, *The Great War for Civilisation: The Conquest of the Middle East* (Harper, 2006), p 400.

78. Ibid., pp 27–8.

79. Ibid., p 66.

80. Karagveuzian and Avron, above n39, p 47.

81. Ibid., p xxi.

82. Norman Stone, *Turkey: A Short History* (Thames & Hudson, 2010), pp 147–8.

CHAPTER 3 : THE EVIDENCE

83. Power, above n18, pp 6–8.

84. Balakian, citing German archives, above n54, p 186.

85. Quoted by Kiernan, above n40, page 411; and see Margaret Lavinia Anderson, 'Who Still Talked about the Extermination of the Armenians?', in Suny, Göçek and Naimark, above n63, p 205.

86. Akçam, above n25, p 134.

87. 9 August, 1915. See Akçam, ibid., p 206.

88. Anderson, above n85, p 205.

89. Ibid., p 208.

90. Ibid., p 209–10. The documents were published in 'Germany and Armenia' and 'The Death March of the Armenian People', by the indefatigable Lutheran pastor and journalist Johannes Lepsius, who had covered the Hamidian massacres and who later testified on behalf of Talaat's assassin.

91. Ibid., p 206.

92. See Hans-Lukas Kieser, 'From Patriotism to Murder' in Suny, Göçek and Naimark, above n63, p 137.

93. Ibid.

94. Ibid., p 143.

95. Ibid.

96. Leslie Davis, *The Slaughterhouse Province: An American Diplomat's Report on the Armenian Genocide, 1915–17*, Susan K. Blair (ed.) (Orpheus, 1989). Quoted by Fisk, above n77, p 400.

97. Balakian, above n54, pp 188, 257.

98. Akçam, above n25, p 306.

99. J. H. Wheat, *Diary*, Australian War Memorial Archives, Canberra, File No: 3DRL/2965.

100. G. Kerr, *Lost Anzacs: The Story of Two Brothers* (Oxford University Press, Melbourne, 1997)

101. See also Daniel Creedom, *Diary*, Australian War Memorial Archives, Canberra, File No: 1DRL 223, 12/1/86.

102. Arnold Toynbee, *The Treatment of the Armenians in the Ottoman Empire*, 1915–16, Misc 31 Cmnd 8325, HMSO 1916.

103. Phillip Knightley, *The First Casualty* (Andre Deutsch 1975), pp 83–4, 104–5. See also David Millers, 'The Treatment of Armenians in the Ottoman Empire: History of the "Blue Book"', *RUSI Journal*, August 2005.

104. See John Horne and Alan Kramer, *German Atrocities 1914: A History of Denial* (Yale University Press, 2001).

105. See Arnold J. Toynbee, *The Western Question in Greece and Turkey* (Constable, 1922, pp 265–6, 50.

106. Republic of Turkey, Ministry of Foreign Affairs website, Presentation by Professor Justin McCarthy at the Turkish Grand National Assembly on the 'Reality of the Armenian Issue' Conference on 24 March 2005, p 6.

107. Ibid., presentation by Professor Justin McCarthy at the seminar on Turkish–Armenian relations, 15 March 2001, p 4.

108. For example, McCarthy, above n66, Chapters 5, 8 and 9.

109. See Justin McCarthy, *The Turk in America* (University of Utah Press, 2010) pp 235–41.

110. Ibid., p 430 footnote 250.

111. Blue Book, above n102, p 3, Despatch from Henry Wood, 14 August 1915.

112. Ibid., p 9 (Dashnak source).

113. Ibid., p 389.

114. There was a lengthy narrative to this effect by Grace Knapp, Mrs Gazarian and other American missionaries – see ibid., pp 32–77.

115. Ibid., pp 285–6.

116. Extract from an interview with Commissioner G. Gorrini, in *Il Messaggero*, 25 April 1915. Blue Book, ibid., p 290.

117. Ibid., pp 479 et seq (Rev. Dikran Andreasian).

118. Ibid., p 627 ('The Deportations of 1915').

119. Ibid., p 633, *Berliner Tageblatt*, reproduced in *Le Matin*, 6 May 1916.

120. Ibid., p 648.

121. Tessa Hoffman and Gerayer Koutcharian, '"Images that Horrify and Indict": Pictorial Documents on the Persecution and Extermination of Armenians from 1877 to 1922', *Armenian Review*, Vol 45, No 1-2, (1992)p 54

122. Wegner diary entry, 19 October 1916, ibid.

123. Balakian, above n54, p 351.

124. Harbord, above n71, p 4.

125. Ibid., p 18.

126. Ibid., p 7.

127. Ibid.

128. Ibid.

129. Ibid.

130. Quoted in dissenting judgment in *Perinçek v Switzerland*, Application no 27510/08, Judgment, 17 December 2013, footnote 26.

131. Ibid., on 21 October 1918.

132. See Jennifer Balint, 'The Ottoman State Special Military Tribunal for the Genocide of the Armenians: Doing Government Business' in

Kevin Heller and Gerry Simpson (eds), *The Hidden Histories of War Crimes Trials* (Oxford University Press, 2013), at p 85.

133. Ibid., p 87.

134. Ibid., p 91.

135. Quoted in Bass, above n16, p 125.

136. See Dadrian, above n34, p 27.

137. Balint, above n132, p 77.

138. See Vahakn N. Dadrian, 'A Textual Analysis of the Key Indictment of the Turkish Military Tribunal Investigating the Armenian Genocide', *Journal of Political and Military Sociology*, Vol 22 No 133, pp 135–6.

139. Taner Akçam, *The Young Turks' Crime against Humanity: The Armenian Genocide and Ethnic Cleansing in the Ottoman Empire* (Princeton University Press, 2012), pp 14, 301–2.

140. Ibid., p 36.

141. Ibid., p 54.

142. Written testimony of Vehip Pasha, delivered to the president of the Commission for the Investigation of Crimes in the Office of the General [Directorate of] Security, dated 5 December 1918, cited in Akçam, ibid., p 199.

143. BOA/DH.ŞFR, no. 55/290, Coded telegram from Interior Minister Talat to the Province of Ankara, dated 29 August 1915, cited in Akçam, ibid., p 201.

144. BOA/DH.ŞFR, no. 54/2406, Coded telegram from Interior Minister Talat to the Province of Diyarbakır, dated 15 July 1915, cited in Akçam, ibid., pp 208–9.

145. Ibid., p 210.

146. Meclisi Âyan Zabıt Ceridesi [Minutes of the Ottoman Chamber of Notables] 3rd Electoral Term, Year of Assembly 5, Vol 1 (TBMM Basımevi, 1990), p 123, cited in Akçam, ibid., pp 193–4, and see generally pp 193–8.

147. Ibid., p 254.

148. Christopher de Bellaigue, *Rebel Land* (Bloomsbury, 2009), p 104.

CHAPTER 4: THE LAW

149. Definitely, in my view. See Robertson, above n38, p 327, and *Mullahs Without Mercy: Human Rights and Nuclear Weapons* (Biteback, 2011), which argues that the Ayatollah's Iran regime committed genocide when it slaughtered atheists in its prisons in 1988, with the intention of destroying them as a group.

150. *Reservations,* above n42, p 23.

151. Schabas, above n23, pp 192–3.

152. The Application of the Convention on the Prevention and Punishment of the Crime of Genocide (*Bosnia and Herzegovina v Serbia and Montenegro*) ICJ Reports 2007, p 43, 26 February 2007. Additionally, in the *Tolimir* case the ICTY held that the targeted killing of three leaders in Žepa constituted genocide: *Prosecutor v Tolimir*, Case IT-05-88/2-T, Judgment 12 December 2012.

153. *Prosecutor v. Krstić*, Case No. IT-98-33-T, Judgment, ICTY TC, 2 August 2001, para 589.

154. Schabas, above n23, p 285.

155. For a British case where the majority of judges considered that where in a statute no clear qualification is given to a noun relating to a number or portion, a 'significant' rather than 'substantial' proportion is appropriate, see *DPP v Whyte* (1972) A.C. 849.

156. See Bloxham, above n60, pp 95–6.

157. *Prosecutor v. Akayesu*, above n47, paras 505–6.

158. *Prosecutor v. Kayishema and Ruzindana*, Case No. ICTR-95-1-T, Judgment, ICTR TC, 21 May 1999, para 115.

159. *Prosecutor v Brdjanin*, Case No. IT-99-36-T, Judgment, ICTY TC, 1 September 2004, para 691.

160. *Bosnia v Serbia*, above n152.

161. *Prosecutor v. Akayesu*, above n47, para 523.

162. *Prosecutor v. Kayishema and Ruzindana*, above n158, para. 9.3

163. *Prosecutor v. Akayesu*, above n47, para 523.

164. Ibid., para 730.

165. See Antonio Cassese, *International Criminal Law* (Oxford, 2008), p 143.

166. *Prosecutor v Blagojević* IT-02-60-T, ICTY TC, 17 January 2005, para 677.

167. See Balakian, above n54, pp 212–16.

168. See generally, Robert Bevan, *The Destruction of Memory: Architecture at War* (Reaktion Books, 2006), pp 52–9 on the destruction of Armenian monuments and buildings, especially churches.

169. *Niyitegeka v Prosecutor*, Case No. ICTR 0 96-14-A), ICTR, 9 July 2004, para 49.

170. *Prosecutor v Kayishema and Ruzindana*, above n158, para 161, and see Schabas, above n23, pp 301–3.

171. *The Prosecutor v. Jelisić*, Case No. IT-95-10-A, Judgment, ICTY AC, 5 July 2001, para 48.

172. See Cassese, above n165, p 141.

173. *Prosecutor v Kayishema*, above n158, paras 158–9, discussed in *Bosnia v Serbia*, above n152, paras 370–76.

174. *Prosecutor v Radovan Karadžić*, Case No IT-95-5/18-AR98bis.1, Judgment, ICTY AC, 11 July 2013.

175. Ibid., para 80.

176. *Prosecutor v Omar Hassan Ahmad al Bashir*, Case No ICC-02/05-01/09 OA, ICC AC, 3 February 2010.

177. *Prosecutor v Akayesu*, above n47, para 477.

178. *Prosecutor v Karadžić & Mladić*, Rule 61 Consideration, Case No IT-95-18-R61, 2 July 1996, para 94, ICTY.

179. *Prosecutor v Kayishema*, above n158, para 93 ICTR.

180. *Karadžić & Mladić*, above n178, para 95.

181. *Bosnia v Serbia*, above n152, para 344, citing *Prosecutor v Krstić*, IT-98-33-T, ICTY TC, 2 August 2001, para 580.

182. *Prosecutor v Blagojević*, ICTY, IT-02-60-T, Judgment, 17 January 2005, para 677, cited with approval in *Bosnia v Serbia*, ibid., paras 294–5.

183. Rome Statute of the International Criminal Court, 2187 UNTS 90, entered into force 1 July 2002, Art 7(2)(d).

184. Ibid., Art 7(1).

185. Bosnia v Serbia, above n152, para 190, citing with approval *Interim Report of the Commission of Experts Established Pursuant to Security Council Resolution 780* (1992), UN Doc. S/35374 (1993), para 55.

186. *Bosnia v Serbia*, ibid., para 190. And see the individual opinion of Sir Elihu Lauterpacht in *Case Concerning application of the Convention on the Prevention and Punishment of Genocide (Bosnia and Herzegovina v Yugoslavia) Further Requests for the Indication of Provisional Measures*, Order of 13 September 1993, ICJ Reports 1993, p 325 at p 432.

187. *Bosnia v Serbia*, ibid., para 90.

188. Akçam, above n139, pp 383–99.

189. See Balakian, above n54, p 274 and Henry Morgenthau, *Ambassador Morgenthau's Story* (Doubleday, 1918), pp 333–8, 342.

190. See *Bosnia and Herzegovina v Yugoslavia*, Preliminary Objections, Judgment of 11 July 1996, ICJ Reports 1993, p 595, paras 27–33, 43.

191. Schabas, above n23, pp 396–7. Thus an *Einsatzgruppen* killing of 859 Jews in reprisal for the deaths of 21 German soldiers could not be countenanced.

192. See *Moinina Fifana et al.*, Case No SCSL-2003-11-A, Appeal Judgment, 28 May 2003, para 247.

193. *Prosecutor v Martić*, Trial Chamber, Review of the Indictment Pursuant to Rule 61, 8 March 1996, para 17.

194. *Lighthouse Arbitration Case* (France and Greece) (1956) 12 R.I.A.A. 155; 23 I.L.R. 659. Permanent Court of Arbitration. 24 July 1956; See generally, Vahagn Avedian, 'State Identity, Continuity and Responsibility: The Republic of Turkey, The Ottoman Empire and the Armenian Genocide', Vol 23 No 3 (2012), *European Journal of International Law* 797.

195. *Bosnia v Serbia* , above n152, para 167.

196. Ibid., para 179.

197. Ibid., paras 142–82.

198. Ibid., paras 399–407.

199. *Prosecutor v Tadić*, Case No IT-94-1-A, Appeal Judgment, ICTY AC, 15 July 1999, para 131: 'In order to attribute the acts of a military or paramilitary group to a state, it must be proved that the state wields overall control over the group, not only by equipping and financing the group, but also by coordinating or helping in the general planning of its military activity. Only then can the state be held internationally accountable for any misconduct of the group. However, it is not necessary that, in addition, the state should also issue, either to the head or to members of the group, instructions for the commission of specific acts contrary to international law.'

200. *Bosnia v Serbia*, above n152, para 385.

201. Ibid., paras 391–3, citing with approval *Military and Paramilitary Activities in and against Nicaragua (Nicaragua v United States)*, Merits, Judgment, ICJ Reports 1986, pp 62–4.

202. Ibid., paras 396–407.

203. Ibid., para 209.

204. *In re Yamashita*, 327 US 1 (1946).

205. *Bosnia v Serbia*, above n152, para 437.

206. Rome Statute, Art 7(2)(d).

207. Ibid., Art 7(1)(h).

208. Interview, *Los Angeles Examiner*, 1 August 1926.

CHAPTER 5: JUSTIFYING GENOCIDE

209. Bloxham, above n60, p 4.

210. De Bellaigue, above n148, p 79.

211. Harbord Report, above n71, p 7.

212. Justin McCarthy, *The Ottoman Turks: an Introductory History to 1923* (Longman, 1997), p 365.

213. Ibid.

214. Quoted by the Turkish ambassador, in a letter to Joyce Quin, 19 April 1999. Website http://www.tc-america.org/terrorism_mccarthy.pdf references this quote. Justin McCarthy, 'Armenian Terrorism: History as Poison and Antidote', *Proceedings of Symposium on International Terrorism* (Ankara University Press, 1984).

215. Ahmed Emin, *Turkey in the World War* (Yale University Press, 1930), p 222.

216. He quotes from another denialist, Salahi R. Sonyel, in 'Armenian Deportations: A Re-appraisal in the Light of New Documents', *T. T. K. Belleten*, Vol 36 No 141 (1972), pp 31–69 (Turkish and English).

217. Available at http://www.mfa.gov.tr/controversy-between-turkey-and-armenia-about-the-events-of-1915.en.mfa , accessed May 2014.

218. Ibid.

219. Ibid.

220. Ibid.

221. Ibid.

222. Ibid.

223. Ibid.

224. Center for Eurasian Studies, Ankara, *The Events of 1915 and the Turkish–Armenian Controversy over History* (undated).

225. Ibid., p 1.

226. This and previous quotations are set out with their sources mostly in German official records, in Vahaku N. Dadrian, *Key Elements in the Turkish Denial of the Armenian Genocide* (Zoryan Institute, 1999), pp 7, 12–13.

227. http://www.mfa.gov.tr/the-armenian-allegation-of-genocide-the-issue-and-the-facts.en.mfa, accessed 24 June 2014.

228. Dadrian, above n34, p 27.

229. 'The message of the Prime Minister of the Republic of Turkey, Recep Tayyip Erdoğan, on the events of 1915', available at http://www.mfa.gov.tr/turkish-prime-minister-mr_-recep-tayyip-erdogan-published-a-message-on-the-events-of-1915.en.mfa.

230. Akçam, above n139.

231. Akçam, above n25, pp 157–8. Constantinople became 'Istanbul' in some form variously from 1453, but officially changed its name on 28 March 1930.

232. Ibid., pp 132–3.

233. See 'Merkel scolds Erdoğan over genocide denial', *Asbarez*, 7 February 2014.

CHAPTER 6: THE POLITICS OF GENOCIDE RECOGNITION

234. 'Armenian genocide recognition: necessary but not sufficient', *Asbarez*, 11 February 2014.

235. Ibid.

236. See Avedian, above n194, p 797.

237. HR 252, 111th Congress (2009–10), Affirmation of the United States

Record on the Armenian Genocide Resolution.

238. 'US attacks Turkey genocide', BBC News, 4 March 2010.

239. 'Turkish EU Minister on the Armenian genocide controversy: we are very serious about this issue', *Der Spiegel*, 16 March 2010.

240. David Matas, 'Prosecuting Crimes against Humanity: the Lessons of World War I', *Fordham International Law Journal*, Vol 13 No 86 (1989), p 104.

241. Anna Patty and Judith Whelan, 'MPs warned off Armenia with Anzac threat', *Sydney Morning Herald*, 16 November 2013.

242. Letter from Julie Bishop to Ertund Ozen (Australian Turkish Advocacy Alliance), 4 June 2014

243. Christian Democrat Party, 'Rev Fred Nile Reminds Australians of the 1915 Muslim Genocide against Christian Armenians', 24 April 2007.

244. See Harut Sassounian, 'Syrian President finally recognises the Armenian genocide', *California Courier,* 30 January 2014.

245. Reagan, on 22 April 1981, declared that 'like the genocide of the Armenians before it, and the genocide of the Cambodians that followed it, and the similar persecution of other people too, the Holocaust should be a lesson to us that we must never forget'.

246. See 'House panel raises furor on Armenian genocide', *New York Times*, 11 October 2007.

247. See Mark D. Kielsgard, 'Restorative Justice for the Armenians, Resolved: It's the Least We Can Do', *Connecticut Journal of International Law*, Vol 24 (2008–9), pp 1–4.

248. White House Office of the Press Secretary, Statement by the President on Armenian Remembrance Day, 24 April 2012.

249. Senator Barack Obama, Congressional record, 'Commemoration of the Armenian Genocide', United States Senate, 28 April 2008, S3438.

250. US Senate Resolution 410, Resolution Expressing the Sense of the

Senate Regarding the Anniversary of the Armenian Genocide. See Harut Sassounian, 'Turkey still haunted by genocide a hundred years later', *California Courier*, 21 April 2014.

CHAPTER 7: GENODICE EQUIVOCATION: A CASE STUDY

251. Memorandum from FCO to Minister Joyce Quin, 8 March 1999, on 'Lord Avebury Letter'.

252. Memorandum, above n6, paragraph 6.

253. *Prosecutor v. Théoneste Bagosora et al.,* Case No. ICTR-98-41-T, Judgment, ICTR TC, 18 December 2008, para 2088: 'With respect to the *actus reus*, the agreement can be proven by establishing the existence of planning meetings for the genocide, but it can also be inferred, based on circumstantial evidence. The concerted or coordinated action of a group of individuals can constitute evidence of an agreement.'

254. Memorandum, above n6, paragraph 9.

255. Draft letter for Joyce Quin to reply to Lord Avebury (undated).

256. Letter from Joyce Quin to Lord Avebury, 9 February 1999.

257. Memorandum, above n6.

258. Ibid.

259. Baroness Ramsey, House of Lords, Hansard, 14 April 1999, Col 826.

260. Letter to the Eastern Department, the name of the sender is redacted, but it is written on behalf of Joyce Quin, 13 April 1999.

261. Letter, Turkish Chargé d'Affaires to Baroness Scotland (Under Secretary of State, FCO), 7 August 2000.

262. Ibid., page 3.

263. Letter from Keith Vaz to Ambassador HE Korkmaz Haktanır, 7 February 2001.

264. The organisers of Holocaust Memorial Day still betray Lemkin's

memory by refusing to mention the Armenian genocide.

265. FCO Background Document re question from Lord Biffen tabled on 25 January 2001.

266. Parliamentary Question Background Document relating to a written question from Lord Biffen tabled on 25 January 2001 – Draft response for Baroness Scotland.

267. Memorandum to Under-Secretary of State Bill Rammell from Simon Butt entitled 'Armenia – Note verbale from Armenian MFA', 19 March 2004.

268. Document entitled 'Armenia: Public Lines' (undated). It goes on to dismiss Ben Whitaker's report, see page 172.

269. Letter from Keith Vaz (Minister for Europe) to Julia Down MP, 12 March 2001.

270. See a letter sent to the Princeton alumni magazine from Professor Bernard Lewis, 5 June 1996: http://www.princeton.edu/~paw/archive_old/PAW95-96/16_9596/0605let.html.

271. See the judgment of the Paris Court of First Instance, 21 June 1995, which cites the *Le Monde* interview published on 18 November 1993 and the 'Clarification offered by Bernard Lewis' printed in *Le Monde* on 1 January 1994:
http://www.armenian-genocide.org/Affirmation.240/current_category.76/affirmation_detail.html.

272. Statement of Professor Bernard Lewis, Princeton University, 'Distinguishing Armenian Case from Holocaust', 14 April 2002: http://www.ataa.org/reference/lewis.pdf.

273. Ibid.

274. Roger W. Smith, Eric Markusen and Robert Jay Lifton, 'Professional Ethics and the Denial of Armenian Genocide' *Holocaust and Genocide Studies*, Vol 9 No 1 (1995), pp 1–22.

275. See William H. Honan, 'Princeton is accused of fronting for the Turkish Government', *New York Times*, 22 May 1996; for a copy of the

letter see http://archive.today/J2cVT, accessed 24 June 2014.

276. Rich Miller, 'History and the power to change it: academic leaders erupt over appearance of Turkish influence at Princeton', *Trenton Times*, 10 December 1995.

277. Lis Verderman, 'Professor Feels the Heat', *Princeton Alumni Weekly*, 24 January 1996, pp 14–15, reproduced on http://www.tallarmeniantale. com/lowry.htm.

278. FCO document titled 'Background: Armenia 1915–16'(undated).

279. Parliamentary Question Background Document, relating to an oral question in the House of Lords. Answer to be given on 14 July 2005 by Lord Triesman. Question 4: What is HMG's view of the article in Turkey's Penal Code that describes affirmation of the Armenian 'genocide' as a crime against the state?

280. *Dink v Turkey,* Applications no. 2668/07, 6102/08, 30079/08, 7072/09 and 7124/09. Chamber Judgment, 14 September 2010.

281. Ben Whitaker, *Revised and Updated Report on the Question of the Prevention and Punishment of the Crime of Genocide*, UN Doc. E/ CN.4/Sub.2/1985/6.

282. See Schabas, above n23, pp 555–8.

283. An undated note of 'public lines' that the minister could take suggested that 'if pressed' he could refer to the views of three prominent historians (Lewis, Lowry and McCarthy) and if asked about the 1985 report (no mention of its author) could say 'Since then we are not aware of it being mentioned in any UN document or forum'.

284. Briefing Note to Geoff Hoon from Russia, South Caucasus and Central Asia Directorate, FCO, 6 June 2006.

285. In 2007 the Committee voted 27–21 to recognise the Armenian genocide. This Resolution 106 was not put to a vote in the House for the reason that it might imperil US national security – i.e. if Turkey reacted by removing US bases and monitoring stations.

286. i.e. becomes convulsed with a nervous spasm whenever the subject is raised.

287. Briefing note, above n284.

288. Geoff Hoon, House of Commons, Hansard, 7 June 2006, Col 136WH.

289. Advisory Opinion, above n12, p 25.

290. *The Applicability of the United Nations Convention on the Prevention and Punishment of the Crime of Genocide to Events which Occurred During the Early Twentieth Century*, International Centre for Transitional Justice (2003), p 4.

291. Background document for Geoff Hoon's visit to Armenia in October 2006 headed, 'Armenia: Relations with Turkey, and the "genocide" of 1915–16 Key messages'.

292. Lord Triesman, House of Lords, Hansard, Written Answers, 29 March 2007, Col WA321.

293. Malcolm Yapp, 'Review article: The History of the Armenian Genocide: Ethnic Conflict from the Balkans to Anatolia to the Caucasus by Vahakn N. Dadrian', *Middle Eastern Studies*, Vol 32 No 4 (1996), 395.

294. Parliamentary Question Background Document relating to a written question from Lord Avebury tabled on 19 March 2007 – Draft response for Lord Triesman.

295. Memorandum from the Russia, South Caucasus and Central Asia Directorate, FCO, to Mr Murphy, titled 'HMG's position on the Armenian genocide claims', 2 July 2007.

296. William Schabas, *Unimaginable Atrocities* (Oxford University Press, 2012), p 63.

297. Document titled 'Armenia: Meeting with Andrew George MP and members of Armenia Solidarity, 16 October 2007', p 2.

298. Ibid.

299. See http://thomas.loc.gov/cgi-bin/query/z?c110:H.RES.106 for the Library of Congress's record of the Armenian Genocide Resolution, H. Res. 106, in the House of Representatives. It was adopted by the US House Foreign Affairs Committee by a vote of 27 to 21 on 9 October 2007.

300. Email from Sofka Brown to Craig Oliphant, 4 February 2008.

301. Erik-Jan Zürcher, *Turkey: A Modern History* (I. B. Tauris, 2004), p 116.

302. Parliamentary Question Background Document relating to a written question from Baroness Finlay of Llandaff tabled on 19 February 2008.

303. Lord Malloch-Brown, House of Lords, Hansard, Written Answers, 4 March 2008, Col WA165.

304. Memo from FCO to Foreign Secretary, 15 July 2009, re opposition to Private Member's Bill promoted by Andrew Dismore MP.

305. Memo to Minister for Europe from South Caucasus Section, Subject: Geoffrey Robertson QC – 'Was There an Armenian Genocide?', 8 December 2009.

306. Briefing the Minister for Europe and Baroness Kinnock, for House of Lords debate 29.03.2010.

307. 'Armenian Massacres 1915–1917', FCO Briefing for Minister of Europe, 17 June 2010, para 26.

308. Ibid., paras 23–4.

309. Ibid., para 9.

310. Para 10, under 'risks', is redacted. Azerbaijan is virtually at war with Armenia over Nagorno-Karabakh.

311. FCO, 'Armenia: Ealing Council Recognises Armenian Genocide', 16 December 2010.

312. FCO, Armenia Digest Message for F.M. to send Remembrance Event, 15 April 2013.

313. FCO, 'Turkey/Armenia', 28 March 2012.

314. FCO, Re Armenian Genocide (from 'Redacted', and sent to 'Redacted'), 20 March 2014.

315. FCO, Centenary of Armenian Massacres 1915–16, 8 November 1913.

316. The relevant documents are in National Archive files: FO383/529; FO608/109; FO608/78; FO608/97; FO608/247.

317. South Caucasus Team Meeting, 21 August 2013, emails to and from Kathy Leach.

318. FCO, 'Armenian Massacres', 21 January 2014 (all names redacted).

319. FCO, correspondence with Kathy Leach, 13 September 2013.

320. Background paper, appended to FCO, above n315, para 15.

321. FCO, 14 November 2013, to: David Lidington, Centenary of Armenian Massacres.

322. Background paper, above n320, para 6.

CHAPTER 8: SHOULD GENOCIDE DENIAL BE A CRIME?

323. Article III(c).

324. See Schabas, above n23, p 579.

325. International Convention on the Elimination of All Forms of Racial Discrimination, 21 December 1965, United Nations Treaty Series, Vol 660, p 195, art 4.

326. UN General Assembly, International Covenant on Civil and Political Rights, 16 December 1966, United Nations, Treaty Series, Vol 999, p 171, art 20.

327. *Cohen v California* (1971) 403 US 15 (US Supreme Court).

328. To paraphrase the opinion of Oliver Wendell Holmes Jr in *Schenck v United States* (1919) 249 US 47.

329. 'Holocaust denier Irving is jailed', BBC News, 20 February 2006.

330. *Irving v Penguin Books and Lipstadt* [2000] EWHC QB 115.

331. 'Suspected Holocaust denier Dr Gerald Toben wins extradition fight', *The Telegraph,* 29 October 2008.

332. For the evolution of the European Court of Human Right's treatment of Holocaust denial laws see Paolo Lobbo, 'Holocaust Denial Before the European Court of Human Rights: Evolution of an Exceptional Regime', *European Journal of International Law* (forthcoming 2014), available at http://ssrn.com/abstract=2428650, accessed 24 June 2014.

333. See Paolo Lobbo, 'A European Halt to Laws Against Genocide Denial?', *European Criminal Law Review*, Vol 4 No 1 (2014), p 74 (footnote 79).

334. *Garaudy v France* (Application No, 65831/01) 24 June 2003.

335. *Lehideux and Isorni v France*, 23 September 1998, Reports of Judgments and Decisions 1998-VII.

336. Decision No 2012-647 DC, 28 February 2012.

337. Spanish Constitutional Court, No 235/2007.

338. See also, *X. v Germany*, Commission decision of 16 July 1982, DR 29, p 194; *H., W., P. and K. v Austria*, No. 12774/87, Commission decision of 12 October 1989, DR 62, p 216; *Irving v Germany*. No. 26551/95, Commission decision of 29 June 1996, which all held that the laws were 'necessary in a democratic society'.

339. *Perinçek v Switzerland*, Application no 27510/08, Judgment, 17 December 2013. The judgment has been recorded only in French, and there is no authorised English translation.

340. Ibid., para 94, citing the Malloch-Brown statement as reproduced in the *British Yearbook of International Law*, Vol 79 (2008), pp 706–7.

341. Three judges – Keller (Switzerland), Popović (Serbia) and Lorenzen (Denmark) prepared the court judgment which the president, Raimondi (Italy), formally signed, casting doubt on whether the genocide was proved. Raimondi separately wrote a *concurrence* with Sajó (Hungary) which contradicted the court's decision on this issue, holding that the genocide was proved, but that (in agreement with the forementioned three judges) it was a breach of freedom of speech to

punish a denialist. A dissent was entered by Albuquerque (Portugal) and Vučinić (Montenegro), who both held that the genocide was proved and the Swiss were entitled to punish its denial.

342. *Perinçek*, above n339, para 111.

343. Ibid., para 116.

344. Ibid., para 112.

345. Public statement from International Association of Genocide Scholars, released 14 February 2014, available at http://genocidewatch. net/2014/04/29/international-association-of-genocide-scholars-2, accessed 2 July 2014.

346. Perinçek, above n339, para 115.

347. Ibid., para 117.

348. Set out ibid., para 115.

349. Ibid., Concurring opinion of Judges Raimondi and Sajó.

350. *Dink v Turkey*, above n280.

351. 'Hrant Dink: Turkey and France can race to see who can jail me first', *Hürriyeti,* 9 October 2006.

352. *Dink v Turkey*, above n280. His family were awarded €100,000 in compensation.

353. *Akçam v Turkey*, Application No 27520/07, Judgment 25 October 2011.

354. Ibid., para 77–8.

355. Amnesty International, 'Decriminalise Dissent', Eur 44/001/2013, March 2013, p 9.

356. Ibid., p 5.

357. 'The Media's 3 Months: 186 Journalists Fired', *BIAnet*, 23 July 2014, available at http://bianet.org/english/media/157385-the-media-s-3-months-186-journalists-fired, accessed 27 August 2014.

358. Milana Knezevic, 'Turkey Presidential Election Shines Spotlight on

Free Speech Challenges', *Index on Censorship*, 7 August 2014.

359. 'The Internet Bill: Is Freedom of Expression under Threat in Turkey?', Al Jazeera, 8 February 2014.

360. 'Why freedom of expression is under threat in Turkey', *The Guardian*, 27 March 2014.

361. 'Why is Turkey's Media Environment Ranked "Not Free"?', Freedom House, 12 May 2014.

362. Ibid.

363. 'Democracy in Crisis: Corruption, Media and Power in Turkey' (Freedom House, 2014), p 3.

364. Maxime Gauin, 'Review of Armenian Studies', No 29, p 127.

CHAPTER 9: REPARATIONS

365. Elie Wiesel, 'Listen to the Wind' in *'Against Silence': The Voice and Visions of Elie Wiesel* (Holocaust Library, 1985), p 166.

366. Colin Tatz, *With Intent to Destroy: Reflecting on Genocide* (Verso, 2003), p 157.

367. Dr Yael Danieli, 'Massive Trauma and the Healing Role of Reparative Justice' in Carla Ferstman, Mariana Goetz and Alan Stephens, *Reparations* (Martinus Nijhoff, 2009), p 57.

368. Ibid., p 45.

369. Ibid., p 61.

370. See Michael Bazyler, *Holocaust Justice: The Battle for Restitution in America's Courts* (NYU Press, 2005), Chapter 1.

371. See ibid., Chapter 2.

372. *Republic of Austria et al v Maria V. Altmann*, 541 US677 (US 2004). In 2005, the parties agreed to end the litigation and submit to an Austrian arbitral tribunal, which ordered the return of five of the six disputed artworks. The sixth painting was found not to have been

confiscated, and therefore not required to be returned. This decision was upheld by the Austrian Supreme Court in 2008.

373. *Application of the Convention on the Prevention and Punishment of the Crime of Genocide (Bosnia and Herzegovina v Yugoslavia)*, Preliminary Objections, Judgment, ICJ Rep 1996, p 595 paras 32–3.

374. *Bosnia v Serbia*, above n152, paras 459–69.

375. Compare my positivist dissent, in the Sierra Leone 'child soldiers' case, with the approach of the other judges: *Prosecutor v Norman (Child Soldiers Case)*, Case No. SCSL-04-14-AR72, Special Court for Sierra Leone, 31 May 2004.

376. Article 28 of the Vienna Convention on the Law of Treaties 1980. This provision codifies the pre-existing international legal position of general non-retroactivity. See *Maviommatis Palestine Concessions Case (Greece v UK)* 1924 PCIJ (Ser A) No 2; *Preliminary Objections, Ambatielos Case (Greece v UK)* 11952 ICJ 40 (1 July).

377. William Schabas, 'Retroactive Application of the Genocide Convention', *University of St Thomas Journal of Law and Public Policy*, Vol 4 (2009), p 41. And see Alfred De Zayas, *The Genocide against the Armenians 1915–1923 and the Relevance of the 1948 Genocide Convention* (Haigazian University, 2010), p 87.

378. *The Crime of Genocide* [1946] UNGAR 72; A/RES/96 (I) (11 December 1946).

379. *United States v Alstötter*, 3 TWC 954, 963 (US Military Tribunal, 1951) (*The Justice Case*).

380. International Law Commission, *Articles on State Responsibility for Internationally Wrong Acts*, Article 31.

381. Ibid., Article 35; *Factory at Chorzow (Germany v. Poland)*, 1928 PCIJ (ser. A) No 17 (Sept 13).

382. Ibid., Article 36; *Gabčikovo-Nagymaros Project (Hungary/Slovakia)*, Judgment, ICJ Reports 1997, p 7.

383. United Nations General Assembly Resolution 60/147, 16 December

2005, UN Doc A/RES/60/147 (2006).

384. See Appendix 2.

385. *Basic Principles*, above n383, Clause 8.

386. Rule 85, ICC Rules of Procedure and Evidence.

387. Carla Ferstman and Sheri P. Rosenberg, 'Reparations in Dayton's Bosnia and Herzegovina' in Ferstman, Goetz and Stephens above n367, pp 494–9.

388. *Ottoman Public Debt Arbitration* (1925) 1 RIAA 529 and *Roselius & Co v Karsten and the Turkish Republic* [1925–6] *AD* (No 26).

389. See generally James Crawford, *The Creation of States in International Law* (Oxford University Press, 2006), Chapter 16.

390. *Lighthouse Arbitration Case* (France and Greece) (1956) 12 RIAA 155; 23 ILR 659. Permanent Court of Arbitration, 24 July 1956.

391. The acts of insurrectionists who then become the government of a new state shall be attributed to that new state – see Haig Silvanie, 'Responsibility of States for Acts of Insurgent Governments', *American Journal of International Law*, Vol 33 (1939), p 78

392. Vahagn Avedian, 'State Identity, Continuity, and Responsibility: The Ottoman Empire, the Republic of Turkey and the Armenian Genocide', *European Journal of International Law*, Vol 23 No 3 (2012), pp 811–13.

393. Ibid., pp 813–16.

394. Pulat Tacar & Maxime Gauin, 'State Identity, Continuity, and Responsibility: The Ottoman Empire, the Republic of Turkey and the Armenian Genocide: A Reply to Vahagn Avedian', *European Journal of International Law*, Vol 23 No 3 (2012), p 821.

395. Akçam, above n139, p 341.

396. Ibid., p 358.

397. *Cyprus v Turkey*, Merits, App no 25781/94 (2002) 35 EHRR 30; Ruling

on Just Satisfaction, 12 May 2014.

398. The court has held that a remedy must be 'practically effective' for it to be available. To determine whether this is the case, in *Akdivar v Turkey* the court held it 'must take realistic account not only of the existence of formal remedies in the legal system of the Contracting Party concerned but also of the general legal and political context in which they operate as well as the personal circumstances of the Applicants' (ECHR 16 September 1996, Reports of Judgments and Decisions, 1996-iV, para 69). A real risk of criminal prosecution would meet this threshold.

399. See Michael Bobelian, *Children of Armenia* (Simon and Schuster, 2009), pp 208–24.

400. *Movsesian et al; Victoria Veersicherung AG et al,* 671 F.3d 856 (9th Cir. 2012).

401. See http://www.anca.org/legal/insuranceclaims/amicus_USG_arzoumanian.pdf for the amicus curiae brief.

402. *Republic of Iran v Barakat Galleries* [2007] EWCA Civ 1374, para 2.

403. De Zayas, above n377, pp 57–8.

404. Special Rapporteur Awn Shawkat Al Khasawneh, *Final Report on the Human Rights Dimensions of Population Transfers*, Sub-Commission document E/CN.4/Sub.2/1997/23.

405. Above n383.

406. De Zayas, above n377, p 79.

407. 'Armenian Mass at church in Turkey', BBC News, 19 September 2010.

408. Return of Churches Resolution, H Res 306, S Res 392; see Armenian National Committee of America, *Return of Churches.*

409. 'Catholicoses Urge Turkey to Return Confiscated Armenian Churches', *Armenian Weekly*, 24 April 2013.

410. See Taner Akçam, 'Anatomy of a Crime', *Journal of Genocide Research*, Vol 7 No 2 (2005) p 268.

ENDNOTES

411. See Tessa Hofman, 'German Eyewitness Reports of the Genocide of the Armenians, 1915–16' in *A Crime of Silence* (Zed Books, 1985), p 70.

412. Lewis Einstein, *Inside Constantinople* (Forgotten Books, 2012), p 2.

413. Hilmar Kaider. *Le Génocide Arménien* (Edipol, 1999), p 82.

414. Einstein, above n412, p 176

415. See Peace Conference FCO file at National Archives, 'Turco German outrages on Armenians and British POW's' Letter from Mr A Delbourgo, 19/02/19.

CONCLUSION

416. Harut Sassounian, 'In major policy shift, Armenia demands lands from Turkey', *California Courier*, 18 July 2013.

417. See 'Football Diplomacy', *The Economist,* 3 September 2009.

418. Nagorno-Karabakh is a mountainous area bordered by Armenia and Azerbaijan which has long been occupied predominantly by Armenians, although it was allocated by the Bolshevik government in 1921 to the Soviet Republic of Azerbaijan. On the break-up of the Soviet Union in 1991 it declared independence, and its Azeri minority fled in the course of a war between the two countries, 1992–4. Since then it has been claimed by Azerbaijan (supported by Turkey) but its independence (unrecognised by other countries) has been protected by Armenia. A protracted diplomatic negotiation (the Minsk process) is currently at an impasse.

419. 'No incentive for Turkey, Armenia to normalize relations', *Al-Monitor*, 3 May 2013.

420. David L. Phillips, *Diplomatic History: The Turkey–Armenia Protocols* (Institute for the Study of Human Rights, Columbia University, 2012), p 68.

421. 'Turkey could deport Armenians', BBC News, 17 March 2010.

422. HR 252 , 111th Congress (2009–2010) Affirmation of the United States Record on the Armenian Genocide Resolution.

423. 'US vote attacks Turkey "genocide"', BBC News, 4 March 2010.

424. 'Turkish EU Minister on the Armenian genocide controversy: we are very sensitive about this issue"', *Der Spiegel*, 16 March 2010.

425. Genocide Recognition Precondition to Turkey's EU Bid, Says Euro-Parliament President', Azbarez.com, 18 September 2012.

426. The ruling also stated that the Genocide Convention does not have retroactive effect – see ICTJ, above n290, pp 5–8.

427. Suny, Göçek and Naimark, above n63, p 4.

428. Ibid., p 9.

INDEX

'Geoffrey Robertson takes us into the courtroom of history for a thrilling cross-examination exposing the hypocrisy and cowardice of the apologists for this colossal crime – the extermination of over half the Armenians in Turkey. Forty-three of our states recognise this as genocide, so why can't the United States?'

TINA BROWN

'Geoffrey Robertson proves the genocidal intent behind the atrocities afflicted on the Armenians. After this compelling book, genocide denial and equivocation can never again be credible.'

AMAL CLOONEY

'With a brilliant display of forensic advocacy, one of the greatest legal minds on the international stage forces a shameful but inconvenient truth upon the world. A shocking indictment!'

HELENA KENNEDY QC

'Geoffrey Robertson, with his usual forensic brilliance, makes the case for justice for the Armenian victims of the 1915 massacre. A must-read for those who want to understand the relationship between victims of unrequited international crimes and justice, not just historically, but also in the here and now.'

SIR KEIR STARMER KCB QC

'A devastating, searing indictment of complicity and cover-up over the extermination of one million people.'
PETER HAIN MP

'Brilliant, forensic and irrefutable … *An Inconvenient Genocide* should be compulsory reading … Very few books are necessary, but this is one.'
THE AUSTRALIAN

'Argues the Armenian corner with informed eloquence.'
MATTHEW PARRIS, *THE SPECTATOR*

'It is not because he comes from an Armenian background that he is drawn to the subject: it is his consciousness as a human rights advocate that guides him.'
NEW STATESMAN

AN INCONVENIENT GENOCIDE

Also by Geoffrey Robertson

Reluctant Judas
Obscenity
Freedom, the Individual and the Law
Geoffrey Robertson's Hypotheticals (Vols 1 & 2)
Does Dracula have AIDS?
Robertson & Nicol on Media Law
The Justice Game
Crimes against Humanity
The Tyrannicide Brief
The Levellers: The Putney Debates
The Statute of Liberty
The Case of the Pope
Mullahs without Mercy: Human Rights and Nuclear Weapons
Dreaming Too Loud
Stephen Ward Was Innocent, OK